THE KINGDOM AND THE POWER

The Kingdom

and

The Power

AN EXPOSITION OF
THE NEW TESTAMENT GOSPEL

Paul S. Minear

Westminster John Knox Press
LOUISVILLE • LONDON

Hardback published in 1950 by The Westminster Press, Philadelphia
Paperback published in 2004 by Westminster John Knox Press, Louisville

Cover design by Jennifer K. Cox

Published by Westminster John Knox Press
Louisville, Kentucky

This book is printed on acid-free paper that meets the American National Standards Institute Z39.48 standard. ♾

PRINTED IN THE UNITED STATES OF AMERICA

Library of Congress cataloging-in-publication date is on file at the Library of Congress, Washington D.C.

ISBN 0-664-22907-7

To
J. L. D.

FOREWORD

THIS valuable contribution to New Testament interpretation is a revision and expansion of a series of addresses by Dr. Minear during the 1950 Annual Midwinter Lectures at the Austin Presbyterian Theological Seminary.

Instituted in 1945 as a service of the seminary to the ministers of the Southwest, these lectures bring to this area outstanding Christians from all lands. It was a privilege to present Dr. Minear in the succession of distinguished Christians who have appeared on this foundation. The men and their subjects have been:

1945 — Ernest Trice Thompson — Christian Bases of World Order.

1946 — Josef Lukl Hromadka — The Church at the Crossroads.

1947 — Paul Scherer — The Plight of Freedom.

1948 — D. Elton Trueblood — Alternative to Futility.

1949 — H. Richard Niebuhr — Christ and Culture.

Ministers and laymen alike will find fresh and challenging insights in this present work of the exceptionally gifted and scholarly Dr. Minear.

DAVID L. STITT,
President.

The Austin Presbyterian Theological Seminary
Austin, Texas

PREFACE

IN THE writing of personal letters, a postscript, if one is needed, is customarily placed last. In the writing of books, however, the postscript comes first and is called a preface. This procedure may be accounted for, in part at least, by the difference in the writer's relationship to the reader. The reader of a letter is usually in a position to understand intuitively the context, whereas the reader of a book does not often share that advantage. Let me, then, use a few paragraphs to sketch for the reader the context of what I have written.

Few writers, I suppose, are able to remain unaffected by the impact of contemporary problems on the communities to which they belong. Who can today be unaware of the earthquake shocks that cause the walls of Western civilization to tremble? Threats to its stability have become so serious as to raise doubts concerning the survival of that civilization. These doubts, in turn, have prompted men to scan more anxiously the story of other societies, looking for some pattern of meaning beneath the obscure events of their birth, maturity, decay, and death. In short, the mind of Occidental man has grown quite obsessed by the need for an adequate philosophy of history.

The Christian Church, in its ecumenical conversations with itself, has been confronted with the task of relating its message to the structure and destiny of civilizations. This task has made imperative a fresh appraisal of God's design for history, and the bearing of that design upon man's disordered world. The Church has recognized that apart from a renewed understanding of its message for men it cannot expect renewed vitality in its mission to men. One of the signs of such a renewal is the rediscovery of the Bible, and, within the Bible, the person of Jesus Christ as the central clue to God's purposes.

Concurrently, Christian theologians from many schools of thought have been impelled to seek a clearer conception of the Christian interpretation of history. The purposes of God for man's corporate activity, his ways of shaping the destiny of individuals and societies, the significance of civilization, the place of the Church in current cultural conflicts — all these are matters on which the theologian must speak, if he is to speak as a contemporary to contemporaries. Yet to speak with authority he too must restudy the Biblical attitudes toward these problems.

During this period Christian historians have become engrossed in the same areas. How is the history of salvation linked to general world history? What do God's saving acts signify for the life of non-Christian peoples? In what ways does the Christian message concerning God's Kingdom transcend the relativities of historical processes? What is the nature of that Kingdom, and how does it enter and redeem the whole fabric of existence? Does it have a unique significance for the modern theologian, the modern church, the modern civilization?

Various movements in recent thought have thus converged at a single point: the effort to recover, to describe, and to apply what may be called the New Testament theology of history. Among historians and theologians one may observe a growing consensus in recognizing the *distinctiveness* of New Testament attitudes toward history, the *centrality* of God's Kingdom in the Christian gospel, and the *necessity* of understanding that Kingdom if we are to grasp God's design for our own times. But although there has emerged a common willingness to recognize these facts, current discussions make even more apparent the absence of agreement with regard to the exact content and relevance of New Testament eschatology. Neither historians nor theologians, whether as individuals or as ecumenical collaborators, have arrived at a common mind concerning the meaning of the Kingdom of God as proclaimed by its first heralds. It is this convergence of interests and this divergence of conclusions that has prompted the preparation of the following chapters.

As a Christian interested in the historical, theological, and ecumenical work of the Church, I have sought to expound the New Testament gospel in its original scope and implications. Because this gospel announces the advent of the Kingdom in the Messiah's ministry, I have tried to describe how that new order manifested its power and glory through Jesus of Nazareth. Because his ministry eventuated in the transformation of individuals, communities, and their world, it has been necessary to trace the course of such transformations. Because his Kingdom advanced through sharp conflicts with all the rebellious forces in creation, it has been necessary to explore in detail the lines of battle and the strategies of opposing commanders. Because the gospel was exciting news of victory, a victory that God shared with men, I have attempted to express not only the joy of the victors but also the reasons why they could be so joyful. Because they through faith discovered the mysteries of God's dealing with all creation, I have aimed at explaining why they could proclaim with such assurance that Jesus Christ is at once the beginning, the end, and the way.

These objectives have made it seem wise to limit the source material, so far as possible, to the New Testament itself. This does not mean that valid understanding of God's purposes has been restricted to a single group of writers, as if they had established, so to speak, a permanent monopoly on the truth. Nor does it mean that I am not greatly indebted to many more recent writers. It simply means that if we are to comprehend the Christian message in its original terms we must listen more attentively than we usually do to the New Testament itself, patiently alert to follow the logic and to catch the accents of the first disciples.

Some readers, however, will ask whether, in fact, the New Testament does proclaim a single message. Are there not many contradictory attitudes and ideas to be detected in this library of ancient documents? In answering this question I have chosen to follow the assumptions and convictions of the writers themselves. They were quite aware of the manifold and hidden ways in which God's Spirit is at work. They knew how diverse are God's gifts, how complex his ways with men. They lost sight of neither the ravines of history nor its mountain panoramas, neither the long stretches of barren plains nor the rushing waterfalls and winding rivers. In them the knowledge of the eternal purpose produced no narrow conventionality of frozen imitativeness but the buoyant freedom of zestful faith. They themselves avoided and protested against any forced uniformity of code, creed, or institution. Any interpretation, then, that forces their thoughts into a formal, external harmony runs counter to their intention. The New Testament echoes a chorus of voices, each singing in its own tongue.

These same writers, however, took for granted the existence of genuine unity, a unity that encouraged the greatest freedom. The varied voices joined in hallelujahs to the same God, in glorias for gifts from the one Lord. Since God's purpose is one, his gospel is also one. Those who have been invited into his Kingdom participate in one body, one hope, one call, one faith, one baptism, one Spirit. Even from their standpoint, of course, this unity was incomplete and would be realized in its fullness only when God's Kingdom had come in its fullness. Unity of Spirit was given to them in their baptism, but it was given to them as a promise from the Messiah which would be fulfilled when his mission had been fulfilled. With regard, then, to the question of whether or not a single gospel may be found in the New Testament, I have been content with their answer.

I have also assumed that their vocabulary was adequate for conveying the good news, and I have therefore limited myself in so far as possible to the major categories and images which they employed in describing God's Kingdom. This should not be taken to mean that non-Biblical forms of expression ought never to be used. At times, however, it may be most helpful to us all to leave our habitual grooves of thought, our conventional modes of expression, in trying to grasp patterns of thought as native to others as they are strange to us. Especially if we are to catch their primal perceptions and perspectives of life, the inner dynamics of their wills, the interplay of their feelings, we need to make the effort to learn their language and to use it. In the case of the early Christians it is particularly desirable to understand the metaphors and symbols that they found most congenial to their message, to ponder not only what they said but also why they said it and how their words disclose the inner orientation of mind and spirit. This again does not mean a frozen and formal language, stiff and stilted. Their language was varied and flexible, replete with a vast range of imagery and color. Within such a vast range each reader should be able to find some spiritual idiom that he can make his own.

This effort to see history as they saw it, from within the horizons of their own situation, demands much more than a repetition of their words. An exposition must make explicit many things which they took quite for granted, subjecting to conscious scrutiny things that they intuitively sensed. When symbols that once were alive have lost their meanings, sustained study must be applied before those meanings can be restored. The basic categories around which they organized their thoughts do not fit readily into the habitual compartments of our minds; we must therefore give more attention to those categories than did they in using them. It is probable that any exposition of their message would sound quite foreign to the prophets and apostles themselves. Nevertheless, a genuine comprehension of the gospel in the terms in which it was first affirmed and proclaimed is, we trust, neither impossible nor fruitless. To this task the Church as a whole perennially addresses itself, recognizing that its own renewal depends upon a renewed proclamation of the gospel. Such a renewal is always accompanied by a double " rebirth of images ": on the one hand, the vitality of ancient symbols is restored when they begin to exert fresh power over our imaginations; on the other hand, modern symbols come to life in a new way when they are used by these converted imaginations to convey the eternal gospel. Faith discovers that an old vocabulary is not so dead as might be supposed; at the same time it discovers that an up-to-date jargon is not so alive as is often assumed. In giving men new life the gospel brings new life also to their language, whether old or new.

So much for the more general context of the ensuing chapters. The more specific and immediate context came in the opportunity to lecture on the theme of this book to various conference groups. By their cordial response and vigorous discussion, these audiences have participated, more than they perhaps realized, in the making of the book. I am thinking with more than perfunctory gratitude of four conferences in particular: Hawaiian ministers and their wives at Camp Harold Erdman on Oahu; college students and their counselors at Camp O-At-Ka in Maine; Congregational pastors at Deering Summer School in New Hampshire; the Annual Convocation audience at the Austin Presbyterian Theological Seminary in Texas. For constant stimulus and candid criticism I am deeply indebted to my colleagues and students at Andover Newton Theological School. There are, in addition, two persons who have shared in this undertaking from start to finish and to whose help no acknowledgment can do justice: my friend J. Leslie Dunstan and my wife.

PAUL S. MINEAR.

Newton Center, Massachusetts
April, 1950

CONTENTS

PART
I

"BEHOLD, THE LAMB"

THE SCROLL THAT WAS SEALED

IN AN eastern province of imperial Rome, the police arrested a man called John as enemy of the state and leader of a subversive movement. They placed him on a lonely penal island, cut off from home and friends. Here he received his ration of food and of slow-footed hours, a time vacant save for hopes and fears. Gone were all freedoms except the freedom to think, to recall what had happened, to ponder what the future might bring. Would his companions also be arrested? Would their movement be exterminated? Would the morrow bring emancipation or death? With such options he could occupy himself to his wit's end.

There may have been still another alternative. He could publicly renounce the "crime" for which he was being penalized. He had been arrested "on account of the word of God and the testimony of Jesus," because he had chosen to share "in Jesus the tribulation and the kingdom and the patient endurance" (Rev. 1:9). But he could disavow this testimony and avoid this tribulation by one simple act. He could recant his "treason." His captors promised him freedom if only he would worship the emperor: "Say yes to the magistrate and avoid the fate of your friend Antipas of Pergamum" (ch. 2:13). To his captors this yes seemed a very easy thing. But not to John. To him such assent would be treason to the King of Kings.

As this prisoner pondered the odds in the situation and as he reflected upon the predicament of his friends, a vision swept into the vortex of his mind. It was a vision of Him who sits upon the throne over all kingdoms, One who is none other than the Lord God Almighty. And in God's right hand he saw " a scroll written within and on the back, sealed with seven seals " (ch. 5:1). The prisoner, of course, knew what the scroll signified. It contained the script for the story of mankind, written by the author of that story. It carried the plot to the drama of human affairs. In it might be read the agelong purposes of God, as those purposes are enacted in tangible events. Each event has its secret, and it was this secret that the scroll contained. To open the scroll was to secure the key to the riddles of destiny.

The scroll, however, was securely sealed. In other words, God's design had been hidden from men. The vision, therefore, gave rise to this query: "Who is worthy to open the scroll and break its seals?" (v. 2). The scroll demanded a reader, someone qualified to penetrate the bewildering labyrinth of life, to clarify its source and its course. The need was urgent, but the query brought the laconic reply: "No one." To this answer there were no exceptions. "No one in heaven or on earth or under the earth was able to open the scroll."

When he realized this rebuff, the prisoner "wept much." And he had good reason, for if this answer were the true one, then indeed was his cause hopeless. It would make no difference whether he died or lived, whether his brothers were purged or pardoned. He had risked his life on a conviction that could not possibly be validated. What was left for him but bleak despair? Thus the angel's message dropped him into the abyss of dismay, where he shared the bleakness of nagging uncertainty with all prisoners, from the days of Moses to the days of Buchenwald.

Moreover, the plight of these prisoners was not far different from the plight of all men, for we all need to know with surety the underlying purpose of our tortuous paths. If the angel's answer was true for John, it may also be the true index of the human situation as such. As in his case, the sentence of our life sooner or later approaches its period. Though we live — and can live — only on the conviction that our particular sentence has some wider meaning, we grow less and less confident of our ability to grasp that meaning with clarity and trust. We seek various values with eagerness, only to find many of them fading, and their transiency induces a fear of ultimate futility. We devote our days to the increase of future security. Today the striving, tomorrow the victory. The coming verdict will vindicate our expectations, or so we wager with the limited stock of daily energy. Yet tomorrow seldom brings the victory we count on, and if it does, the victory is often a hollow triumph indeed. We yield to the future its right to judge the present; yet when tomorrow arrives we find its verdict as inadequate and uncertain as today's. The dream that shored up our wavering efforts fades, and only another dream can reactivate our spirit. But as the wedding procession of many tomorrows yields to the funeral procession of many yesterdays, each new hope comes with greater tentativeness. We may begin in despair to distrust every future verdict, or we may with defiant optimism resolve to compel a favorable verdict. We may gain a wry pleasure from using the skeptic's excuse that " history is a box of puzzles with a lost key." Or we may employ in bitterness the sardonic axiom that " history is a mother who devours her own children."

The problem becomes even more acute when we have wagered all our treasure on a single hope. Suppose that we have yielded our hearts to will one thing only, to serve one Lord only. Then suppose that this one loyalty brings the threat of death. Then suppose that this threat places in final jeopardy the fulfillment of that one hope. We would now be ready, with the prisoner of Patmos, to appreciate the enigma of the closed scroll, in its full import. Is that scroll legible? If so, does it narrate a single inclusive purposeful story in which the events of a single life — of my life — have a part? If so, what is its true beginning and where does it end? What is its central plot? And who is worthy to decipher its runes and to divulge its mysteries? Who is qualified to judge the seething turbulence of the human ocean?

What wisdom and power such a judge must possess! Consider, if you will, the intricate tangle of threads that meets at a given moment and place — let us say, at the intersection of two busy streets in any city. Look at the men, the women, and the children who come and go, shopping, talking, momentarily touching each other's lives, yet continually occupied each with his own world of plans and hopes. Follow each person through his ordinary or dramatic career, his parents' dreams, his birth, the casual and incidental experiences of his childhood, adolescent conflicts and friendships, courtship and marriage, the lengthening chain of sorrows and joys, the efforts and expectations expressed in the routines of work and play. Record, if you can, the complete inner and outer biography of this person, then of that one, and of that one. Then convey the inner core of meaning involved in all these separate stories.

Perhaps, you may say, it is easier to generalize and to deal with masses. Let us be content if we can detect the pattern in the tapestry woven by masses of men. But even when one deals with large segments of the social saga, one's imagination staggers at the effort to encompass the career of races, classes, nations, and civilizations — their habits, governments, arts, forms of work and worship, their transient achievements and their oblivion. Where does one go to find the tokens of an over-all design? How can one trace these tokens through the long aeons in the evolution of suns, stones, animals, and societies? Our eye span is not wide enough to take in all the kingdoms of the earth. Whether we contemplate the rise and fall of a civilization or of a single individual, our mind may well be overwhelmed with the sense of impenetrable mystery. If we are to challenge the " No one " of the prophet's word, we must do it with some recognition that we thereby accept a tremendous burden of proof.

Or perhaps, fearing to shoulder such a burden, you point out how fortunate it is that not many of us are called upon to wrestle with these intricate riddles, fortunate that men may spin out their fourscore years without torturing themselves by examining its pattern or its meaning. Yet the fact that we are men and not beasts means that, willingly or not, we cannot evade such questions. Whether we like it or not, our answers are actually given in our everyday tasks and pleasures, in our working and loving and fighting and dreaming. The only problem is whether those answers are profound or puerile. In every activity we move by a sense of direction. The compass that points the hiker one step along the way is the same compass that guides the globe-circling plane. And unless our bearings are accurate we are lost, however safe we may feel. If none can be found to read the compass aright, then it is our whole existence and destiny that are threatened.

Some grounds for confidence, however, may be found in man's innate sense of direction, in knowledge slowly accruing through generations of conversation with the ways of nature and of society. Man has demonstrated unusual powers of hope, perseverance, and instinctive reliance on the goodness and wisdom of things, even when he is least able to understand the outcome of his toil and tears. We should by no means be scornful of the tested instinctive wisdom of the common man. Yet neither should we deny that this wisdom often fails to afford trustworthy guidance on ultimate issues. Today we observe masses of men most confident of their shibboleths and most willing to fight other masses whose confidence in opposite shibboleths is equally firm. Millions read black where other millions read white, and the conflicting versions spell mass slaughter. When they reach this impasse, those who reflect are bound to doubt their own instinctive power to read and interpret the course of events. As in the case of John on Patmos, this doubt is most agonizing when we are compelled to make choices in which the whole world is ranged on one side and only a paltry minority is left on the other. Such choices do come, and when they come, we realize with a shock that the truth of the matter may be hidden from both sides.

May we not, then, in such an exigency vest our confidence in the steady and rapid increase in the knowledge of history on the part of our scholars? By their patient, impartial digging, they have unearthed a larger quantity of dependable objective knowledge concerning nature and history than ever before. Never has so broad a range of historical experience been covered by scholarly exploration. In no previous generation has so much time, energy, money, and talent been devoted to scientific historical research. Never have the tools and methods for studying the past and the present been so precise, so sharp, so accurate. Never have the accumulated data been so accessible to all sections of the public. These advances and achievements must not be minimized in a mood of self-pity for our present plight.

The field of historical science has witnessed triumphs as striking as those of the physical sciences, though less widely heralded. Objectives hitherto unattained by any previous generation have been quietly attained. But these goals that have been reached, like those of the engineer and the chemist, have not been such as to unseal the scroll of destiny. The best historian, today as always, finds that his knowledge does little more than underscore the ultimate riddles of life.

Even in more limited areas there is justification for the conclusion that such knowledge is not enough. For example, objective historical knowledge appears strangely unable to counteract human prejudice and passion. Policies that lead to war are not genuinely controlled by knowledge of former wars. Policies that lead to inflation are not controlled by the history of former inflations. In an age that needs to learn from the past, the layman turns away from history to historical fiction, becoming ever more cynical of the disciplined wisdom of the historian. In reaction, the historian becomes more skeptical of his own trade and bitterly resentful of the indifference of the masses. Well he knows the tragic truth of Hegel's thrust: " The only thing men learn from history is that men never learn anything from history." In time of crisis the most " impartial " historians are enlisted as the brain trust for one of the competing mass movements, giving their signatures, perhaps unwittingly or unwillingly, to the propaganda devices which are major weapons of those movements. There are repeated cries for more and better history-teaching in public schools, but it must be American history, or Russian history, or democratic history. And there must be periodical expurgation of previous textbooks.

This generation that has collected an unprecedented body of historical data has also produced an unprecedented diversity in interpretations of history. Modern man has passed from a period in which the meaning of history was taken for granted, absorbed in latent form in the subconscious axioms of the body politic, into a period that is subject to a veritable epidemic of competing philosophies of history. The nearer a civilization comes to its death pangs, the more diverse and conflicting the philosophies of civilization that it spawns. Such philosophies strike the best-seller lists, enter into dining room discussions, and become the stock-in-trade of jesters and newscasters. So it develops that everyone who discusses current affairs becomes a philosopher of history, and coteries form around the more vociferous and persuasive interpreters. Fearing at any moment the eruption of volcanoes, men carry with them a portable seismograph and try to interpret the movements of the nervous needle. Almost hysterically they follow its jerky course. And they choose their authorities by finding a name of importance to support their own graph. What names one can play with: Marx, Freud, Heard, Sorokin, Toynbee, Du Noüy, Dewey, Spengler, Hegel, Croce, Nietzsche, Kierkegaard, Sartre, Bergson, Whitehead, Pareto, Haushofer, Huntington! . . . And what erudite and esoteric terms can be employed: Existentialist, Idealist, Marxist, Organicistic, Tychistic, Geopolitics, Realpolitics, Psychoanalytic. . . . Under these conditons any of these interpretations may become a fad.

It must be admitted, of course, that these names and types of interpretations circulate more widely in academic discussions than on the

street. But one should not forget the unofficial and semiofficial interpreters of history. There are those who read the scroll of history by
taking the measurements of the Great Pyramid or by consulting the
stars. There are those who substitute their favorite columnist in the
day's paper or the "best" commentator on the radio. Some predict
man's fate according to the chemical constitution of the soil, by the
deficiencies in his diet, or by the shape of his neuroses.

Why this pandemonium? Why should a civilization with such extensive knowledge be so befuddled by its own ventriloquists as they
shout their uneasy omens? Ancient Romans studied the entrails of
birds; are modern Americans much better off? Could this be evidence
that our civilization has lost its unity, its sense of direction, its nerve?
Does it mean that men are becoming dimly aware of the vulnerability
of all existing securities? Does the fluctuating popularity of current prog-
nosticators bespeak an inner despair concerning the ability of any commentator to depict the shape of things to come? Make no mistake.
Men are today as feverishly absorbed in reading the rune of history as
people have ever been. One has only to note the fluctuations of the
stock exchange and the instantaneous reactions of world economy. Or
to catch the mood of New Year's speeches and to watch the poignant
way in which, responding to current headlines, men veer from optimism to pessimism and back again. Note the speculative elements in ad-
vertising, public relations, education, business, sports. In this constant
hubbub of oracles we are more tolerant of self-appointed sibyls than we
are willing to admit the problematic character of all prophecies. The
land of pilgrims has become the home of insurance companies. Yet
the more insurance against the future, the more dread of that future.

Modern *thought* may be characterized by a growing awareness of
the ultimacy and the insolubility of the puzzles of temporal happenings. Modern *action,* on the other hand, may be characterized by its
effort to slash through all the knots at one stroke by elevating to the
throne of final purpose the temporary and partial interests of a particular human community. Men who are haunted by the inaccessibility of
a final design for living are impelled to seize by Promethean action the
control over their own destiny. But such despair-driven efforts not only
draw upon them the nemesis of deeper despair and more frantic action, but the whole cycle of frustrated activity increases and confirms
the skepticism of the thinkers. These self-appointed makers of history

demonstrate, to be sure, the truth that life is composed of responsible choices that must be made before all the evidence concerning their results can be weighed by the analysts. But the desperation with which they proceed to make history indicates the subconscious dread that this evidence will not be wholly favorable. In reaction against their headstrong violence, the thinkers are tempted to delay decision until they have arrived at a coherent understanding of history and are in a position to make wiser choices. They are therefore doomed in advance to the derision of actors who are already committed to partial and self-chosen goals, and to the disdain of other thinkers who recognize the oversimplification that is required of any system. It is a time when the laws of overstatement are effective with men thirsting for remedial action. By the same token it is a time when the laws of understatement are effective with scholars who have learned from inspecting the countless fallacies that are paraded confidently as the truths of history. The actors become more and more hysterical and hasty until their avowed concern for truth becomes swallowed up by their preoccupation with pragmatic expediencies. The thinkers, as they view this degeneration of action, become more and more afraid of precipitate choices, more and more detached from the hurly-burly. Consequently their wisdom dries up into a barren tossing of words back and forth from one expert to another. The outcome is obvious: action is divorced from wisdom and wisdom is sterilized by its inaction. Yet the men of thought are perforce men of action, and the men of action are perforce men of thought. Both thought and action give expression to an interpretation of history; both are dependent on the truth of that interpretation.

When they begin to examine and to test their interpretation of history, they become involved immediately in at least ten major riddles. These may be characterized by comparing history to a road down which humanity moves in its polyglot caravan.

1. The first we may term the riddle of the *road*. From what beginnings to what end does creation move? Is there unity of direction midst all the devious turnings, and if so, what is this direction? Shall we think of the road as a horizontal plane, an escalator, a toboggan chute, a race track, a spiral staircase? Or does humanity, like a caterpillar truck, lay its own road over unexplored terrain?

2. Then there is the riddle of the *wheels,* whose revolutions appear to produce the changes in the human situation. Does the process move

through regularly recurring stages? What are the rhythms and patterns that hold true for the entire caravan, or for the separate parts of that caravan? Through all the changes are there laws of change that do not change?

3. The character of the *motive power* is itself another enigma. What are the major forces that give history its momentum toward this end or that? Are these forces personal or impersonal, accidental or providential? Does the god of Fate or the god of Chance sit at the controls? Or is the power self-generated and self-propelled?

4. The fourth riddle is that of the *milestones* by which pilgrims in transit measure their progress. Man's history, whether that of the individual or of the group, is punctuated by events, strategic happenings that make such a difference that we say that things will never be the same again. Yet we may doubt our ability to locate the decisive turning points. One needs only to look at last year's papers, or to recall his own enthusiasms of a decade ago. How may we know when something really happens in what happens? How may we " carve history at the joints "?

5. Then there is the problem of the *landscape*. The environment of the traveler may change so rapidly that he cannot adjust himself to it, or it may change so slowly that he becomes bored. At one stage he is ready to exclaim, " History never repeats itself." At another, he confesses, " The more history changes, the more it remains the same." Man participates in the transient and in the enduring, but he is baffled when he asks which is which.

6. The *pilgrims* in the procession are in themselves a puzzle. They are the actors in events, for whom events have their significance. Some individuals and some groups, however, loom above the rest as the chief bearers of meaning. Each is inclined to assert a manifest destiny of its own. Yet to which individuals and to which groups does the future really belong? Is the civilization, nation, race, or class the chief unit in terms of whose destiny the chief meaning is to be discerned? Or is history simply a cosmic *Who's Who,* recording in final form the biographies of innumerable individuals? Or is it merely the stage where star actors read their lines? When and how does a person or group achieve historical significance?

7. Then we encounter what may be called the riddle of *traffic congestion*. In this strange pilgrimage everyone seems to be going in a

different direction. The lines of march crisscross at every step. Conflicts
and struggles arise and no traffic controls are available. On every side,
individuals and groups fight for the road. Are these endless contentions
real or illusory? Are all the cross-purposes incorporated in a higher
purpose, or is the survival of the fittest the only law of progress? If
so, what is true survival, and how is true fitness determined?

8. For many passers-by the primary problem is the riddle of the
individual's destination. For him, history is his own biography, a
story that is different from every other story. What is the relationship
between the plot of this story and the plot of the whole? When does an
incident in private history become truly historic? How does the inner
history of man — his hopes and fears, his intentions, his struggles with
conscience — enter into the arena of public events?

9. Each pilgrim also finds himself involved in the riddle of *freedom*.
He assumes that he is able to choose and to act. But he discovers too
that this freedom is not so unhampered as he may have thought. It is
limited by necessities implicit in his birth, his flesh, his race, his wealth,
his hormones, his present situation. So also is it with any class, race, or
nation. What is the relationship of freedom to these conditions? How
may the boundary of freedom be extended? By what is his freedom
actually limited, and by what is his necessity transformed into liberty?

10. The problems of his freedom and his destination are realized
most keenly when man approaches each *crossroad*. He is now called
upon to select one of the options afforded by the immediate situation.
Each day confronts him with the demand to do something, and every
deed starts a chain of effects, foreseen and unforeseen. Refusal to act is
itself an act. His actual conception of the purpose of life is embodied in
what he does. So he persistently puts to himself the question: What
shall I do; how shall I act in this situation? And in answering that
question all other problems reach a sort of tentative solution, however
problematic.

Anyone who has the impulse to open the scroll of destiny must solve
such problems as these ten. The list could be expanded, but the reader
is doubtless already weary, not to mention the fatigue of the philosopher of history. When a man starts out to reduce these puzzles to some
kind of coherence, he immediately tangles himself in a double predicament. In the first place, he must select a single event, or a limited
sequence of events, that discloses the structure and meaning of all

events. Yet he can discover no mountain high enough to afford a clear view of the entire sweep of history. He cannot himself experience more than a tiny fragment in the middle of one life story. In an endless landscape he must detect the watershed of meaning. In an aeonic epic he must select the episode that epitomizes the plot. But how can he make this selection? All happenings are localized; all are bound to become dwindling specks in the receding landscape of the past. In its transience each event appears to inherit a fate similar to that of all other events. Where, then, shall we look for that uniquely decisive series of happenings which will reveal the all-inclusive purpose and grain of existence? This part of the predicament we shall call the *relativity of the historical action.*

Let us assume, however, that the interpreter has been able to localize such a decisive series of events. Immediately he is confronted with the second part of the predicament, which we may term the *relativity of the historical actor.* The interpreter himself is strictly localized. He is a pilgrim who trudges but a short distance along the road before he dies. His moods shift. His thoughts are affected by everything that happens to him. His mind is shaped by a special set of circumstances: family, environment, education, the " accidents " of race and nation and class. He can free himself from some of the prejudices that warp his vision, but there are many prejudgments of which he never becomes conscious. Can any single interpreter claim to have the eyes to read the script so accurately as to get the true key to its plot?

And if no single man can boast the required qualifications, can one trust the composite judgment of a hundred experts? The experts are willy-nilly members of some parochial segment of society. An honest and able Marxist interpreter of history, using the same data and methods, will produce a very different interpretation from that of an equally able and honest capitalist interpreter. Neither an American nor a Russian 'can give the whole truth about Russo-American rivalries. Will an American be able correctly to assess the ultimate significance of his own culture, or the culture of Burma? Can a soldier or sailor give the true story of an entire global war? However objective and impartial a psychologist or sociologist may be, he himself, his methods of study, his categories of thought, his conception of ends, and his criteria of judgment are those given him by some segment of his own culture and generation. And we are all so intimately and passionately involved in the meanings and purposes of our existence that we may well ask whether we can sit as impartial judges on a supreme court. It is the habit of such judges to eliminate themselves from hearing cases in which their own interests are deeply involved. Must we so withdraw from any case that affects not only each day's work but also eternal life? Certainly every man is equally involved in the problems we have itemized. Each of us when drawing the map of life is inclined to produce something that resembles the lines on a railroad map, lines that show how much more direct and central is the route of this road than that of its competitors.

Small wonder, then, that our interpretations of history diverge so radically when all our interests and activities are so confusingly a part of the anarchy of our age. Small wonder that many would-be interpreters seek passionately to escape their dying culture, supposing either that truth is open only to a nonpartisan or that no meaning at all will emerge from the infernal welter of things.

Yet we cannot join these self-exiled malcontents. We cannot forget that even for them the problem remains. Man ceases to be man apart from the conviction that the course of his life marks a real journey and that the milestones in his career bear some importance. When that conviction is undermined, man's spirit withers. So too with the work of a historian. However cynical he may be concerning the meanings imputed to existence, his work as a historian rests upon the assumption that the experience of the human caravan has meaning and that knowledge of the past is not without value. Our condition is this: having seen men whose lives have been snuffed out to no obvious purpose, having seen the most glorious achievements of the race turned into rubble, having accepted the possibility of a sudden atomic death for ourselves, our nation, our culture, our civilization, we are wondering how anyone can discover the purpose that underlies such catastrophic events. To whom shall we go when our seers and sages share our own bewilderment?

Looking back at the Patmos vision, as John risked death for himself and for his community, for all that he counted dear, we can now appreciate the eagerness of his question: " Who is worthy to open the scroll? " And we can grasp the somber sadness of the answer: " No one in heaven or on earth or under the earth." The seven seals have kept the secrets of the scroll from our eyes as well as from his.

2

THE OPENING OF THE SCROLL

IN THE vision of John on Patmos there were two scenes. After the first, the prisoner was in tears because he knew of no one who could tell him what he most needed to know. Had that scene been the only one, there would be many who would, with some reason, protest the unrelieved pessimism of the prophet. Others, more charitable, would explain the morbid defeatism as a mood produced by abnormal, enforced isolation. But there follows a second scene which transforms John's mourning into joy, a joy even greater than that which would have followed his release from custody. Another heavenly messenger appeared and commanded him to cease his weeping. Someone had been found who had overcome all the obstacles, and who was therefore worthy to open the scroll.

Who is this person? " The Lion of the tribe of Judah " (Rev. 5:5). When, however, the prophet looks for this lion, he sees only " a Lamb standing, as though it had been slain " (v. 6). And he hears resounding through the corridors of heaven a new song, chanted by thousands of angels, the twenty-four elders, and the four living creatures: " Worthy art thou to take the scroll and to open its seals . . .

> " Worthy is the Lamb who was slain,
>   To receive power and wealth and wisdom and might
>   And honor and glory and blessing! " (vs. 9, 12).

In the end, the antiphons to this hymn are sung by " every creature in heaven and on earth and under the earth."

Who, then, is this Lamb? There is no doubt of his identity. This is none other than Jesus, " the Root of David," " the faithful witness, the first-born of the dead, and the ruler of kings on earth" (ch. 1:5). He it is who walks among the churches and holds their destiny in his hands (v. 20), who has received power over all nations (ch. 2:26), and holds the keys of Death and Hades (ch. 1:18). He it is who stands at the door, knocking and waiting for the invitation to enter (ch. 3:20).

Yes, the identity of the Lamb is clear. He is no exotic fanciful denizen of the clouds, but a person whom John has met before. John and his companions are the servants of this man, sharing his temptations, his patience, and his power. Jesus loves them and comes to them. They know that he knows their thoughts and their works, their toil and their loves. His servants are those who give witness to the fact that Jesus has freed them from captivity and has made them to be a Kingdom, ruled by his invisible majesty (ch. 1:5, 6).

How, it may be asked, did this Lamb receive the power to read the text of creation's story? The hymn of the angels makes the reason clear:

> "Thou wast slain and by thy blood didst ransom men for God
> From every tribe and tongue and people and nation,
> And hast made them a kingdom and priests to our God" (ch. 5:9, 10).

It is through his suffering that the Lamb has become the conquering Lion (vs. 5, 6). It is through his death that he has become the first-born from the dead, and has received power to free men from sin and death. This power enables him to issue promises that will be fulfilled surely and quickly:

"To him who conquers I will grant to eat of the tree of life, which is in the paradise of God" (ch. 2:7).
"Be faithful unto death, and I will give you the crown of life" (v. 10).
"I will give some of the hidden manna" (v. 17).
"I will give him the morning star" (v. 28).
"I will make him a pillar in the temple of my God" (ch. 3:12).
"I will grant him to sit with me on my throne" (v. 21).
"They shall reign on earth" (ch. 5:10).

This vision of the Lamb transforms the sadness of John into blessedness. Having glimpsed the glory of the King of Kings, however, he is not permitted to suppose that the vision is intended only for himself, as consolation for private grief. He is commanded to communicate with those friends who, like him, have entered into tribulation because of their fidelity to Jesus. He must tell them of the manifest power of the slain Lamb to wipe all tears from their eyes.

For many modern readers, unfortunately, his letters have themselves become a sealed scroll, almost impossible to decode. Even for men of John's day, the text could be fully deciphered only by servants of the Lamb. Many of these latter, though they could understand the message from John, preferred to transcribe it into simpler words. Their songs of triumph to their victorious King were transposed into many keys with different texts. Yet all their songs echoed the same jubilation over the same news.

To consider another version of the music, we may scan a letter from another prisoner, the letter to the Ephesians.[1] This message begins with a paean of praise to God whose power is immeasurably great and whose inheritance is inexhaustibly glorious (ch. 1:18, 19). From the foundation of the ages and through all the ages yet to come, this God has created all things and has retained the right to control and govern all things. He has at his disposal "every spiritual blessing in the heavenly places" (v. 3). He can bestow all wisdom and insight into the mystery of his will. He has a plan for the "fullness of time" which includes the unification and reconciliation of all things (vs. 9, 10). This God is none other than the Father of Jesus Christ.

In his eternal plan God has appointed Jesus as the ruler over all authorities, placing all things under his feet. He has "filled" him with the divine fullness, his austere authority and gracious love, his world-encompassing wisdom and all-reconciling power. In Jesus, God has chosen to accomplish all things "according to the counsel of his will" (v. 11).

The power-laden act in which this purpose has been accomplished is the resurrection of Jesus from the dead and his enthronement in heavenly places (v. 20). God has transformed the place of lowest humiliation into the place of highest exaltation. The scope of this transformation is not restricted to Jesus only, but includes all things in heaven and on earth. In Jesus and through him, God has chosen other men to be his sons (v. 5). In Jesus they receive forgiveness and holiness, power and grace. Through Jesus they are filled with all the fullness of God, for they become nothing less than the body of Christ (v. 23).

This fullness includes "all wisdom and insight" into the mysterious purposes of God for all creation (v. 9). It also includes a work to be done, a love-impelled participation in the unification of a shattered and broken creation. In Christ they are now "destined and appointed to live for the praise of his glory" (v. 12). By word and deed, they must proclaim the mystery of God's design and the progression of Jesus' triumph. What God is now doing in Jesus provides the context and the energy for every memory and hope, every thought and desire. Christ's servant lives at the point where God is manifesting and extending this redemptive program (ch. 2:10, 19–22).

By means of Jesus and his servants, God removes every vestige of curse from the destiny of a tormented humanity. He dispels the despair that feeds on the frustrations and calamities of history. He moves into every diseased situation with a proclamation of healing and an assurance of peace (ch. 1:7). No ruler on earth can evade or defeat the plan that Christ is carrying to completion. And no servant who knows and trusts that plan can respond otherwise than by gratitude, joy, love, and peace, placing all his affairs within this single grand design.[2]

This paraphrase of the opening paragraphs of Ephesians is by necessity condensed, but not so condensed as the original. The vocabulary of our summary must strike the modern reader as heavily theological, studded as it is with ponderous abstractions and sententious pronouncements. It is, however, no more inclusive in its assumptions and no more sweeping in its affirmations than the original. Whatever may be the reactions of the reader to the visions in Revelation and the beatitudes in Ephesians, he should remember that these are messages from prisoners who are risking life itself for these convictions. In their minds, they are words whose truth measures the distance between irretrievable ruin and indestructible hope.

Even their adversaries must admit that there has never been a claim more colossal in its audacity than such claims by the prisoners of the Lord Jesus Christ. Some of these claims may hold little meaning for many readers, whether ancient or modern. Some may appear entirely unjustified. For one reason or another, men have hesitated to accept their truth on the basis of these ancient documents alone. But these hesitations should not conceal the fact that these *are* the claims and that they are expressed *with complete confidence* not only by these two prisoners but by the New Testament as a whole. Whether it be trusted or not, their proclamation is as astounding as any that has ever been uttered.

If this seems an exaggeration, consider again the facts. Each of these prisoners was powerless, despised, and alone. Yet each announced that God had committed to him a secret hidden from the beginning of time. He insisted that others might grasp this secret only on the terms that God has laid down. He declared that the character of this secret had been unveiled in the crucifixion and resurrection of an obscure Galilean. He asserted, with unwavering conviction, that all future developments and all human situations lie within the span of this one mystery. What daring! What madness! How unprecedented! How offensive! Each prisoner knew that the Lamb had been slain by the powerful and the wise. He knew that the Lamb's followers received little but ridicule and resistance. (His imprisonment kept him from forgetting that.) He knew how intolerant it sounded to exclude unbelievers from this saving knowledge of the eternal purpose of God. He knew that others viewed the glorious dreams of the Church as pathetic megalomania. Nor was he himself immune to the arrows of doubt and the torment of aloneness. The stronger his faithfulness, the more it was tested by the tensions in the midst of which he lived. Yet he was qualified by the testing of his faith to write to other disciples who were caught in the same dilemmas.

Those who first read the letters of John or Paul stood on the same battle line between Christ's Kingdom and the world. In fact, if we had access to their minds, we should probably find that they were more distressed by the disaster befalling their leaders than were those leaders themselves. They had accepted the fact that the Lamb had suffered for them, but they had not yet fully understood that the disciple of this Messiah must suffer with him. They did not relish the way in which the cross continued to tear them loose from the world. They were unnerved by a gospel that made them the object of derision and ostracism. Their hearts needed a daily ration of iron, because what happened to their leaders might quickly happen to them.

The author of Ephesians is therefore impelled to urge his readers "not to lose heart over what I am suffering for you, which is your glory" (ch. 3:13). Realizing that such courage can be nourished only by a power not their own, he prays that God

"may grant you to be strengthened with might through his Spirit in the inner man, and that Christ may dwell in your hearts through faith; that you, being rooted and grounded in love, may have power to comprehend with all the saints what is the breadth and length and height and depth, and to know the love of Christ which surpasses knowledge, that you may be filled with all the fullness of God " (vs. 16-19).

This correspondence between the two prisoners and their friends serves to define the frontier that separated them from their contemporaries. On one side was a tiny group of men united by loyalty to the Lamb. Their tangible resources were quite inadequate for carrying on a global conflict. But their intangible resources were known to be adequate: God's spirit in the inner man, Christ's presence in the heart, a love that surpasses knowledge, a power to comprehend the heights and depths. Over against them as enemies stood everyone else, supported by tangible resources and made confident by the wisdom of the world.

The frontier had been created by a strange series of episodes woven together into a single story: the coming of Jesus, his baptism and temptations, his authority to forgive sins and heal sickness, his controversies with the rulers, his death at their hands. On the yonder side of the frontier men supposed that this was the story's end, however just or unjust the verdict of the judges. They accepted Jesus' death as, at the least, a mark of his weakness, a sure sign that he was unqualified to heal the world's malady.

Here lay the frontier, invisible save for the signs of visible conflict. Yet how could there be a meeting of minds across that invisible barrier? The very event which to those on one side signified God's invincible love signified to those on the other side an outrageous folly. How could the helpless prisoners expect their captors to accept the name of this Lord as the only name by which men may be saved? Did not the preaching of Christ crucified simply make the barrier higher? [3] Yes, that was the logic of the situation. Yet the servants of the Lamb were not free to change the core of their message. In the cross God invited all men to inherit the gift of unsearchable riches. And that invitation sufficed, on occasion, to attract even persecutors of Jesus' band across the frontier. The proclamation itself carried a strange power to overcome even its strongest adversaries.

Such a reversal of logic must prompt a question concerning how such power operated. What were the steps by which this transition took place? Perhaps it is unfortunate that we do not have full transcripts of their stories, giving in neat order the psychological stages by which the frontier was crossed. We suppose that each "displaced person" described his exodus in his own terms, and that there was no single stereotyped experience common to all. In so far as an underlying pattern existed, The Epistle to the Hebrews suggests the recurrent elements. First of all, a man heard "the word" as uttered by some delegate of Jesus, who asserted that his message had been authorized by God himself (ch. 2:3). This message was accompanied by various "signs and wonders," explained as works of the Holy Spirit dispensed according to God's mysterious will (v. 4). The word and works bespoke the assurance that God had crowned Jesus "with glory and honor because of the suffering of death, so that by the grace of God he might taste death for every one" (v. 9).

The right response to this message was "repentance from dead works" and confidence in the God who thus had revealed his purpose. Following this response the initiate received instruction in the "first principles of God's word" (chs. 5:12 to 6:5). He was taught the meaning of baptism and "the laying on of hands." He was told the implications of Jesus' death and of his own baptism as regarding "the resurrection of the dead, and eternal judgment." This, however, was more than could be communicated by words of the human teacher alone. Repentance and faith were accompanied by inner enlightenment and a taste of "the heavenly gift." Men "partook" of the Holy Spirit, and in doing this were enabled to apprehend "the goodness of the word of God and the powers of the age to come." This "hope" released in them an energy for work and a constraint to love (ch. 6:10).

This description in Hebrews is clearly intended to cover the various experiences of many disciples. It is too broad and too retrospective to indicate clearly how a single disciple may have thought and felt at each stage of transition. To focus attention upon the story of an individual pilgrim we might venture to particularize the story as follows:

A certain man had been going about his normal routine of sleeping and eating, working and playing. He had been absorbed in his own concerns, reacting to everyday events in terms of the mind of his natural associates. He had been acquainted with the average quota of joys and sorrows, hopes and disappointments. At times dimly conscious of the deep-seated malaise of men, usually he had been protected from despair by the cushioning rationalizations of his friends. One day a stranger appeared with an unprecedented message. He had been sent from God — or so he said — to tell the story of the most astounding transformation in human affairs. He called attention to various things that were happening, interpreting these occurrences as the work of God's hand, as surface manifestations of a deeply mysterious leavening. The leaven was nothing less than the leaven of a new age, a divine Kingdom, which had begun with the career of a Galilean named Jesus. Then the stranger told the story of Jesus' life, beginning with his baptism by John and ending with his death outside the walls of Jerusalem. The story had a momentum of its own that carried the narrator from one incident to another, from one teaching to another, from one conflict to a deeper one. It implied the innocence of Jesus and the guilt of his adversaries. It reached its climax in the apparent triumph of the adversaries, but, according to the narrator, an amazing miracle had followed this death. "God has made both Lord and Saviour this Jesus whom you crucified. It is the power of this Saviour that is now at work in your midst, accomplishing these strange things" (cf. Acts 2:22–36).

Such tidings must have provoked many questions, some of which would require conversations spread over many days. Among the initial reactions would be this: What does all this have to do with us? And the answer: You belong to those who crucified him. You too resist the Holy Spirit. You are also enslaved, like Jesus' adversaries, by ignorance and sin. Such an accusation would prick the conscience and arouse self-defense. Such folly, to believe in the resurrection of a criminal, and to suppose that a dead man actually saves the world! Can our ailing society be purged by such means?

But the witness would be ready for these objections. He met them everywhere, not least in his own soul. His answer would therefore have the ring of genuine sincerity: " So we also thought. And by thinking thus we were deceiving ourselves. But God made us see our blindness and reversed our faulty judgments. God has sent us as his witnesses. We know what he can do. Through us he is offering you health, forgiveness, and life. You too are invited into the Kingdom."

" What should I have to do? "

" Repent, so that your sins may be forgiven."

To this demand the natural response would be curiosity: What sins do you refer to, and what does repentance mean? Or the response would be resentment against the unjustified charges. Resistance took protean forms. But this resistance was in certain cases counteracted, through various processes, by an attraction, a contagious power, coursing through the apostle's words. The message began to exert a strange influence which penetrated the shell of self-defense. It uncovered a sense of guilt, it tugged at the subconscious awareness of a hollow existence, it fanned a submerged hope for freedom and release. It spoke to the inner caverns of the heart where ultimate questions had been confined and ultimate fears had been inhibited. The cross began to evoke the consciousness of a central need which had not yet been satisfied.

It began also to heal the wounds and dispel the isolation. " The Spirit of God moved upon the face of the waters. And God said, Let there be light: and there was light " (Gen. 1:2, 3; cf. II Cor. 4:6). A man repented because the word of the cross had broken through the shell surrounding his soul. And in the repentance he experienced a new release. Peace and joy began their mysterious encroachment. Day began to break.

We began the venture of visualizing the path a person might take in crossing the frontier of faith. But we must give up the undertaking, partly because the story in all its ramifications is too long, and partly because the imagination is too inert to weave together the countless threads into a single coherent strand. We have followed the pilgrim only to the threshold, and even in this we have compressed the journey into words that are unsatisfactory when sundered from the inner meanderings of the spirit. A full-length biography would be required to tell the whole story of any disciple's pilgrimage.[4] And no disciple is wholly satisfied with another's description of the same pilgrimage. The first Christians were strangely reticent in autobiography.

Each individual's story included a long path of preparation, with many episodes that at the time must have seemed quite fortuitous. The realignment of loyalties may have been gradual in some cases and rapid in others. The powers of attraction and repulsion may have worked largely in the subconscious minds of some and in the conscious thought of others. Yet, however winding the road that led to the boundary, hard and sober reflection must have been required to step across that boundary, because of the radical sternness of the demands and the dangers that discipleship entailed. These left little room for sentimentality or vague toying with general ideas. One who was destined to inherit the new life came to realize his destiny by many advances and many retreats. As he moved nearer to the line, his doubts and fears may well have increased. If Peter's story is any indication, the process of arriving at an understanding of the mission of Jesus covered months of the most diverse experiences. For him the path to faith was no smooth, short, straight line.

If the journey toward faith was too complicated to be fully charted, the journey in faith baffles the teller even more. The period of instruction lasted the rest of his life, and the range of instruction covered every situation he encountered. This was a period, too, that included and utilized every relationship to the community and to the unconverted. It included whatever happened to the soul of a man in and between the meetings for worship, in and between the observances of the Supper of the Lord. The circle of faith would gradually come to embrace all the thoughts, feelings, and duties of the pilgrim. What was taking place was the moving of the story of Christ from the outermost periphery of a man's life to the innermost center, where it became the " image " of the whole drama of the disciple's experience. The chain of episodes that marked the Master's faithful journey was paralleled by the episodes that marked the path of his followers — their call, baptism, temptations, struggles to do God's will, their confidence in trial and faithfulness unto the end.

En route, the story of faith incorporated the whole story of their life. Looking backward they could compress the time and select the crucial moments. En route the experience of conversion may have taken months of backward and forward movement. But in retrospect it was the radical and decisive nature of the transition that impressed the converts. En route, their understanding of the mysteries of God may have been very confused and partial, adequate only to meet the exigencies of the day. In retrospect, they were overwhelmed by the evidence that a gracious Providence had guided their steps. It was in retrospect that the assurances of the apostles would take on luminous meaning as they saw in their own lives the evidences of the love of Christ, the Spirit working in the heart, and the power that had been able, over and over again, to withstand the assaults of the enemy. It was in fresh and clear memory of what God had done through Christ that they apprehended the breadth and depth of man's story. It was thus that they became confident of having a sufficient clue to the mysteries of history.

Before leaving this subject, it may be well to recall the discussion of the preceding chapter. There it was noted that the difficulties in reading the scroll of history involve the reader in a double predicament: each action in history is relative, and each actor-interpreter is likewise relative. This double predicament is, of course, a single predicament with two sides. Action without an actor is inconceivable. Any happening becomes significant, becomes a historical event, only to the eyes of those who participate in it. The eyes are conditioned by the event; the event is conditioned by the eyes. The true meaning of history can be discerned only by specific interpreters viewing specific events in which they are themselves active. And that meaning must ultimately be affirmed or rejected by a single person viewing a single series of events. In all his relativity he must judge events in all their relativity, and at the same time both he and they must be freed from those limitations.

In announcing the " plan of the mystery," New Testament writers accept these terms and affirm that they have been fully met. In one act and word, God has overcome the double relativity without erasing it. He has acted in a localized event in such a way as to disclose the purpose of all events, so that in their response to this event men define their relationship to God, or, rather, he defines the only true relatedness to him. Furthermore, he has acted in this event in such a way as to correct the astigmatism of the eyes, so that mortal man, in the midst of his transiency and provincialisms, may comprehend the plot of the whole story. He has done this by drawing man into direct participation, the event of disclosure being thus consummated in the event of participation.

As a consequence of God's deed, both the human story and the human eye are altered. The story is altered, because after this event history can never be the same again. The eye is altered, because after this event the man who participates therein can never be the same again. Of this event two things may be said: The action altered alters all, and the eye altered alters all. God acts to fulfill a single purpose, but this act has this twofold consequence: a new age and a new man. And neither consequence is intelligible unless one considers its counterpart as well.

One succinct description of this divine deed appears in the letter to the Ephesians. God's purpose for creation he has set forth and

> "accomplished in Christ when he raised him from the dead and made him sit at his right hand in the heavenly places, far above all rule and authority and power and dominion, and above every name that is named, not only in this age but also in that which is to come; and he has put all things under his feet and has made him the head over all things" (ch. 1:20–22).

Plainly this declares that God has overcome the relativity of all historical events in this one historical event of the death-resurrection of Christ.

The passage just quoted is, however, excerpted from a context that is essential for its understanding. Immediately following it, the author declares that this event finds its true counterpart in the transformation of the historical participants:

> "*And you he made alive, when you were dead* through the trespasses and sins in which you once walked, following the course of this world, following the prince of the power of the air, the spirit that is now at work in the sons of disobedience. Among these we all once lived. . . . But God, . . . even when we were dead through our trespasses, *made us alive together with Christ* . . . and *raised us up with him, and made us sit with him in the heavenly places in Christ Jesus*" (ch. 2:1–6).

In the terms that we have been using this means that God has overcome the problem of the relativity of the historical actor. And this victory is accomplished *in the same event* in which he overcame the problem of the relativity of the historical event. "You he made alive [with Christ], when you were dead." These two "resurrections" and these two "deaths" are inseparable aspects of a single purpose, although presumably they do not take place simultaneously, as men reckon time. The act of raising Christ from the dead is one step in a divine intention that is not complete until disciples are made alive with him. It is in the disciples that an event that was begun in Christ finds its wholeness. The primacy and priority belong to the act of raising Christ. It is this act that is the content of the gospel, a message that comes from God, though couched in the fragile, variable words of men. Whenever this message is accepted in faith, the act of raising Christ is continued in the act of raising the believer. The Lamb is worthy to open the scroll because he is the central figure in this decisive double event. And because he is central here, he constitutes for the disciple the central figure in every situation that he may face. The meaning of each episode, as well as the meaning of the whole drama, is rightly determined only by reference to the continuing work of this man whom God has made the pattern of a new humanity.

As we reconsider the material presented thus far in this book, the broad outlines of our task may become clear. We have noted the riddles that arise when men ask questions about the beginning, the course, and the end of history. The posing of ultimate questions seems to produce insuperable obstacles to the answering of those same questions. Yet in the New Testament (as illustrated by Revelation and Ephesians) we meet men who are placed in a position where it is impossible to ignore such questions. More than this, we meet men who testify that the usual obstacles have been surmounted through a unique activity of God. Ordinarily one might suppose that for these prisoners the riddles would be peculiarly frustrating. Yet the extremity of their predicament, instead of resulting in frustration, contributed to a sure confidence in what lies " beyond the veil." A frontier had been crossed where fear was replaced by courage and ignorance was supplanted by adequate understanding of God's design. The character of this frontier constitutes the key to understanding that design as they understood it. How, then, may we proceed to explore that invisible boundary line?

We must begin with the double event that transpires on the frontier itself: the death-resurrection of Jesus and the death-resurrection of his disciple. Beginning here, we must explore the sequence of episodes in the story of Jesus, looking backward from the frontier to retrace the important stages in his journey and looking forward toward the completion of his mission among men. Beginning at the same point, we must explore the sequence of episodes in the story of the disciple, looking backward along the path over which he arrived at the gate and looking forward along the path set before him by his new leader. The evidence for both the journeys comes to us from the firsthand narratives of the disciples, who stand, as it were, on this side of the boundary. That evidence, according to their confession, is more trustworthy by virtue of the fact that they are running the same race that Jesus had run. By its intrinsic nature, that evidence demands at least two things of the investigator. In the first place, he must grasp the interrelationship at every point between the story of Jesus and the story of the disciple. And in the second place, he must give full weight to the pivotal events, measuring what happened in those events by contrasting the human situation before and after they took place.

These two obligations suggest the structure of succeeding chapters. The character of God's eternal purpose is dealt with in three major sections. The first of these describes the turning point where Jesus himself initiates a new beginning: the beginning of the gospel (Chapter 3); the beginning of new life for the disciple (Chapter 4); and the beginning of a new age for all mankind (Chapters 5, 6). In each of these areas, the significance of the turning point is measured by contrasting the periods before and after death-resurrection. The second major section discusses the end of Jesus' mission, the coming event that defines the promise of the gospel (Chapter 7), the goal of the disciple's pilgrimage (Chapter 8), and the harvest of all creation (Chapter 9). The third major section describes the path which disciples follow en route to this new end. Here we seek to understand how Jesus determines the duties and provides the energy for their journey, how his presence in each successive situation effectively redeems that situation, how each step of the disciple manifests the power of that Kingdom over which Jesus rules (Chapters 10, 11, 12).

The intrinsic nature of the New Testament confession adds one further requirement if the student is to comprehend its truth. Over and over again, his messengers reiterate the conviction that God shares his wisdom and power only with men who " repent, and believe in the gospel." Except to those who share the faith of the Church, the message of the gospel must appear to be nonsense. What shall we do about this warning? Thus far in these first two chapters, the writer has maintained a pose of at least a tentative neutrality, viewing the claims of faith from the historian's balcony. Now he is faced with the warning that he cannot cross the frontier unless he becomes, tentatively at least, an immigrant to the new city. He cannot apprehend the mysteries of faith without surrendering to that faith. Moreover, what holds true for the narrator holds true also for the reader. We can perhaps assess the *scope* of the Christian claims from a distant mountaintop. But according to Christian witnesses, we can apprehend the *truth* of those claims only along the trail.

What, then, shall the narrator do? To be a good historian he must enter fully into the thoughts and feelings, the memories and hopes of the characters in his story. Otherwise he cannot tell their story accurately. Yet to enter the territory of faith he must himself cross the frontier, and that means that he will cease to speak as a disinterested observer and will speak as a believing witness. It may be that now his report will seem to be prejudiced or meaningless to those on the yonder side of the frontier. However the reader may solve this dilemma, the author has chosen to accept the conditions laid down by the nature of the territory to be explored. As far as possible he will enter into the perspectives of the New Testament witnesses, seeking to grasp the inner and outer dimensions of their experience, as seen from within. Not content simply to hear *what* they said, he will listen for what lies behind the words, that is, what had happened to them to make them want to say what they said. He will consider himself a member of the apostles' own community and occasionally speak in the first person plural, even at the risk of alienating the reader who insists on preserving a fancied objectivity.

This procedure involves other risks. To use an ancient language as his own makes any modern writer sound affected and stilted. Then too he may use the assertions of faith as means of enhancing his own superiority or to ward off legitimate criticism. Indeed, he may falsify the testimony at the very moment when he is most confident of his affinity with the ancient witnesses. Nevertheless, these risks must be taken, because the alternate path leads away from any genuine apprehension of the truth.

PART
II

THE ETERNAL PURPOSE

CHAPTER

3

THE BEGINNING OF THE GOSPEL

JESUS is Lord " (I Cor. 12:3). So runs the initial confession of his disciples, in its simplest terms. Yet these simple terms carry far-reaching implications. The term " Lord," for instance, points in two directions: It affirms at once the master status of Jesus and the slave status of the confessor. The confessor testifies that he has been bought with a price and is now the possession of this Lord. To Jesus belongs final and exclusive sovereignty over the slave's existence. Henceforth his work is done " *in* the Lord," his recompense is expected " *from* the Lord," all gifts from God come " *through* the Lord," all hopes depend upon the coming manifestation " *of* the Lord."

Moreover, the confession, " Jesus is Lord," is the joint affirmation of a band of slaves, a community with various assignments " but the same Lord " (v. 4). The unity of the Church is constituted by the fact that it serves this one Lord. Its confession is a seal of this unity. Where the sovereignty of Jesus is actualized in word and deed, there is his body, the Church.

More than this, for this community the title " Lord " implies a very high status. Jesus holds power over all creation, for he is the Lord *of Lords*. Through him all things exist (ch. 8:6). Under him all things have been subjected. To him every knee will bow, " in heaven and on earth and under the earth " (Phil. 2:10). Jesus is Lord because God has made him such, because he is now our Lord, and because he will be manifested as the ruler of all the powers in heaven and on earth.[5]

The affirmation of Lordship in this full meaning of the term is first uttered after the death of Jesus. It is this " Jesus . . . , whom you crucified" (Acts 4:10; 5:30) whom "God has made . . . both Lord and Christ." In this event of death-resurrection Jesus becomes the "first-born" of a new humanity. In him God begins the work of renewing creation. To him is given the power to mediate eternal life to others. In the story of Jesus' exaltation the disciple discerns the greatest revolution in the history of God's dealings with his people.

To comprehend the scope and strategy of this revolution, however, the disciple must keep in mind the episodes in Jesus' life preceding the cross. For it was not an unknown, anonymous figure who had died; it was "this Jesus whom you crucified." The crucifixion was not an incidental or accidental circumstance; nor was the exaltation merely a particular expression of a general law. The significance of both derived from the previous ministry of Jesus. The death had been foreshadowed throughout that ministry at every point of tension between Jesus and the world. His humiliation on the cross was the terminus of a line of *descent* that began with the earliest recorded decision of Jesus. Every subsequent decision pointed forward and downward toward that lowest point. God's exaltation of "this Jesus," therefore, was a special disclosure of what his mission had been, a verdict concerning all that Jesus had said and done. Conversely, the cross was the terminus of a line of *ascendancy* on the part of the spiritual powers that rule the world.[6] It marked the visible triumph of these powers, the fruit of efforts that began in the wilderness and ended on Calvary. Rebellion against God, as manifested in resistance to Jesus, moved forward in constant accelerando and crescendo. God's exaltation of Jesus was therefore a specific judgment upon the sinfulness and futility of the powers that had opposed Jesus. To understand the significance of Jesus' death and resurrection, then, we must recall the story of the career that found its consummation in this single event, where the lowest point on the line of descent was revealed as constituting, in God's eyes, the point of highest exaltation, and where the pinnacle of the world's rebellion was shown to be nothing less than its final self-judgment.

A. Before the Cross

The disciples who had known Jesus before the cross have transmitted their memories in the writings now found in the New Testament. But before these memories were committed to writing, they were transfigured by the light thrown backward from the cross. The writings are all confessions of faith ín Jesus, confessions that were made possible only by God's revelation of him as Lord. Only his exaltation could make God's purpose in the line of descent clear. This did not mean, however, that these memories of earlier events were either obliterated or falsified, because the true meaning of the resurrection could be grasped only if the story of previous happenings were preserved. This story therefore remained an integral part of the witness of believers. Let us, then, review this epic of the Messiah's descent.

Where does the story have its beginning? The answer depends upon the exact reference of the word "beginning." If one asks concerning the date when Jesus' victory was first declared openly, the answer must be the moment of revelation when the risen Lord appeared to his disciples. One may, however, have in mind the time when God had begun to prepare the disciples for this disclosure; in this case, the story should start with the first public preaching of John the Baptist and of Jesus (Mark 1:1-15). On the other hand, the questioner may have in mind the personal consciousness of Jesus: When did he first become aware of a distinctive mission? When did he first decide to be loyal to it? In the nature of the case, this question is hard to answer because the Gospels preserve the disciples' memories rather than those of Jesus himself. According to the Gospel of Mark, the conscious acceptance of his mission accompanied his baptism in the Jordan. An earlier episode is given by Luke in his account of Jesus' visit to the Temple as a boy (Luke 2:49). Another vista is suggested if one inquires as to when God began to prepare Jesus for his later mission, and when the redemptive purpose became visible in earthly happenings. An answer to such an inquiry is furnished by the birth narratives in Matthew and Luke, with their imaginative interpretations of earlier events in the light of later developments. If one is concerned with ultimate beginnings, of course, in the preparation of mankind for Jesus' work, the story must include the divine pledges made to the prophets and the fathers (Heb. 1:1 f.; I Peter 1:10 f.). The line does not, however, start even here. Because in Jesus God's eternal intention is disclosed, the ultimate commencement for the whole story is the dawn of creation (John 1:1-4).

One may earnestly debate the merits of these diverse ways of asking and answering the question, but in the process of debate he moves quickly beyond the ambit of New Testament concern. The first Christians did not try to fix a single starting point on the time line of world history. They were engaged in proclaiming God's eternal purpose, as that purpose had been unveiled to them in the life and death of the Messiah. In the Messiah's story they discerned the genuine epitome of creation's story, and were enabled to trace the pattern of God's redemptive activity " from the foundation of the world."

A succinct sketch of this pattern is given by the apostle Paul in his letter to the Philippian church (Phil. 2:1-12),[7] a passage in which Paul is clearly dependent upon a common tradition. In this passage, the movement of redemption has a constant direction — forward and downward. The span of Jesus' life was a span of humbling himself, of becoming so obedient as to die the death of the cross. The first decisive act was the self-denial in " taking the form of a servant." This initial step cannot be limited to a single point of time, because it included all the consequences of that step. Each later step moves forward toward lower depths of humiliation, toward positions of less prestige and power, less wisdom and popularity. The story as a whole is the dynamic progression in humble love of the perfect servant, the entire mission being embraced within the expression " the form of a servant." The man, therefore, who grasps the meaning of the whole line of descent can thereby sense the truth that is hidden in each episode of the story.

He was " born in the likeness of men," subjecting himself fully to the conditions of ordinary human existence. He was " born of woman " (Gal. 4:4), appearing as a helpless babe in a lowly family amidst the simplest surroundings. This form of humiliation was genuine; to his first associates there was nothing artificial or synthetic about his humanity. After his death, believers might affirm that he had been " rich," yet this affirmation of wealth underscored the fact that " for your sake he became poor" (II Cor. 8:9). Unless the poverty were authentic, the act of humiliation could not have been " for your sake "; to save his brothers, he must be made like them " in every respect " (Heb. 2:17). Just as death came by man, with its consequence that all men die, so also the resurrection of the dead comes " *by man,*" with its consequence that " in Christ shall all be made alive " (I Cor. 15:21, 22). The promise of new life for humanity is thus predicated upon the full humanity of him by whom the new life comes.

Jesus was born as a son of Abraham. As a son, he was an heir of the covenants that God had made with Abraham. He worshiped the living God of Abraham, Isaac, and Jacob. He trusted in the promises that God had made: "In thee shall all the families of the earth be blessed." He looked forward to the time when men shall "sit at table with Abraham, Isaac, and Jacob, in the kingdom of heaven" (Matt. 8:11, 12). He was a trustee of the mission to which God had called Abraham. Since his humility and obedience were in direct line with the vocation of "my servant" Israel, his vindication in the resurrection was a fulfillment of the promise that God had given to the fathers.

Jesus was born "under the law" (Gal. 4:4), under the enduring agreement that God had established with Moses at the exodus of Israel from Egypt. In keeping with the law he was circumcised; he was nurtured at home and synagogue in the traditions so zealously guarded by Israel's teachers. He learned to celebrate the festivals, to repeat the Shema, to recount the stories of God's mighty acts, to pray and to praise in the idiom and manner of his people. With the contrite poor of many generations, he oriented his daily activity around the commands and promises of the Torah and the Psalms. This full identification with "my servant" Israel meant for Jesus an intimate sympathy with the sorrows of that servant. The "back" of that servant had been scarred by many lashes. For generations, Israel had suffered defeat, frustration, heartbreak. The burden of tragedy had rested most heavily on those humble folk who trusted most fully in God's power to redeem his people. With their agonies and their trustful patience Jesus aligned himself. With them he confidently awaited the Day when God would establish his Kingdom and bring his sons within its borders.

Thus was the carpenter's son prepared for that day when a prophet appeared in the wilderness, announcing the imminent arrival of the long-delayed day of redemption. Here sounded the voice of one who was preparing in the desert "a highway for our God." Here was Elijah, sent forth at the end of the old age to herald the new (Mark 9:13). At last God's justice would spring forth in triumph, terrible but glorious. He would winnow the chaff and burn it. Even then, the ax was laid to the root of the trees (Luke 3:1-14). So near was the final judgment of God; so near was the final decision by men.

"What then shall we do?" was the question men asked of John. And the answer was clear and sharp: "Repent." No one was exempt from this demand, nor was any cranny of man's life immune to its thrust. Repentance must be wholehearted; it must be immediate; it must produce fruits. The reality of repentance is, in God's eyes, the only proof that a man is a true son of Abraham (v. 8). In other words, the only gate into the long-expected Kingdom is to be found at the point where God's final judgment is greeted by man's full repentance.

That was the greeting given by Jesus to John's call. In the message of John, Jesus detected the authentic voice of the Most High (Luke 7:24-28; Mark 11:27-33). And his response was wholehearted obedience to it. By subjecting himself to John's authority, he subjected himself to God's demands. And in this unfettered act of genuine meekness he received a divine approval of that act. He detected God's seal of blessedness and heard God's mandate to join in the work of preparing the nation for the new age. He must go to " the lost sheep of the house of Israel " (Matt. 15:24). The moment of repentance was the moment of commission; it was also the moment when the Holy Spirit began to mediate to him and through him the powers of the coming age (Mark, ch. 1). The appearance of these powers instigated greater temptations, which in turn called for a deeper meekness. The tempter could be overcome at each step only by the power of lowly obedience. Each victory meant, in earthly terms, going lower down. But the line of descent in historical action secretly pointed to the line of ascent in divine glory.

It was through such meekness that God gave to Jesus power to see what was concealed from others by their lack of full repentance. In the healing of the sick, the freeing of captives, the forgiveness of sins, he discovered that the joys of the new age were already superseding the agonies of the old age (Luke 7:18-23). He detected in the exodus of demons the entrance of a higher power into the demons' parish. Satan had fallen from heaven and these events on earth were the results of his eviction (ch. 10:17-19). The new day was dawning in a way wholly unexpected; its powerful signs were discernible even in the midst of men who did not recognize them. These were momentous events, marks of a deliverance that prophets and kings had long hoped to see. Here was good news indeed, far more startling and far more emancipating than the message of John: " The law and the prophets were until John; since then the good news of the kingdom of God is preached " (ch. 16:16). Yet this blessedness was accessible only to the meek and visible only to the penitent.

In Jesus himself this meekness was tested in a dramatic sequence of trials of which the story of his wilderness wrestling with Satan was both a forecast and epitome. One form in which Jesus' faith was put to the test was the fate that befell John the Baptist. Jesus never ceased to look upon John as a prophet sent from God, as the Elijah of the new Day who would prepare Israel for the final judgment. Jesus was convinced that John had been faithful to God's commission. Yet what had happened to him? He had been arrested, imprisoned, and executed (Mark 6:14-29). This disaster must have plunged many of John's disciples into deeper despair. They had scattered, for all of them, including Jesus, were as worthy of Herod's wrath as was John. And with this execution and dispersion John's message of a coming Day of Justice must have appeared to his contemporaries as hopelessly discredited.

Not to Jesus, however. He humbled himself to accept John's death and the likelihood of a similar fate for himself. The death of his revered teacher was not a brake but a spur to greater activity. He began to preach the good news even more publicly and provocatively than John had. Into the cities where Herod's power was greatest he carried his incendiary message, most of his work being done within a few miles of Herod's capital. His humble obedience seems to have driven out any trace of defensiveness, fear, and self-pity (Luke 14:31-33). This was the work to which God had called him. The death of John strengthened rather than weakened his faith in the *good* news. The danger in which he himself stood merely confirmed the power of the new age over all the fears of the old.

The citizens of Galilee, however, were astounded that he should press this mission at such a place and time. How anomalous the message under those circumstances! For Jesus, in the face of such a defeat, announced that God was using that defeat to inaugurate his reign. God has opened his eternal city to publicans and harlots, centurions and Zealots. He invites them all, without regard to their previous behavior. God does not wait until they have met what *they* consider to be the necessary conditions and specifications for a new age; he simply brings his Kingdom near to them now, transforming the situation in which they stand, revolutionizing all their conceptions of present actuality or future possibility (vs. 15-24). Life in his Kingdom is a free gift, infinitely out of proportion to any of the earthly goods that men may seek or possess. Yes, one must humble himself to accept such a message as true, to accept such a messenger as coming from God, to accept a manner of life that poses such an ultimate conflict with the present order.

That is precisely the initial requirement which God has demanded through Jesus: " Repent, for the kingdom of heaven is at hand " (Matt. 4:17). The Kingdom is the highest good, the fulfillment of God's promises to all generations. It is so good that it counterbalances all risks, allays all anxieties, heals all wounds, cancels all sins, and provides the highest blessedness to the poor, the hungry, the homeless, and the outcast. Yet the gateway to this blessedness is extremely narrow, so narrow in fact that not many are willing to venture into it. The repentance that Jesus required is no simple matter, for it touches the nerve center of all attitudes and actions. Let us glance over the range of staccato commands that indicate what the act of penitence implied.

We begin with the imperative of self-denial which Jesus directed to all who heard him: " If any man would come after me, let him deny himself and take up his cross and follow me " (Mark 8:34). Akin to this command are several axioms that punctuate the whole teaching of Jesus: [8]

" So the last will be first,
    And the first last "
        (Matt. 20:16; 19:30; Luke 13:30; Mark 10:31).

" Whoever exalts himself shall be humbled,
    And whoever humbles himself shall be exalted "
        (Matt. 23:12; 18:4; Luke 14:11; 18:14).

" For whoever would save his life will lose it;
    And whoever loses his life for my sake and the gospel's will save it "
        (Mark 8:35).

These same alternatives, so sharp and clear and simple, are presented also in pictures. There are the twin stories of a carpenter building a tower and a king making war (Luke 14:28–33), neither of them able to complete his enterprise because he had not counted the cost in advance. The same will be the fate of the disciple who at the outset does not renounce all his possessions. Or the picture of the Pharisee and the publican is thrown on the screen of one's mind (ch. 18:9–14). Both pray in the Temple, and in their prayers they reveal opposite attitudes toward God, toward self, and toward others. Here the possession that must be renounced is the good opinion of oneself, the prestige of piety and orthodoxy and decency.

Jesus also stated the implications of humility in terms of forgiveness. Here again the commands admit no exceptions or amendments: " Love your enemies, do good to those who hate you, . . . pray for those who abuse you. . . . Give to every one who begs from you. . . . Judge not, . . . condemn not, . . . forgive " (ch. 6:27-38). Again one hears from Jesus the axioms that correspond to these commands:

> " With the judgment you pronounce you will be judged,
>   And the measure you give will be the measure you get "
>   (Matt. 7:2).

> " If you forgive men their trespasses,
>   Your heavenly Father also will forgive you;
> But if you do not forgive men their trespasses,
>   Neither will your Father forgive your trespasses " (ch. 6:14, 15).

These axioms and commands are communicated in story form as well. Consider the parable of the steward, who was graciously forgiven a huge debt, but who stubbornly refused to forgive a trivial obligation. His lord delivered him to the jailers. " So also my heavenly Father will do to every one of you, if you do not forgive your brother from your heart " (Matt. 18:23-35). In this instance as in that of self-denial the necessity of forgiveness is equally vigorous, whatever may be the form in which indebtedness has made one man superior to another.

Another corollary of repentance is obedient love. True humility is loving and true love is humble. The central command of all is this: " You shall love the Lord your God with all your heart, . . . and with all your strength, and with all your mind " (Luke 10:27). This command is understood in its rigor when a fundamental truth is related to it:

> " No one can serve two masters;
>   For either he will hate the one and love the other,
>   Or he will be devoted to the one and despise the other.
>   You cannot serve God and mammon " (Matt. 6:24).

The image of humble obedience is depicted in the story of the servant plowing in the field, who, after his day's work, serves supper to his master (Luke 17:7-10). The same alternatives are sharply outlined in the parable of the two sons, both assigned a task by their father (Matt. 21:28-32).

The son who obeys God with his whole heart will seek first God's Kingdom. He will watch night and day for its coming. He will store all his treasures where no moths can devour them and no rust corrode them. This, it may be added, is no pious advice or vague sentiment, but the sternest demand, and a demand that is reinforced by inexorable logic:

"Where your treasure is, there will your heart be also" (Matt. 6:21).

"No one who puts his hand to the plow and looks back is fit for the kingdom of God" (Luke 9:62).

The disciple will remember Lot's wife (ch. 17:32). He will recall the pictures of the sentry on duty, the virgins waiting for the bridal proces-sion, the householder watching for the thief, and the stewards readying themselves for the master's arrival (Matt. 24:45 to 25:30; Mark 13:33-37). His heart will have the resilience of expectant patience, of eager soberness, of faithful hope.

The demand for instant and unwearying alertness is linked closely to injunctions of complete confidence and trust. The disciple must be-lieve with his whole heart in the coming of that Kingdom which he seeks with his whole heart. He is enjoined to "ask, . . . seek, . . . knock" (Matt. 7:7-11). Knowing that it is God's gracious intent to give him the Kingdom, he must have faith, even though it be as small as a mustard seed. Such knowledge and such faith are grounded in the truth that "all things are possible with God" (Mark 10:27); and that God wills only the good for his children. The disciple remembers that even the hairs of his head are numbered (Matt. 10:29-33), no sparrow dies without the Father's concern, and that the care of God is much more trustworthy than the affection of a father whose son asks him for a loaf of bread or a fish (ch. 7:9-11).

The integrity of the Father's love must be reflected in the integrity of the son's response. This integrity requires not only that every deed be exactly equivalent to a pure intent and that every word be proportioned to an undivided will. It even requires that the disciple himself be un-aware of any good deeds he may do. In giving alms he must keep his gift secret even from himself, his right hand not aware of what his left hand is doing (ch. 6:1-18). In fasting his face must be radiant with unaffected joy. His inward relationship to God must be kept hidden from all. The basis for such perfect integrity, such full obedience, is expressed in such axioms as these:

" No one is good but God " (Mark 10:18).

" Each tree is known by its own fruit " (Luke 6:44).

Even more striking is the image of humble goodness which is sketched in the parable of the final judgment, where the reward of infinite blessedness is given to those who are unaware of any merit of their own (ch. 25:31–46). In this picture we glimpse again the publicans who continue to pray at every moment, " God, be merciful to me a sinner! " Here again we note the penetration of the " downward movement " which constitutes the way to life:

" Whoever would be great among you must be your servant,
    And whoever would be first among you must be slave of all"
        (Mark 10:43, 44).

Such is an all too brief résumé of the cardinal demands of Jesus. Welcomed into the Kingdom are the poor, the hungry, the meek, the sorrowful, the merciful, the pure in heart, the ostracized, the burden bearers. Excluded by their own choice are the rich, the complacent, the haughty, the secure, the double-minded, the superior, the self-righteous (Matt. 5:3–10; Luke 6:20–26). The disciple of the Kingdom sees himself standing before God for a final accounting. Here and now he renounces all that he has, he forgives all debtors all their debts, he responds in a single allegiance to one Lord, he forgets to compare himself with other men, being aware of his sin and unaware of his righteousness. He knows that he stands at the threshold of eternal life. Here and now he seeks for that pearl of great price, he hopes for God's gift and confidently awaits it, plowing steadily down the furrow with eyes fixed on the joyful end.

Nor can he persist in this course with any easy or transient sentimentality. The heavenly hope is associated with an earthly prospect that enforces soberness. For he is moving downward along the path of repentance which John had opened, the end of which in John's case was martyrdom. And he is following in Jesus a teacher who warns him constantly of the cost of following this path.

As one listens again to the words of Jesus in this setting of historical realism, one senses a mysterious depth to which no description can do justice. He may call such teachings *absolute,* because they exert an exclusive and unlimited claim upon his will. He may call them *radical,* because they are so unconventional and rigorous, because they probe so deeply into the roots of his being. He may call them *ultimate,* because he cannot discern any horizon of duty lying beyond them, because he cannot move beyond them until he has succeeded in fulfilling them. The teachings themselves encourage lowliness of spirit, because in all honesty a man can hardly claim to have obeyed them fully. Should he make such a claim, he merely proves that he has misunderstood and disobeyed them all. Another word one may apply to such teachings is the word *integral.* Jesus' commands are integral (1) in the sense of constituting God's single and whole requirement, (2) in the sense of engaging the response of the entire man, his heart and all its fruits, (3) in the sense of coping with all conceivable conditions and situations a man may face, and (4) in the sense of applying equally to all men in view of their common position before God. In listening to Jesus a man becomes aware of a lack of integrity in himself. He does not now love God with his whole heart, but tries constantly to serve two masters. Yet Jesus' word opens the way to a true integrity, to an undivided mind and eye and heart.

Whatever words one may choose to characterize Jesus' message, one cannot ignore the fact that, to Jesus, God's command places a single, all-inclusive, inexorable choice before those who seek to enter the new age of glorious joy. Unless a man in his full integrity repents for his lack of integrity, he will not see that Kingdom. Yet, paradoxically, it is God's *gift* that thus both sets the task and opens the door to its fulfillment. God's Kingdom is already at work, powerfully turning and overturning men's lives. It is God who gives one the new possibility of integrity and wholeness, by his Spirit's expelling the demons that torture men's souls. His blessedness is not only *a* possibility now confronting men; it is *the* possibility, the only true possibility. Jesus is the messenger who announces that God has willed to give men the Kingdom. And the announcement of the gift sets the task for men. God's gracious activity manward demands man's activity Godward. The integral response of repentance is a person's fullhearted expression of gratitude and trust.

Now, perhaps, we can review the varying ways in which men reacted to Jesus' proclamation, not forgetting the concrete historical situation to which that proclamation was addressed. For most of his hearers, the announcement of such a gift was too good to be true, coming in the midst of irreconcilable hostilities and indescribable frustrations. For most of them, too, the task was too burdensome to be accepted. " If these are the requirements, then who can be saved? " Both the gift and the task prompted skepticism, ridicule, fear, and resistance. Men were attracted and repelled, baffled and offended. Inevitably the work of Jesus provoked questions. Perhaps these questions would not have been so troublesome had not Jesus spoken with clarion authority. Had this conception of the gift and the task been the idle opinion of a stray fanatic, had the news been announced with the hesitant " perhaps " of an irresponsible meddler, they might have been quickly dismissed. But they were spoken with prophetic assurance as a directive coming from heaven.

" Who, then, is this? "

" A carpenter from Nazareth." . . . " The son of Joseph and Mary."

" But why is this carpenter so foolhardy as to announce the arrival of God's blessed Kingdom in the midst of this cursed world? Why is he so insistent that we must, if we are to receive this gift, renounce everything else? "

" He is a prophet, like John the Baptist or Elijah."

" Then where are his credentials? How may we know that he is not a false prophet? What can vouch for him? "

" His works."

" But these works may be due to the fact that he is an instrument of Satan."

The Gospels make it clear that Jesus spoke with an authority not his own. It is also clear that the nature of this authority baffled his listeners. Instead of presenting the expected credentials, he merely pointed to the work of John the Baptist. He announced that he had seen Satan fallen from heaven, yet they could not see what he saw or hear what he heard. The seed that had been planted was germinating secretly; the leaven that was at work was working silently. With such credentials they were unsatisfied. Why should they trust his guidance on the crucial issues of salvation or damnation? Some there were who sensed the genuineness of his commission and who followed him. Yet they too were unable to capture in titles or credentials the hidden impulse lying behind his work.

Such hiddenness seems to have been intrinsic to the Kingdom he announced and to the character of his work. At least Jesus accepted this ambiguity as essential to his mission. He was more concerned with men's failure to apprehend the " downward movement " of his ministry than with their failure to grant him appropriate titles. In fact, there remained about his status the same quality of hidden mystery that characterized the Kingdom which he proclaimed. Seldom if ever did he give a straightforward answer to their questions about his credentials. He seems to have desired to avoid titles, to have been unwilling to have his authority reduced to honorific terms. At times his answers to their questions seemed evasive and intentionally equivocal. The question of his status could not be avoided, but the question was usually raised on a level where it could not be answered. He did not repudiate the terms that men applied to him, but neither did he approve them as satisfactory. When his followers ventured their own stumbling guesses, he tried to suggest that those opinions were not yet understood in a way appropriate to the level of his descent. " The Son of man must suffer " (Mark 8:31–33).

What is clear in the gospel records, however, is the concentration of Jesus upon matters of response rather than upon matters of rank. Of first importance was God's act in bringing the Kingdom into their midst; of first importance was their response to it. Acceptance of an exalted position did not in Jesus' mind precede faith in the Kingdom; rather, faith in God's goodness and faithful obedience to God's commands opened the way to a sharing in Jesus' mission and his authority. Acceptance of his message and appropriate action was the only form of recognition that Jesus sought. Some called him Lord without doing his will. These he rebuked. Others were genuinely loyal, but were unable to put into words the grounds of the Master's authority. They humbly accepted both the inestimable gift and the inexorable task. They simply gave their silent witness: " Once I was blind; now I can see."

Those who were drawn into the Kingdom's orbit through Jesus' work comprised a motley company: lepers, harlots, beggars, Pharisees, publicans, soldiers, Zealots, fishermen, housewives, the lame, the palsied, the blind. Accepting God's Kingdom as the focal point for present decisions, they repented and were healed. And each act of penitence produced a new situation in which more thorough penitence was required. Each act of mercy led to new occasions for more thorough-going forgiveness. Each self-denial led farther down the road where more complete renunciation was required. Jesus made it clear that no one moves into a position where he becomes exempt from God's mandates, and that no situation lies beyond the realm where God's will is sovereign. He made it clear that the command is inexorable precisely at the point where it appears most difficult, at the point where the boundaries of God's Realm are being extended over rebel territory. Love is not true obedience to God if it is limited to those who love one in return. Only in love for the enemy, yes, for the greatest enemy, does one become a son of God. It is where man's roots are sunk most deeply into the soil of the old age, that repentance and faith serve to transplant those roots into the soil of the new era. Where obedience appears to be most impossible, there God's power appears. There the disciple is taught that with God all things are possible.

It was in this area where both the gift and the task appeared to be impossible that Jesus' authority was " proved." It was here too that his own personal obedience was tested to the uttermost. Because he was obedient, his work propelled him into positions of greater and greater temptation and danger. Seeking God's Kingdom first and loving God with his whole heart, he found antagonism mounting, even among those who professed to be disciples. In hostility to him, those who had been enemies submerged their usual hostility to one another. Romans and Jews, Pharisees and Sadducees, Zealots and conservative businessmen, all united to protect their conflicting interests from this common threat.

The Nazareth carpenter, however, detected in these tensions the signs, not of God's weakness, but of his power. His faith in the new age mounted in proportion to the apparent folly of that faith. His obedience to God's mandates surmounted the apparent impossibility of fulfilling those mandates. He suffered because he was obedient, and the more he suffered the more he learned obedience by what he suffered. As the fateful drama moved to its climax, so did his demonstration of the Way that he had taught: humility, forgiveness, trust, expectancy, unconscious goodness, self-denial, gratitude, and joy.

As he moved through the gathering storm, his concern was not so much for himself as for others. In fact, he used all the dangers he faced as scenes for instructing his disciples concerning what lay ahead of them, trying to prepare them to continue his own work. Their blindness was not wholly healed, for they could not discern in this path of rejection the mark of God's grace and the road to glory. Nor did this training, in the first instance at least, prove to be successful. All along he sought to make the odds clear: "Whoever of you does not renounce all that he has cannot be my disciple." And all along he showed them where this road led. Yet along that road many wavered, begging to be excused for one reason or another. Each defection made clear that the disciple's obedience was not total, his humility not deep enough to undermine the world's standards of greatness. But there were eleven who endured in his company, down even to the last meal with him, and to the struggle in the Garden. These stoutly protested their ability to see the thing through. The Master utilized his last few hours with them in the effort to prepare them for what lay ahead, to arm them for the coming test. But when Jesus was arrested, they all fled. There was one, to be sure, who followed the captors into the judgment hall, but here even this man denied that he had ever known the captive.

The servant of God, and he alone, "became obedient unto death, even death on a cross" (Phil. 2:8). He was alone. Others stood around, but the usual channels of communication were closed. No longer could he convey to them in words the mystery of God's Kingdom, present in their midst. His mission to the lost sheep of the house of Israel was terminated by those whom he came to save. Extended to all, the invitation had been rejected by all. No one was able, apart from the helpless captive, to gauge the priceless value of God's gift or the austere implications of God's demand.

The struggle that took place in Jesus' heart cannot be put into words. In the idiom of their day, those who later came to apprehend the terror and splendor of that hour described it as a final conflict between God's servant and God's foe, Satan. Satan now had all earthly power in his hands, and he used that power to tempt his enemy. Can Jesus now maintain the truth of his message in the light of the failure of his mission? Can he now practice the total meekness and mercy that he demanded of others? Can he trust in the future fulfillment of the promise on which his life has been wagered? Will he continue to believe that all things are possible with God? We do not know the story of Jesus' suffering in its fullness. But those who told the story were guided by two convictions: that the trial of Jesus' faith was carried to the maximum intensity and that the victory of his faith was complete.

His obedience was made perfect by what he suffered. This was Satan's hour, to be sure; the powers of darkness dominated the world. But it was also the hour of Satan's final defeat by God's humble servant.[9]

B. After the Cross

The crucifixion of this servant made it impossible for other men to escape the same dilemma that Jesus faced. The story of his death made a choice inescapable for every person who heard it. This death was no casual incident, soon to be forgotten, for it was the death of one who had proclaimed life. It was the end of one who had announced a new beginning. He had asserted with authority that God's Kingdom had drawn near and that man's destiny is determined by his response to this Kingdom. His death did not silence the message, although it raised a final question mark over its validity. Will men now believe in the good tidings? Will they now affirm that God has begun to establish his new age? Will they trust that Satan has been permanently evicted from heaven? All who heard the story were confronted with such questions.

This is one reason why the account of Jesus' death accents the remarks of Jesus' adversaries, for even the crude and brutal charges of his executors pose the same issue. The soldiers mocked him with their cries, " Hail, King of the Jews! " The high priest unctuously intoned, " It is expedient for you that one man should die for the people, and not that the whole nation should perish." Bystanders leered at the spectacle and cried, " He saved others; he cannot save himself." His own people gave way to frenzied shouts, " His blood be on us." [10] The judge asked of Jesus in mock seriousness, " What is truth? " The world assumed, in these bitter and sarcastic thrusts, that it knew the answer. Its verdict was rendered, in fact, in the act of crucifixion. The Kingdom of God as proclaimed by this prophet could be nothing more than a pathetic illusion. Thinking himself divinely guided, Jesus had been completely, though perhaps innocently, deluded. Thus the enemies of Jesus are included in the epic of his death, not because the disciples had a special animus against any class, clique, or race, but because they sense in the attitudes and actions of these " culprits " tendencies that are representative of all men and because these actors in the drama give an unintended testimony to the love of him who had become " the slave of all."

The Passion story suggests further that the resistance to Jesus is an index of Jesus' power to challenge their complacency. For example, the minds of even the brutal soldiers are not free from the suspicion that Jesus is no impostor. Their very taunts seek to stifle a vague uneasiness that haunts them. Perhaps this man is after all a true servant of the Most High God. Perhaps he has been sent to bring salvation to men. Perhaps his Kingdom is, in spite of appearances, the true destiny for men. At any rate, the story of Jesus' death makes it certain that *if* his mission *were* divinely sanctioned and guided, the whole world has betrayed itself, condemned itself for blindness, disobedience, anxiety, insecurity, pride, and total rebellion against its Creator. If the sign of the cross prevents the world from recognizing in Jesus its deliverer, it means that such a sign is either a final disproof of Jesus' message or a final revelation of the world's self-deception.

The latter alternative, of course, is the one that God attested to certain disciples of Jesus. God's verdict reversed the world's judgment. He exalted his humbled servant, Jesus, and gave to him a name above every other name, in heaven or on earth. He made " both Lord and Christ, this Jesus whom you crucified." He performed a mighty act which brought the Kingdom nearest to men at the very point where it had seemed most distant. At the place of lowest descent God gave his final *Amen* to Jesus' faith as that with which God was well pleased, to Jesus' hope as the highest fulfillment of God's own promise, to Jesus' love as the measure of God's merciful treatment of men. In naming the Crucified as King of the new age, God validated Jesus' teachings as the transcript of his eternal purposes. Henceforth the death of Jesus marks the limit of the power and wisdom of the world, the place where God's power and wisdom extend their conquest over the world. By accepting this position of greatest humiliation, Jesus had taken the road to highest exaltation. He had both proved his Sonship by what he suffered and had been adopted as Son because of that suffering. The least of all and the servant of all had become in fact the greatest of all and the Saviour of all.

So stupendous and revolutionary was this event that those who glimpsed its meanings were either tongue-tied or impelled to sing alleluias. All words became inadequate, save as pointers to what the powerful love of God had accomplished. Death had been conquered by life, sin by righteousness, corruption by incorruption, rejection by election, defeat by victory. God had glorified Jesus and had anointed him with the oil of gladness. God had set him in the heavens as the bright and morning star. He had made him a life-giving spirit, the first-born of many brethren, a new man who serves as the Second Adam, or the pattern of a new humanity.

How did this transformation take place? The disciples spent little time in conjecturing what happened to the physical body of Jesus. They were strangely unconcerned with objective, external proofs of a miracle that had made all things new. They made no effort to trace the sequence of thought or feelings on the part of Jesus himself. Such matters lay beyond the ken of men who did not yet know the actual experience of death. In such matters they were content to bow before a grace-veiled mystery, content to ponder the fact and meaning of the greatest miracle of all.

A miracle it was — of that the first apostles were certain. And they were equally certain that it was God's doing. "The very stone which the builders rejected has become the head of the corner." To an equal degree were they certain that the working of this unheard-of wonder was "for our sakes." In Jesus, God has won a victory over all his foes for the sake of all his creatures, that they might share in the life and love of his only begotten son. Moreover, the story of the conquest identified the foes who had thus been bested. They were not the men of flesh and blood who had driven the nails into the cross. They were the invisible powers who had blinded and goaded these men into such actions.

One of the defeated enemies was described as sin. The Messiah had appeared in the guise of a sinner, and had been openly placarded as such. He had been condemned by the defenders of "righteousness." He had borne on his shoulders the infinite weight of the world's guilt, his execution being the measure of this burden. But the resurrection revealed the true character of sin. Here, where sin's sovereignty was greatest, it had been defeated — by Jesus for all his servants.

"The power of sin is death." Death is thus another of the invisible foes to which through fear men have become enslaved. It was their deception by death that trapped men, for they had considered it as a sure index of impotence and infamy. Therefore it was only by destroying this illusion that God could free them. Only in and through the death of the Messiah could his triumph over death become accessible to men. In the exaltation of the crucified Messiah, the impotence of this adversary was vouchsafed.

Sin and death hold dominion over the world. It is this dominion that makes of the world a rebellious colony, where a beachhead of loyalty must first be won, if the colony is to be won back to its original allegiance. Jesus came " into the world " for this very purpose, although the world did not receive him. The hostility of the world was registered throughout his ministry, for the world is ruled by other " laws " than that of meekness and mercy. Jesus sought to establish a Kingdom ruled by God's " laws " in a world ruled by antithetical " laws." His Kingdom was not of this world, although it can only approach men by challenging the sway of the kingdoms of this world. Their hostility became total in the cross. Nevertheless, the sacrifice of God's Son for the sins of the world is intended to save the world in the only way it can be saved — through repentance and faith. Only when the world is reconciled to God does it become the sphere where God's sovereignty can be realized, and that is the work to which the risen Lord is assigned, a work the success of which is assured by the victory on Golgotha.

These three foes — sin, death, the world — are not three but one. And one way to underscore their unity is to describe them as the realm where Satan is sovereign. He is the *de facto* ruler of the world, the one who enslaves men by the illusions of sin and death. He is the one who encompassed Jesus' death, as the climax of all temptations. He, therefore, is the enemy who is most decisively defeated by the miracle of God's power working through the faithful obedience of God's servant.

Such, then, are some of the terms in which the first Christians appraised the scope of the gospel. Such are the categories that indicated for them the meaning of the confession, " Jesus is Lord." These are the ways in which they told the story of redemption. Both the confession and the story centered on the total transformation which God had wrought throughout the whole range of created life. And this transformation is concentrated in the doxology, " Thine is the kingdom and the power and the glory, forever."

Since the whole of this book deals with the implications of this doxology, we must be content here with this brief sketch of the beginnings of the gospel. The following chapters will deal in greater detail with these hostile areas that were subjugated by the cross. It is hoped that the ensuing discussion will make clear the fruits of the victory that God won when he raised Jesus from the dead to be the Lord of Life.

4

THE REBIRTH OF THE DISCIPLE

THE testimony to the crucified Jesus as Lord of Lords was in the initial instance a most astounding confession, one that required a complete reversal of the attitudes of those who made it. So great a change was required that the confessors must think of themselves as reborn. Only those who were "raised with Christ" could utter with complete assurance their witness that the death of Jesus marked victory instead of defeat. Nonbelievers viewed the same events from an opposite vantage point. To them, nothing had happened. The balance of political power, the jockeying of economic rivalries, the pressures of social institutions, the scourges of war and famine, the gossiping of trivial people over daily occurrences, the drab monotony of small-town life — all these remained as they had been before, unaffected by what had taken place on Golgotha. To them it was absurd to suppose that the most decisive turning point in all history had happened on that skull-shaped hill.

But to a tiny minority, the humiliation and exaltation of Jesus loomed upon the horizon as the most decisive and revolutionary act of God, the act that alone reveals God's purpose in all his acts. To members of this minority, the event when they "died with Christ" and were "raised with Christ" became the most significant moment in their own personal histories. This humiliation and exaltation were, like that of Jesus, a divine act. In both events, whether in the public or the private story, they saw the same divine mind and hand at work. God in his goodness, in executing his purpose, had given life to his Son and to the other sons who were reborn in his likeness. We must inquire, therefore, into the nature of this turning point in the life of the disciple. This we can do best by recapturing the previous and subsequent situations.

A. Before Faith Came

The previous period was for the original followers of Jesus summed up laconically in the terse words, " They all forsook him, and fled " (Mark 14:50). Satan had asked and had received permission to " sift " them like wheat (Luke 22:31). One approach to understanding the *status quo ante,* therefore, is to explore the query, " Why did they forsake him? " The Gospel writers show keener interest in this question than in the question, " Why did Pilate execute him? " To their minds, Peter's denial was more revealing than Pilate's vacillation and more culpable than the blind hostility of the priests. This indicates that the early Christians were more susceptible to the same obstacles that caused Peter to stumble. In his tussle with the devil they saw a replica of their own struggle; in his temptations the clearest image of their own.

During his ministry Jesus had indicated the signs in which the Kingdom's presence might be discerned: " The blind receive their sight, the lame walk, lepers are cleansed, and the deaf hear, the dead are raised up, the poor have good tidings preached to them." And to these signs Jesus had appended the prophetic beatitude with its concealed barb: " Blessed is he who takes no offense at me! " (ch. 7:22, 23).

The disciples had been confident that they belonged among the blessed. And there was much to support their confidence. Did they not worship the same God? Did they not place his Kingdom first? Had they not repented and proved their sincerity by great sacrifice? Had they not left their occupations and their families to throw in their lot with Jesus? Had they not participated with him in preparing men for the new age? Had they not demonstrated their authority to heal the sick and to drive out demons from their entrenched positions? Had they not suffered obloquy and ostracism by Jesus' enemies? Had Jesus not declared their eyes to be blessed for seeing the signs of approaching redemption? In all these ways they had recognized in Jesus the beginning of the long-awaited Kingdom. Yet it was these disciples, and their leaders in particular, whom Satan " sifted." The very temptations that had occasioned Jesus' victory occasioned their defeat. In what ways, then, do the records set forth the dimensions of that defeat?

There is, for example, the account of Peter's recognition of Jesus as the Messiah. The accent of this story falls on Peter's temptation rather than on his wisdom, for when Jesus tried to make it clear that the Son of Man must be rejected and killed, Peter had objected: " God forbid, Lord! This shall never happen to you." Jesus recognized in this reply the work of Satan, but Peter had been blind to what this meant (Mark 8:27-33). On each occasion where the Master tried to prepare his disciples for the suffering which his mission entailed, they had betrayed an obtuse stubbornness. Their very love and loyalty to Jesus — misconceived, to be sure — had caused them to stumble. Unable to comprehend the Master's path of suffering, they had been quite unable to accept the same path for themselves (chs. 8:34 to 9:13). He taught them that " a disciple is not above his teacher," but this was a lesson they had not been able to grasp.

Jesus taught them by parable and sign that only those who become as a little child may enter the Kingdom. Again they had misunderstood (ch. 10:13-16). And when he declared that " it is easier for a camel to go through the eye of a needle than for a rich man to enter the kingdom of God," they had boggled over the austerity of his requirements (vs. 23-28). When they had heard such declarations, they had been alarmed about their own prospects. What would they be paid for their sacrifices? Their blindness concerning the " downward movement " had been made obvious by their rivalries for leadership and their request for chief seats in the Kingdom. Nor had this blindness been removed by Jesus' repeated warning that " he who is greatest among you shall be your servant."

Then had come that dramatic gathering at the Last Supper, where the Lord announced the imminent fulfillment of his mission and tried to explain the significance of his death. He alone saw the tentativeness of their obedience: " You will all fall away." They had protested their loyalty, unaware that they misunderstood the deeper ranges of his intention. " One of you will betray me." Once more they had shown astonishment and confusion. " Before the cock crows . . . , you will deny me." To this had come a vehement rejoinder: " If I must die with you, I will not deny you." Peter thus had spoken for all the disciples (ch. 14:29-31).

Then had come the fateful hour in which " the sheep will be scattered." Into the Garden Jesus had taken the disciples, leading the most faithful trio farther than the others. Here he made his final decision, with the adversary's power at its maximum. Now the greatest conceivable temptation assailed him, a temptation that was mastered only in prayer and by an act of utter humiliation and trust. Here he gave his followers but a single command: " Remain here, and watch." But the three sentries had fallen asleep. They had not known that the most fateful battle in human history was being fought and won. To them nothing of importance was happening. So they were unable to watch even one hour. Sharply awakened when Jesus was arrested, " they all forsook him, and fled " (vs. 32–50).

This, then, is the deeply etched portrait of the disciple before faith came. One is impelled to ask, " Why did they stumble? " Many answers are more or less obvious. They were cowards, their flesh was weak, the pressure of misfortunes was too great to endure, the power of Jesus' adversaries was too great, their support of Jesus would not have changed the outcome. The most obvious answers, however, are not the significant ones. The more significant reasons arise from the fact that this event affronted the logic of their minds. The God who permits such a thing to happen to his most faithful servant cannot be the supreme power in history and the supreme lover of his children. The Kingdom that purports to come among men through such an event can hardly be considered a gift of the highest blessedness. What sort of Kingdom is it that is introduced by such disgrace and impotence? What sort of God surrenders his chosen servant to the power of his rivals? The messiah who shows no better qualifications than these for receiving " power and wealth and wisdom and might and honor and glory and blessing " is surely not the true messiah for whom men have been yearning. What sort of messiah is it who is crucified by the very forces from whose tyranny he must deliver men?

During his ministry Jesus had taught the law of the Kingdom, and had himself exemplified his obedience to that law. His death revealed to his disciples both the possibility of obeying that law and the cost of such obedience. His life was the measure of its possibility in the existing order of things.

On the other hand, the disciples' failure was the measure of its impossibility in the existing order, that is, in what they later came to call the old age. It disclosed their unwillingness to pay the cost and to share

its fruits. They were unwilling to center all their hopes on that Kingdom which Jesus preached. They could not wholly repent and break
away from the past, relinquishing the chains that bound them to their
earlier hopes and fears. They could not seek the Kingdom first, their
eyes set wholly on the furrow's end, their " loins girt " in eagerness to
welcome the returning Lord. They could not forgive " from the heart "
either Jesus or his enemies for exposing them to this predicament. They
could not place complete confidence in his power to move mountains
nor submerge all anxieties for the future by trusting in God's promise
alone. They could not remain wholly unaware of their own goodness
which God had treated so shabbily, or be wholly unconcerned over the
rewards for their sacrifices, or be entirely convinced of the integrity and
goodness of Jesus. Like the builder of the tower, they found that they
could not complete the structure they had started to build. They had
insufficient resources. They were not yet prepared to become last of
all and servants of all.

Another way to assess their predicament is to ask *why* they interpreted this particular historical event in this particular way. Jesus
had been able in this situation to see his relation to God as central
and determinative and to discern the significance of his relations with
men as dependent on this God relationship. His disciples were blinded
because they viewed their relations with men as central and determinative and their relation to God as dependent on these human associations. Jesus had placed the mandate of God above the commonly accepted expectations of men; his disciples reversed the order. Jesus had
trusted his Father with power to transform the most forbidding
historical situation into a redemptive act for which, even in that extremity of temptation, man's response should be one of gratitude and
joy. This trust, with its consequent gratitude and joy, the disciples
could not share. For they looked at this historical situation from the
perspective of the present age, while Jesus had looked at the same
situation from the vantage point of the coming age. He had calculated
earthly appearances in terms of heavenly realities; they calculated
heavenly hopes in terms of what they assumed to be the realities of
earth. He had laid up treasures in heaven; they, when the alternatives
became sharpest, preferred the treasures on earth. He had lived and died
in fulfillment of the fundamental axiom, " He who humbles himself
will be exalted "; they were alienated from him in his death, follow-

ing rather the principle by which the rulers of the Gentiles lord it over men (Mark 10:35-45).

Thus the crucifixion of Jesus revealed the fact that their mind was conformed to this present age, their wills subject to the rulers of this age, their hopes derived from the promises of this age, and their ability to discern the signs of the times distorted by the perspectives of this age. This made them sons, not of Jesus' Father, but of his adversary, whose wiles had succeeded in tripping them up. It is the mind of the world that reasons in this fashion: " Before the Kingdom can come, there must be drastic visible changes in the tragic plight of men. War, injustice, poverty, sickness must be removed. The happenstance of Jesus' death does not really change the human situation. Ergo, this incident has no special importance, however just or unjust Pilate's sentence of Jesus." Their interpretation of the central event thus became a reflection of their kinship to the world, a proof of their unconscious enslavement by the world. It was this kinship to the world that is disclosed in those who crucified Jesus, and it was this same kinship that operated among the disciples when they were " offended " in him. They had been unable to see aright. So much for the situation that prevailed before faith came.

B. After Faith Came

When God disclosed to them the fact that he had won the victory in Jesus as the Messiah, three things simultaneously happened. In the first place, the shame of Jesus was transformed into his glory. The message and mission of Jesus received divine validation precisely in the event where, in the world's eyes, they had been invalidated. The powers of the Kingdom had proved to be greatest where men had seen nothing but ignominious failure. The work that Jesus had assigned to his followers now received a divine countersignature. This Commission, undertaken with such eagerness before they forsook him, held now an utter urgency and an inescapable compulsion. Their denial of him had been reversed by God's own approval of him.

In the second place, whereas they had been blind, they now were enabled to see. When they remembered how Jesus had tried to prepare them for his death, they realized how blind they had been, but they realized too that only his death could cure that blindness. They remembered with special poignancy his prediction that they would deny and betray him, but remembered too that at that final gathering in the shadow of the cross he had prayed for them that their faith might not fail (Luke 22:32). They recalled how at the table where he had foreseen their treachery he had promised that they would eat again with him in his Kingdom. Knowing their weakness and sin, he had chosen them in spite of their weakness and sin to share in his temptations and in his triumph. But now the risen Lord had been manifested to them as Victor. In what form he appeared to them remained a mystery, but they knew that he was among them as a life-giving Spirit. He came into their midst while they were fishing, discussing things among themselves, or pondering the meaning of the Scriptures. At first they did not recognize him, for their eyes were still " holden." They were " slow of heart to believe." But he appeared and spoke to them in ways that broke down their resistance. Again he broke bread with them, reminding them of the covenant he had made. He opened again the Scriptures, explaining from them why it had been necessary for the Messiah to die. Then, as soon as they recognized him, perceiving the truth of his victory and accepting again his Commission, he vanished from their sight. But his appearance had been sufficiently luminous with heavenly glory to shine into their hearts and to transfigure their whole existence.

Shining into their hearts, it made them see the proportions of their own treason and the specious rationalizations by which the world masks such treason. They had acted in ignorance, but this ignorance ceased to be excusable once the truth was disclosed. Supposing that they had saved their lives by their flight from Gethsemane, they discovered that they had actually been " dead through the trespasses and sins." [11] They had adopted

" the course of this world, following the prince of the power of the air, the spirit that is now at work in the sons of disobedience " (Eph. 2:2).

And they were induced to confess their slavery to this " prince ":

" Among these we all once lived in the passions of our flesh, following the desires of body and mind, and so we were by nature children of wrath, like the rest of mankind " (v. 3).

The " old nature " which had belonged to their former manner of life had been corrupted by deceitful lusts, so that their minds had become futile and darkened. Their hearts had become callous, unconsciously alienated from the life of God (ch. 4:17–24). Whenever Moses had been read, a veil had dropped over their minds so that they could not listen aright (II Cor. 3:12, 13). This had resulted in a deceptive confinement under the law, which therefore was shorn of its power to mediate freedom and life (Gal. 3:21–24). Held under the law as immature children, they had been "slaves to the elemental spirits of the universe" (ch. 4:1–3). All the sacred memories inherited from the fathers had thus proved futile (I Peter 4:17, 18).

In the third place, the revelation of *Christus Victor* meant the end of their slaveries to the world. The first step required that they be made conscious of their blindness and of their responsibility for that blindness. They had judged that Jesus' death was an evidence of his sin and impotence. This judgment was now seen to be a mark of their own blindness, because Jesus' death was disclosed as the supreme instance of God's righteousness and power. This meant that while they had been imprisoned in their own sin, Jesus had died for them, as the means of healing their blindness. This humbled them, for they had shared the guilt of those who killed God's Son. But at the same time it freed them, by sharing with them knowledge of sin and power over it. By forgiving them their sin and including them in his righteousness, God had enabled them to die to that sin. By repenting of their sin and receiving God's forgiveness, they had now been given a share in the Messiah's victory *in, through,* and *over* sin. Thus the power of the resurrection was manifested in their hearts. Thus they were "raised with Christ."

In their sin they had really been dead, though supposing themselves alive. In Jesus' righteousness, he had been made alive, though they had supposed him dead. So when their eyes were opened to grasp the meaning of his sacrifice, all their seeing was transformed. Now they could see how the devil, through their fears of death, had subjected them to lifelong bondage, and how Jesus, through his death, had destroyed "him who has the power of death, that is, the devil" (Heb. 2:14, 15). How they had feared death! But the fear had been the mark of the devil's power and of their own ignorance. How Jesus had conquered that fear! His death had proved to be life, an eternal gift lying beyond the assaults of what men called death. And this life, when they once received it from the living Christ, freed them from the previous tyranny and ignorance. Henceforth by faith in him they could participate in his victory *in, through,* and *over* death. They could die to death and arise to life. Having now done what was impossible before faith came, they could say,

> "We were buried therefore with him by baptism into death, so that as Christ was raised from the dead by the glory of the Father, we too might walk in newness of life" (Rom. 6:4).

This baptism into death was renewed whenever they sat at the Table of the Lord, where they received the cup of the new covenant in his blood. "The cup of blessing which we bless, is it not a participation in the blood of Christ?" Each day of their new discipleship became an invitation to emancipation from slavery by taking up the cross.

Many surprising changes were wrought in them by this new discipleship. The sheep that had fled when the shepherd had been struck down reassembled in the city that had witnessed their flight. They appeared in the Temple daily, proclaiming their message boldly to the very men who had condemned Jesus. Here the power of Jesus came upon them to heal. Commanded by the political and religious rulers to desist, they were constrained to obey a higher authority. Imprisoned for their disobedience, they rejoiced in gratitude and trust. About to be executed by stoning, they proclaimed to their executioners the gospel of God's judgment and forgiveness. Wherever they were and whatever the odds against them, "they did not cease teaching and preaching Jesus as the Christ" (Acts 5:42). Just as Jesus had responded to the Baptist's death by vigorous announcement of the Kingdom's approach, so his disciples responded to the Master's death. Like him, they now could see the Holy Spirit at work on all sides, and especially in places where the opposition was keenest. As they followed the narrow road of humiliation, from one step to a lower one, they witnessed the flight of demons and the dawning of peace.

Another indication that the new age had dawned was provided by their ability now to fulfill the commands that Jesus had given. Now they could see how Jesus' death was a genuine fulfillment of the Sermon on the Mount, proving how narrow is the gate to eternal blessedness. Through that gate Jesus had passed alone. The cross had been the stone on which they had stumbled. But by making this stone the head of the corner, God had himself repeated the Sermon on the Mount from the site of Golgotha. What had seemed a human impossibility thus became not only a divine possibility but an immediate mandate. To take up his cross, the disciple must climb the same hill that Jesus had climbed. The teaching of Jesus, ratified as the law of God's Kingdom, now held for them an absolute authority. Each facet of Jesus' teaching could now be seen in its most radical bearing.

What, for instance, did repentance now mean? In the light of the cross, it meant a willingness to humble one's self wholly, to put to death the desires and attitudes of worldly superiority, to " die " with Christ to the fear of ignominy and death. And what did obedience mean? Jesus' example gave the answer. And what did forgiveness mean? God's cancellation of the bond held against them became the measure of their attitudes toward enemy and friend alike. What did trust in God's integrity mean? Such unshakable joy and confidence as Jesus had displayed along the path to the cross. And what was the mark of perfect love? The perfect humility, the unconscious goodness, of Him whose only thought was the goodness of God and whose only motive was in love to become lowest and last of all.

Yes, the resurrection of Jesus raised these demands to the level of the highest law. But it also made available the power for their observance. Those who accepted Jesus' yoke and carried it in his spirit found it easy. By sharing in his death and resurrection, they could put off the old nature and put on the new; they could exchange the mind of the world for the mind of Christ. To be sure, the old nature and the old mind were not easily shed; nor could they be dispensed with once for all. Daily the battle between the old and the new was resumed. But victory was always at hand, for the mind of Christ was accessible and his grace was constantly at work in their hearts. Never in their own power, but always in the power of Christ, could their freedom be gained.

When they found that this power at work within them was able to accomplish things far beyond their ability to ask or even to think, they knew with greater assurance that they had been reborn after the pattern of the new man. The new day had dawned and they had been delivered from darkness. They had been transferred from the kingdom of Satan to "the kingdom of the Son of his love " (A. S. V.).

"You are not in darkness, brethren, for that day to surprise you like a thief. For you are all sons of light and sons of the day. . . . So then let us not sleep, as others do, but let us keep awake and be sober" (I Thess. 5:4-6).

That which made them sons of the Day was the continuing link between Jesus' humiliation-exaltation and their own. This link they often described as due to the Holy Spirit's activity. The Holy Spirit had been "poured out" on them as the first fruits of the Kingdom, and they had a share in all its gifts. Among its more basic gifts were faith, hope, love, peace, joy, and life. But it also brought gifts specially adapted to the particular station of each disciple. Every disciple had a mission to perform. The world was no longer simply a realm of darkness in which they had been trapped. In so far as it exerted the power of a tyrant over their hearts, they must die to it. There could be no appeasement. In this world they must "work out" their own salvation "with fear and trembling." But in so far as the world was the prison where the tyrant held others in bondage, it remained the arena in which the reconciling work of Christ must be continued by the stewards of the mystery. Each disciple must love the world as Jesus loved it, though this meant being hated by the world as he had been hated. He must fulfill the same duties in the world and for the world. He had been called by Christ for a redemptive purpose. Only by faithful obedience to this purpose would he actually become a witness to the resurrection, would he actually bear about in his body "the marks of Jesus." Those who gave merely a cup of water in Christ's name and those who gave their lives for his sake could together say,

"We are his workmanship, created in Christ Jesus for good works, which God prepared beforehand, that we should walk in them" (Eph. 2:10).

Such works, works done *in* the Lord, would never be vain, for they were in fact works *of* the Lord (I Cor. 15:58).

Thus was all history transfigured to the eyes of the disciple, although all history remained the same to the eyes of the world. The world continued to view the cross as a rock of offense. The world continued to accept the sovereignty of Satan, being deceived by his logic. It continued to interpret every historical incident in terms of its desires for superiority; its pride in its institutions; its walls of division between the strong and the weak, the wise and the foolish, the slaves and the free. It assumed that it was quite able to read the scroll of destiny, deriving knowledge of God from an objective analysis of external events. It continued to interpret the meaning of life in terms of what men wanted from life and what they feared from death. These wants must be fulfilled and these fears avoided before the purpose of history could be realized. Thus God's will was made contingent upon man's wisdom and his will-to-power. Thus actually men were living by false gods, denying themselves any sound hope (Eph. 2:12).

Yet those who had shared in the power of the resurrection were fully convinced that Jesus' victory signalized a transfiguration of all creation. A new age had dawned which represented the final epoch in all history. To the description of this transition the next two chapters are devoted.

Before moving ahead, however, let us recall a matter mentioned at the outset of this chapter. There we noted that the early Christians who told the gospel story found in the experience of Peter an epitome of their own movement from sin through death to life. We have been considering the rebirth of the original band of disciples, but we have treated their experience as typical for later disciples as well. In fact, it is quite impossible to draw a sharp line between the story of the first disciples and that of the later converts. This is true for two reasons: the state of the narratives and the purpose of the narrators.

First, let us consider the narratives. The modern historian, who is interested in recovering exact sequences, seeks to discriminate between the confessions of the first disciples and those of a subsequent generation. For some purposes such discrimination is altogether wise and necessary. The state of the records, however, makes this task extremely difficult. It is likely that not one of the existing documents comes to us directly from the hand of those who associated with Jesus during his ministry. The four Gospels, to be sure, contain authentic echoes from that period, but in their present form at least they come from the second generation of the Church, and reflect the perspectives of that generation. In the portrait of Peter, which we have used, is to be seen a composite portrait of discipleship, drawn by others than Peter, and based on the accumulated experience of several decades. The earliest firsthand testimony that has survived comes from Paul, who was not one of the original Twelve. What, then, is the historian to do? Surrender the task of reconstructing the experience of death-resurrection on the part of the original band? Or conjecture the dimensions of that experience on the basis of later and indirect testimonies? We have, for the purposes of this book, chosen the latter alternative. In depicting the situation before and after the coming of faith, we have pieced together the evidence that comes directly from Paul and indirectly from the earlier disciples. This is done, we trust, not because we ignore the need for historical discrimination, but because we are here tracing the portrait of the typical disciple rather than the individual life story of a particular disciple.

Some justification for this procedure is offered by the second factor mentioned above, namely, the purposes of the narrators. Those who told the stories that are preserved in the New Testament were convinced of the kinship of their experience with that of the original band. They tell the story of Peter, for example, in such a way as to say to all later disciples that if they had been present in those situations, they would not have been less blind or fearful than Peter. And those who heard the story of Peter proved, in one way or another, the truth of this assumption. If they rejected the gospel, they indicated by their rejection that they have stumbled over the same stone. If they hesitated and postponed decision, they thereby associated themselves with the hesitant and fickle companions of Jesus. If they accepted the gospel, it was not without genuine inner resistance to the implications of the cross. For these reasons, the apostle in the book of The Acts could accuse men of crucifying Jesus, men who had not been present at his trial (Acts 2:36). The writer of The Epistle to the Hebrews could accuse faithless Christians of crucifying the Son of God " on their own account " (Heb. 6:6). And the apostle Paul in writing to Roman Gentiles could declare that the cross is a revelation of the wrath of God against all who do not serve the true God (Rom. 1:18–31). Thus the Passion story had the power to demonstrate the solidarity of all men in the sin of the original disciples. To be sure, men differed in the points over which they stumbled, the features of the message by which they were offended, the words with which they rationalized their guilt, and the metaphors in which they described the revolution which faith incited. But once faith came, they recognized in Peter the story of their own rebellion, their own blindness, and their own forgiveness.

" Were you there when they crucified my Lord? Were you there?

. . . Oh! Sometimes it causes me to tremble, tremble, tremble." The disciple of later generations trembles because he sees himself in the disciple of the first generation. He sees the offenses that caused him to stumble in the period before faith came. And he sees in Peter's temptations the same temptations that continue to beset him even after he has begun to follow Jesus.

5

THE KINGDOM OF DARKNESS

WHEN Jesus' disciples called him "Lord," they pointed to a single event with a triple implication: God had made him Lord by raising him from the dead; God had raised them with Jesus to be servants of this Lord; God had begun a new creation, transforming the world into a Kingdom under the sovereignty of this King. Nor had this triple affirmation been arrived at by an easy process of observation and reasoning, since they had been made keenly conscious of the apparent absurdity of faith in such a Messiah. In spite of tremendous doubts, they were impelled to recognize in what God had done a radically new beginning in three interlocking stories: the story of Jesus, the story of the disciple, and the story of mankind. In a preliminary way we have explored the ramifications of the first two of these transitions. Now it is necessary to explore the transition from the old to the new age.

We cannot, of course, analyze the transition without keeping in mind the key that God provided by which his sons may understand the design in all creation, namely, the event of Jesus' humiliation-exaltation. If we recall the ten riddles set forth in Chapter 1, it becomes apparent that this key applies immediately to some of them. What individuals and groups are the chief bearers of historical destiny? Answer: Jesus as Lord of the coming age, with those who, as his Body, participate with him in the inauguration of that age. When and how does private history achieve a unique significance for public history? Answer: In the decisions of faith — the faith expressed in Jesus' decision in Gethsemane and in the decision of the disciple to die with Christ. What is the meaning of conflicts among men in history and how are they resolved? Answer: Just as the conflicts, in so far as they are truly significant, are a continuation of those revealed by the cross, so is their resolution provided in the exaltation of Jesus as Lord of all.

For the disciples, as for us, these far-reaching problems are localized within the context of daily associations and choices. Honesty demands that we recognize the narrow span enclosed by our lifetimes, the paper-thin depth of our experiences, the limited scope of our imaginations. Yet in recognizing the pin-point smallness of our existence, we are conscious of the total compass of the world's life. We seek for some firm connection between the small and the large. We instinctively want to be present in those happenings where history is being made. We want to be related as closely as possible to individuals and to groups who are actually shaping the future. We are filled with suspense whenever events on the personal path seem to coincide with events that have a bearing on world-wide issues. We can bring ourselves to accept whatever suffering serves to advance the victory of true and permanent peace. It is the absence of connection between our immediate choices and this wider circle of meaning that casts the cloud of unmeaning over our hearts.

In this context we can perhaps appreciate the stupendous daring of the early Christian witness that a new age has actually been initiated by the God of all power. He has made Jesus the pioneer of a new humanity, revealing in him the "manifest destiny" of all men and institutions. Through his continuing work in the disciple and the community, Jesus is advancing his Lordship over every earthly and heavenly power. In him all barriers among men crumble, all conflicts find resolution. His struggle with rebellious creation is the only struggle that possesses final significance. All other clashes, whether among nations, races, classes, or religions, are but the empty recurrence of rivalries that can never be resolved apart from their relation to God's battle in Christ with his adversaries. All other victories are momentary and illusory apart from his victory.

Such statements as the one just made sound too sweeping to be convincing, too negative in their denial of meaning to historical values to be palatable. Yet our primary concern is to be faithful to the New Testament, so that the question is not the persuasiveness or palatability of the interpretation, but only its accuracy. It can hardly be denied that such writings as Romans (chs. 1:18 to 3:20), Revelation (chs. 7 to 9), Acts (chs. 3:17-23; 4:5-12), and the Johannine Gospel (chs. 3:16-36; 5:19-47), give ample evidence for drawing the sharpest contrast between light and darkness, life and death, the Kingdom of God and the kingdom of Satan. But on the other hand we should not overlook a vital qualification in the statements of the foregoing paragraph, the qualification expressed in these words: "Apart from their relation to God's battle" and "Apart from his victory." It is the believer who affirms that such victories as unbelievers seek are intrinsically momentary and illusory; but in saying this the believer knows that nothing happens entirely unrelated to God's victory. God's battle encompasses and permeates all lesser conflicts because his proceeds at a deeper level than all others. His is not a struggle "with flesh and blood," men pitted against men for human securities, with the outcome determined by superiority in human resources. The final conflict is that which proceeds between God and the devil, between Christ and the "rulers of this present darkness" (Eph. 6:12). This conflict proceeds in the three interlocking realms which the cross has revealed to be *one* realm: it is precipitated in the invisible realm where Jesus met and overcame, during his brief ministry, all the powers of the adversary; it begins and continues in the heart of each man who hears the call of God as proclaimed by the Crucified; it proceeds in that heavenly realm where the sovereignty of Christ is arrayed against all the spiritual authorities that rule the present evil age. Victory in any one of these three realms carries with it a victory in all. The disciple, for example, who accepts the invitation to share the sufferings and the glory of the Messiah becomes a participant in the battles of the Messiah against his adversaries and a participant as well in the triumphs of the Lord. To these disciples the apostle can say: "All things are yours, whether . . . the world or life or death or the present or the future, all are yours; and you are Christ's; and Christ is God's" (I Cor. 3:21-23).

Such at least are the testimonies of those who had become slaves of the meek Jesus. In his meekness they discerned a transcendent power and glory; in the story of his humiliation they heard the news of God's triumph over all his adversaries. As they reflected upon this news, they detected in it the strategy by which God reclaims for himself, through the humble obedience of his servants, the realm that has been enslaved by other gods and lords. To grasp the scope of these testimonies is not difficult, but to comprehend how they could be so certain of their truth is less easy, and to understand the ultimate truth itself is still more difficult. As aids to this understanding, we may well ask three questions: the character of the cosmic situation before its transformation; the means by which God accomplishes its redemption; the structure of the new realm where God " is all . . . in all." The present chapter examines the first of these; the others will receive attention in the succeeding chapter. The exploration of the first question, i.e., the alignment of sovereignties in the period before the Messiah's triumph, cannot proceed far without coming to terms with two key images by which early Christians articulated their experience of reality. One of these refers primarily to time — the old aeon or age; the other refers primarily to sovereignty — the power of Satan. Each may receive separate treatment, although in the end the two images coalesce.

A. The Old Age

Let us begin by discussing the meaning of the term " age." Some such category of measurement is necessary for any interpretation of history that distinguishes one epoch from another. For example, the term is used by geologists to mark off the various periods in history according to the strata of the earth's surface. The *azoic age* is the period when the earth appears as a separate planet. Here lie the beginnings of the atmosphere, the oceans, the separate continents. But as yet there are no signs of life. Many aeons later comes the *Cretaceous age,* or the age of chalk. By now the earth's surface has altered enough to support the life of dinosaurs, archaic mammals, trees, and flowering plants. Many aeons later comes the *ice age,* which is characterized by the rise and recession of the last continental ice sheets. During this age man appears, and challenges the larger, more powerful animals for a place on the earth. In this struggle, the Neanderthal man and the Heidelberg man use stone tools (*the old Stone Age*); then other types of men appear and support themselves by the use of metals, fire, and domesticated animals (*the new Stone Age*).

Other examples lie close at hand. The anthropologist may distinguish different epochs by such terms as Nomadic, Pastoral, and Agricultural. The economic historian may focus attention upon the changes in modes of production or the modes of commercial organization. The political historian may separate one age from another in terms of a prevalent type of political system: "the age of city-states" or "the age of empire." During a monarchical period, the separate periods may be marked off in terms of the ruling families, such as "the age of the Antonines." The cultural historian, on the other hand, may cut across political and economic stratifications with such categories as "the age of the Renaissance."

One must ask what is the common element in the connotation of the term "age," in all these various classifications. In all of them the term serves to distinguish the new from the old. It serves to locate an emergent force or pattern that influences the structure of human relationships. The contrast between the old and the new, however, is significant only when both the old and the new are placed within the continuum of a larger and longer process, whether it be the history of Western civilization, the history of mankind, or the history of the solar system.

What criteria serve to distinguish the new from the old? Different sciences, with different objects in view, will adopt criteria appropriate to those objects. But we notice that seldom do purely chronological or geographical factors serve to define the boundaries of an age. Men who live in the same place and time may belong to different ages. More central in all scales of measurement is the character of human relationships. The degree to which these relationships are affected seems to be the measure of change, and the factor that seems to produce the greatest change is held to be the hallmark of the age. The analyst must locate the primary cause for the greatest change. He may find this cause in the tools of production, the mode of social organization, the dominance of a particular hierarchy of authority, the pervasiveness of a particular mentality, or the sway exercised by a given system of values. Whatever may be the efficient cause of the greatest change in human relationships will determine the way in which the historian "carves history at the joints." And in all the ways so far reviewed, the relationship of men to God is considered of either marginal or negligible importance.

It is obvious that the outlook of the analyst will affect his appraisal of the boundaries of an age. His position in society, his interests and hopes, his conception of social dynamics, will condition his location of the "joints." One observes, for instance, that the various ways of periodizing the past command agreement in proportion to two factors: the distance in time from the present point of judgment; the extent to which entirely objective and nonspiritual criteria are utilized (e.g., the character of the earth's surface). The nearer one comes to the present, and the more one takes mental and spiritual quotients into account, the less agreement will be found in mapping the ages. How, for example, does one locate " the modern age " and " the modern man "? Different answers will be given by the geologist, the anthropologist, the sociologist, the cultural historian; and these answers will in part reflect conflicting criteria. Or if one wishes a more dramatic demonstration of this fact, let him ponder contemporary efforts to assess the signs of a new age. Each crisis is identified as such because it appears to presage a drastic change in human affairs. And wherein lies the primary cause of the pending changes? What exactly is meant by the clichés: " atomic age," " supersonic age," " plastic age "? Whoever seeks to discover the true boundary between the old age and the new finds himself in this dilemma. He cannot chart the boundaries with precision unless he first knows the ultimate meaning inherent in both the old and the new. On the other hand, he cannot reduce the manifold data of history to this ultimate meaning unless he is first able to divide the totality of history into an intelligible sequence of epochs.

Having observed what is involved in defining the term " age," let us return to the perspective of the New Testament. Here we immediately note a far-reaching contrast, for it is assumed that the primary power to define the separate ages belongs to God. Here it is assumed that the prime differentia between one age and another is located in the character of the divine-human relationships. These relationships provide the continuum within which the sequence of ages proceeds. From everlasting to everlasting, God remains the only true sovereign of all his creatures. No man can escape from dealing with him, though he take " the wings of the morning, and dwell in the uttermost parts of the sea." Moreover, within this continuum of God-relationship, all decisive changes from one epoch to another are initiated by God. He ordains the times and the seasons, setting the limits to the bounds of man's habitation. Embraced within his design are the manifold alterations in social institutions, the oscillations in the fate of nations, the growth and decay of cultures. This design is motivated by his loving-kindness and accomplished by his power.

Furthermore, it is assumed that true knowledge concerning the transition from one age to another is communicated by divine disclosure, by the acts of God as interpreted by his Spirit. Only by standing before God in faith can man know in which age he is standing; know, too, how man is transferred from one age to another. This is what has happened in the activity of the Messiah. In the story of Jesus, God has revealed the "turning point" between the ages, indicating the conditions of the old and the conditions of the new.

The character of the old age was disclosed to the first disciples through their initial misunderstanding of Jesus' Messiahship. Why had they first stumbled over the offense of the cross? Because they had been unable, like Jesus, to reorient their lives around the coming age. Because they had repudiated Jesus' mind: his faith, his hope, his love. Why this inability? Because they had belonged essentially to the old age, "the present evil age." Their mind had been conformed to its pattern; their faith, hope, and love had been corrupted by its standards; their judgment of power and greatness had been borrowed from its institutions.

As they pondered the fact that God's Son had died *alone,* repudiated by the whole world, they realized the *oneness* of this epoch. The old age had actually enforced a cohesive solidarity of rebellion against God (cf. pp. 67 f.). Because of this oneness in rebellion, the disciples came to view the "age of darkness" as embracing all the various periods of past history. Those who share the mind of that age constitute a single "body" which might be called "the old man," "the first Adam." Because the sphere of solidarity in sin was so inclusive, they could ignore many of the relative distinctions among men and institutions, distinctions that from any other vantage point might loom large.

As they examined the structure of this old age, they discovered in it at least five interdependent qualities. Life in the night is known by the source and direction of men's *hopes,* the structure of their *minds,* the *fruit* of their deeds, the *slavery to earthly authorities,* and *their subjection to the invisible powers* that govern the kingdom of darkness. Let us glance at each of these in turn.

1. The men who were delivered from the old age were prompted to confess that they had not sought God's Kingdom first of all. They had been anxious for food and clothing, for security, or for social priorities and prestige. "We all once lived in the passions of our flesh, following

the desires of body and mind, and so were by nature children of wrath, like the rest of mankind" (Eph. 2:3). To be sure, they may have deceived themselves into thinking that they were seeking God's righteousness, but their desire to defend their own rights had hidden all manner of secret sin. They had wanted the wrong things, or the right things for the wrong motives. They had set up their own goals of attainment, trusting in their own right and power to achieve them. They had devised their own methods for realizing these goals, using their relationship to other men as the means for gratifying their own superiority and security. Whatever the form of their sin, they had lived by their own hopes, by the directives issuing from their own divided hearts.

2. According to their minds, they had been assured of their own righteousness, but these minds had been conformed to "this age" (Rom. 12:2). This mind judged what was good in God's eyes to be evil. It judged God's goodness and God's power in terms of what men considered to be good and powerful. It was complacent about its ability to measure the first and the last, the greatest and the least. Perchance it claimed to love God with "the whole mind," but this love stemmed from a double mind and a double heart. Life in this age had blinded them to the depth of this duplicity (cf. pp. 72 f.).

3. Because God remains the sole arbiter of life, the fruit of such blind hopes and maladjusted minds was vanity and futility. "We were dead while we lived according to the course of this age." God could not fulfill men's hopes except by showing their sterility. Those who hope for life according to the mind of the world must first be disenchanted of that hope. They must die to their expectations. The sentence of death therefore lies over the whole of the present evil age. Yet that verdict is at bottom the condemnation preferred by men against themselves. Behind the sentence, however, the disciples had come to see the mercy of God: "The creation was subjected to futility, not of its own will but by the will of him who subjected it in hope" (Rom. 8:20). Both the darkness of the dying aeon and the brightness of the new aeon were manifested in the crucifixion of Jesus.

4. In their hopes and their minds, men are dependent upon social institutions and upon the human agents on whom those institutions have conferred authority. Through these institutions and agents men are induced to adopt certain scales of superiority, in terms of which

individual ambitions are nurtured. The law, the synagogue, the Temple, the prevailing distinctions between races and classes — all these served to shape the private judgments of what was desirable and right. All exerted the power to enforce these judgments with appropriate rewards and penalties. They induced men to conform to prevailing attitudes by applying the pressures of wealth or poverty, fame or infamy, success or failure. False hopes and false fears were vested with a false ultimacy by man's dependence upon his communal attachments. The cross underscored the strength of these bonds. It proved, through the reaction of men against its truth, that the dependence on the mind of social institutions pre-empted the primal reliance upon the will of God. It proved, in other words, that the whole age is characterized by subconscious subservience to earthly authorities.

5. Behind each human institution, behind each agent of that institution, appears an invisible source of its authority. The men who govern the synagogue or the state die, and even the institutions themselves decay, but the principle to which they appeal remains constant. It is this intangible power that permeates the hopes of men, the mind by which they judge values, the harvest for which they labor, and the whole web of communal affiliations. The power that thus determines their spiritual existence is *de facto* king. Viewing the old age most broadly, therefore, the earliest Christians called it the kingdom of Satan, for in it all allegiances are integrated into one lordship which has usurped the throne of God. Sons of disobedience make themselves sons of Satan rather than sons of God. Satan's effective sovereignty and man's alienated heart — these twin conditions constitute the age of rebellion. We should look more closely, then, at the character of this sovereignty and the ways in which men come to be enslaved to it.

B. The Power of Satan

The continuance of Satan's rule depends upon the success of his deceptions. He is the tempter par excellence because he is the father of lies. To maintain his control he must work indirectly. Because he is intangible and his very existence is doubtful, he must utilize visible agencies whose reality can scarcely be doubted. He therefore governs men through a highly developed bureaucracy that conceals his hand.[12] Some highly respected entity like the law is encouraged to claim for itself a greater control over destiny than it has been given by God. When a man accepts this claim as ultimate, he begins to worship the creature rather than the Creator. This unwitting idolatry makes him a citizen in Satan's empire. Any form of social organization, because it is the vehicle of human desires and loyalties, may become an instrument of the evil one. He may extend his reign through the policies of a political dynasty or king, through the demands of an economic system or employer, through the rationalizations of a philosophy or its teacher, through the control of behavior by prevailing mores and morals, through the sanctification of the existing order by religious cultus. This does not mean that social institutions are inherently evil, since they have been created and ordained of God for the service of man (Mark 2:27). But for men who live in the old age, Satan has made these agencies into instruments of coercion. The point at which bondage is created is the point where man's heart yields its allegiance to the fraudulent claims made in behalf of some tangible earthly authority. When this happens, the ruler of darkness, worshiped by a desirous but deceived servant, defrauds God of his rightful glory and challenges his power. Let us analyze the patterns of social organization which Satan corrupts with his persuasive but illegitimate maneuvers. In this analysis, we should note carefully the interdependence of authority, superiority, and power.

In any society the common life is stabilized by being organized into a hierarchy of authorities. Each person is placed under the authority of others; he is at the same time given authority over others. To him others are subjected; he is subjected to others. The gift of authority coincides with the gift of power, whether the sword be sheathed or unsheathed. And every sword wields control to some degree over the historical futures of men. It has the right to impose sanctions, rewards for obedience, and penalties for disobedience. Where two authorities conflict in their demands on a man, the authority with the greater power will be the winner. And in most social arrangements, the authority who is conceded the right to take away one's life becomes by that token the supreme power.

Furthermore, authority resides not only in the person in whom it happens at the moment to be vested, but also in that which gave him such authority. One Army general replaces another without a break in the system on which the authority of both is based. The authority of the agent derives from the office. The authority of the office, in turn, derives from the community that establishes and supports that office. Nor does this socially granted authority survive on a short-term basis alone. The elemental needs of all societies cause them all to develop regular modes of meeting those needs. All societies have systems of subordination that regularize family relations, economic relations, and relations with neighbors. Even if one moves from a polygamous to a monogamous society or from a nomadic to an industrial economy or from a Micronesian clan to a megalopolitan nation, he does not escape the necessity of holding some position on the scale of status. The principle of authority, the existence of superior-inferior relationships, the exercise of power — these together constitute prime factors in shaping man's life story, from before his birth to after his death. These permeate all his thinking, feelings, and actions, from the most intimate daily contacts to the most remote affiliations with society and history.

As one reflects upon this skeletal structure of power, several observations command quick acceptance. In the first place, all authority is, in its source and support, invisible. No historical exercise of authority can be wholly reduced to visibility, and one has extreme difficulty in tracing it to its ultimate origins. It transcends space and time and any particular human community which may, at a particular place and time, be its channel.

In the second place, all authority is manifested to men through the medium of visible agents, whether priests, bankers, policemen, or mothers. These agents are as persons subordinate to the authority vested in them, but they *are* agents and must be treated with respect appropriate to their assigned province.

In the third place, all authority calls into play spiritual activity. It is exercised through persons. It relates the spirit of one to the spirit of others as embodied in social patterns of behavior. Never does the execution of authority become entirely mechanical. A response is always necessary if the right of the superior is to be recognized. Should this right be successfully and continuously repudiated by either underlings or overlings, it ceases to exist as an authority. A living system of societal arrangements presupposes active command and active obedience.

In the fourth place, the authorities that most thoroughly condition personal destinies are the authorities that give expression to elemental needs — familial, economic, legal, religious. These are most universal and most constant in their impingement on ordinary daily routine. Accordingly it is in his relationships to these authorities that man finds either the greatest slavery or the greatest release. Yet these are the relationships in which the principle of authority has seeped most deeply into the subconscious texture of life, so that man may be entirely unaware of the controls exerted by this authority.

In the fifth place, for him who becomes conscious of his relationship to others above or below him in the ladder, a limited range of attitudes is open. With reference to his superiors he may adopt (*a*) the policy of voluntary subjection or (*b*) the policy of voluntary rebellion. Whichever the policy, it may be motivated either by self-centered fears and hopes or by other-centered love. With reference to his inferiors, on the other hand, he may either (*a*) rule or (*b*) abdicate. And he will do what he does either from self-centered desires or from other-centered love (cf. Chapter 12). His choice of attitudes toward both inferiors and superiors will finally depend, not upon the personal agents, not upon the institutions they represent, but upon his own personal choice within the range of options offered to him. He may suppose that his attitudes toward superiors and inferiors are wholly determined by their respective offices, but that supposition is untrue. This supposition merely hides from himself the fact that he chooses this fatalistic attitude as the ground for evading his responsibilities.

In the sixth place, the response of abdication or of rebellion may succeed in supplanting one set of human agents through which an invisible authority operates, but it will not cancel that invisible authority itself. A woman may be divorced by seven husbands, but the elemental obligations of family life are not thereby abrogated. A man may surrender citizenship in one nation and migrate to another, but he remains subservient to some political sovereignty. The government of a nation may disintegrate and another government take its place, whether the change be for better or worse, but the existence of political duties and the operation of political sanctions will not evaporate, leaving nothing in their place. Contrary to utopian aspirations, neither the family nor the economy nor the state nor the law ever " wither away."

Any profound interpretation of history must therefore deal with the infinite complexities in the organization of power at two major levels. In the first place, it must come to terms with the immediate tangible associations of a particular superior with a particular subordinate (e.g., this husband and this wife, this master and this slave, this king and this citizen). In the second place, the interpretation must comprehend the ultimate intangible connections between these agents of authority and the principles of authority on which the daily associations are based (e.g., the relation of both husband and wife to the institution of marriage; the relation of both master and slave to the economic system). The total situation embraces not only the associations of this worker to this employer, but also the association of both worker and employer to the conditions determined by a given economy or to the principle of subordination to be found in all economies. Such an assessment of the human situation results in the discovery that " slavery " at the latter level is more binding, more decisive, and more permanent than " slavery " at the former level.

It is significant that Christ's emancipation proclamation gives priority to slavery at this deepest level. From what sort of rulers does Christ free men? From those rulers to whom *both master and slave* are subject. Many different names are used to denote these invisible lords whom men obey: authorities, powers, the elemental forces, rulers in heavenly places, spiritual hosts, angels, thrones, dominions, principalities. The variety of titles accents the diversity of factors which we have seen to be inherent in the relation of inferior to superior. Implicit in all these categories, however, are the six aspects of authority which we have just analyzed. To accent the factor of invisibility, the term " heavenly " is often used. To accent the fact that all these relationships involve voluntary personal associations, the term " spiritual " is often used. These various titles also indicate the elemental, universal, and constant character of the power that these realities exert over human destinies. Men may be freed from subservience to one of these authorities only by the imposition and acceptance of an authority that is at once more elemental, more universal, and more powerful. Yet never is an authority considered to be implacable and mechanical — each authority receives its spiritual sovereignty in part from the consent of the governed.

It is well to observe that to the followers of Jesus the sharpest battle for sovereignty does not lie between one organized religion and another. The paramount conflict is not waged by apostles against rabbis, by Christianity against Mithraism, by theism against atheism. The gods who were formally worshiped by Gentiles in public temples and grottoes are seldom mentioned in the New Testament. The disciples of Jesus have been made aware that God's battle line follows a different contour from the familiar rivalries of recognizable religious cults. The course of history is for them charted, not by the gods of the pagan pantheon, but by the powerful rulers of darkness that indirectly build their invisible temples among men. These demonic powers, to be sure, infiltrate the official religious institutions, however laudable may be their laws, sacraments, sacrifices, and festivals; but the sphere of Satan's power is much wider. Mammon is a more dangerous antagonist than Mithras, Caesar than Isis. They were aware, as many moderns are aware, that the powers that really determine the course of history are pervasive cultural affiliations that are now alienated from God, having become his rivals for the souls of men.

In using the terms " mammon " and " Caesar " they were expressing a vital distinction between individual rich men and emperors on the one hand and the pervasive claims of wealth and imperial power on the other. And it is primarily through these latter that Satan succeeds in blinding men. In his use of the principle of political authority as vested in a particular government, for example, he encourages nationalistic pride, so that the fancied hopes of the nation will be placed first of all by its citizens. He insists on the peculiar national virtues and excellencies, as compared with other nations. He exalts the rights of the nation as inalienable, creating prejudice against any limitation of sovereignty and stirring up strife whenever absolute sovereignty is threatened. The prestige and security of the nation are made the primary consideration by which every act of the individual is justified or condemned. The climate of public opinion is so rigged by propaganda machines that people nervously avoid any deviation from the lock step. Thoughts and feelings, as well as behavior, are policed by invisible censors. When any danger to the present fortunes of the political unit appears on the horizon, it is accepted and heralded as a major crisis. This crisis, in turn, justifies the overruling of man's duties to God and to his neighbor by the interests of the nation. In the name of that nation promises are given to the populace that are too rosy ever to be kept, and threats of disaster too dire to be executed. Allegiances narrower or wider than allegiance to the nation are submerged by the latter allegiance. And what holds true for the nation holds true, also, for other types of earthly authority. There is no form of communal organization from which Satan's activity is excluded.

Satan's success, however, depends upon men's response to such exorbitant claims. They must fear the penalties and hope for the rewards that the group has at its disposal. They must identify their own pride, virtue, and rights with those of the group. They must view their personal lives within the horizons common to the herd, without challenging those horizons by their abnormality. They must strive for personal superiority according to the rules of the game, content with the limits set to their ambition and proud of their progress from the bottom of the ladder. Thus they turn the social conventions into chains, making them the inviolable laws of an invisible authority, although they are presumably dealing only with men.

Even mammon and Caesar are among the lesser gods, whose power is quite tangible, however diffused through the fabric of society. The more subtle sovereignty is exerted by heavenly forces less tangible and more ultimate, forces whose existence goes back to the roots of creation. Yet even the most elemental and powerful among such rulers are creatures and not creators (Col. 1:5-18). As creatures, all of them are agents of the purpose of God and are finally subordinated to his power. Men are now subservient to them, but God can free men from this subservience, because he is ruler of all thrones and princedoms. They are created by God, yet they have rebelled against his authority, claiming to have an ultimate power over men. They permeate all the activities of man — political, economic, ethical, religious. The right of Jesus Christ to rule over all other heavenly rulers is vindicated not alone by his superiority over Osiris and Astarte, or by his ability to conquer mammon and Caesar, but by the manifest defeat of all other invisible powers that exert controls over human hearts and communal loyalties. In short, Jesus does not exercise his power in the first instance by taking captives captive; his power is vindicated as ultimate only when he takes captivity captive (Eph. 4:8).[13]

Glancing backward over our exploration of the character of the old age and its sovereignty, perhaps one now finds the meaning of the key images clearer. At least it should be obvious that the primary connotation of the term " age " does not derive from measurable objective factors of time or space. The primary connotation derives from the dominant status of the God-man relationships. To be sure, the old age has a certain length, an element of persistence, of duration, of dynamic sequence; but these elements are not measured primarily in terms of centuries or calendar years. The same reality may be designated by the terms "an evil . . . generation" or "the night."[14] Or it may be characterized by the inclusive epithet "the old man" or "the first Adam." Another virtual synonym is the term "world," so long as the primary meaning of this term is not defined by geographical or numerical extent. It is the mind of the world and the desires of the world that constitute it as the world. Whether one uses the temporal term "age" or the spatial term "world," what is actually definitive is the blindness and sin of men, their mistaken dependence upon the false ultimates of corporate entities, or, in short, their obedience to Satan. These images are simply different ways of describing the existing relationship between the creature and his Creator. Any change in this basal relationship affects all the others. A decisive and final transition in this latter realm cuts across all the other realms, because they are in reality one, the night of man's alienation from God.

What has been said of the pervasive evil that permeates the world, of the meaninglessness of historical conflicts apart from their bearing upon God's design, may easily be taken as expressions of extreme world weariness and dismal defeatism. When the key images of age, world, death, and the devil are viewed from non-Biblical perspectives rather than from the vantage point of faith, they are the source of vast misunderstanding. The old age is not a period that includes automatically every human being and every social institution. It is not a realm utterly removed from God's presence and power, utterly corrupted by its allegiances and hopelessly blinded by Satan's deceits. Throughout the range of space and time God remains the only true Lord. All the hosts of darkness are subjected to him, even Satan receiving from him permission to tempt men by wielding apparently invincible power over men. The war is a civil war, not an international war. Through all its shifting course, God's purpose remains steadfast, and this purpose holds a promise for all creatures. His truth remains true, though every man be a liar and deceived by his own falsehoods. His power determines the future, though men accord that power to other lords. He remains faithful, though all his creatures turn faithless. In terms of his all-comprehending design, this age is therefore an age of promise and of preparation. Though all men have sinned and come short of his glory, it is he who has shut them all up in the prison of sin in order that he might have mercy upon all (Rom. 11:32). Though all creation is made futile, it is subjected to futility through his will. And he has subjected it to futility in order that the whole creation may be " set free from its bondage to decay and obtain the glorious liberty of the children of God " (Rom. 8:21). The age of bondage is thus in his plan the age of promise, the age of hope, the age of preparation. Where enslavement is greatest, there the word of liberty is most vigorously proclaimed.

But where may men hear this word of liberty in the confusing turmoil of earthly strife? The answer must include all creation itself. His eternal power is manifested in what he has made. It is manifested in the stubborn testimony of man's conscience, in man's awareness that all is not right with his efforts at self-fulfillment, in man's experience of frustration and vanity. The whole age hangs under God's condemnation, and his judgment is present in all that happens, could man but see it. God's purpose, his command, his promise — these have all been declared to men by the various covenants God himself has provided: the covenant formed with creation itself in its beginning; the covenant with Adam in his beginning; the covenant with Abraham and his descendants; with Moses and the children of Israel at the Exodus; with David; with the prophets. The covenants are good and true, though in an age of rebellion they have become tools to convict man of his sin in forsaking them.

God also has spoken to every generation through his servants the prophets. Living by faith and hope, they manifested God's promise of the coming age (Heb., ch. 11; Rom., ch. 4). Wherever God's word came to the prophet, there he declared the judgment and the promise under which the whole age stood. These promises were expressed as a word of imminent judgment and of ultimate hope. The prophet stood as a sign of the covenant that had been broken and of the covenant that God would restore when he turned " the hearts of the fathers to the children." Man's heart is now alienated; but there will come a time when God will purge the hearts, forgive the sins, and create a perfect relationship between himself and his sons. Thus the old age bears within itself, within its sinning and its dying, the assurance of a coming renewal. At its boundaries have always stood men who by the Spirit could anticipate this coming salvation, though they could not depict its form or date. These messengers recognized the preparatory character of their age, and in so doing actually belonged to the coming age. They were the heralds of the fullness of the time when God would take his great power and reign. The community of the coming age includes all those who by faith lived from the new age into the old (Heb., ch. 11). In that age "many will come from east and west and sit at table with Abraham, Isaac, and Jacob in the kingdom of heaven" (Matt. 8:11).

Such an understanding of the old age was communicated to those who heard God proclaim the vindication of Jesus as Messiah. They could understand the previous period now because they had themselves been transferred into the new Kingdom. They could grasp its dimensions as a time of God's judgment and promise. And since they had received a share in the age to come, they could estimate from the signs of dawn what the new Day would mean. In the following chapter we shall give attention to their understanding of the means by which God redeems the evil time, and the character of the realm where his will is done on earth as it is in heaven.

6

THE DAWN OF A NEW DAY

THE supreme antagonist of God in his program of emancipation and reconciliation is Satan, or the devil, who asserts his ownership of the souls of men through their fear of " spiritual hosts . . . in the heavenly places." The final struggle, a struggle that permeates all creation, is this conflict between God and his adversary; but the arena for the battle is always the souls of men. It is in this arena that God accomplishes his victory in the Messiah. We must ask, then, how the Messiah carried out his mission, and what were the means he used for emancipating men from the rulers of darkness.

A. THE POWER OF JESUS

The kernel answer has already been suggested. In the first place, he humbled himself. This meant that he voluntarily accepted a place on the lowest rung of the ladder of earthly power. He became last of all. To establish his right to command the obedience of other men, he did not use the prerogative of power and authority which other " heavenly rulers " used. At no point did he demonstrate his superiority over others by utilizing means that the rulers of darkness use (Mark 10:35–45).

In the second place, he subjected himself to all earthly agents of these invisible rulers. He did not lead a human rebellion against the rampant injustices of social institutions. He accepted the authority that the Creator had given to Pilate, to the Sanhedrin, to centurions, tax collectors, and wealthy landlords. He carried this subjection so far as to accept all that these earthly rulers could do to him. He accorded to them the power to feed or to starve him, to permit or to prohibit his activity, to allow him to live or to cause him to die.

In the third place, his voluntary subjection was motivated throughout by love of his earthly superiors, which included all men. There was no self-regarding fear of their power, no self-regarding pity of himself or his fate, no self-regarding program for escaping from his earthly position to a higher earthly seat. Rather, he was ready to die for those men whose earthly position gave them power to put him to death.

In the fourth place, this way of humble love toward all, this power over fear, this selflessness of hope and ambition, were the counterpart of his singlehearted loyalty to God. He feared God alone. He depended for sustenance on God's care alone. He found God's will accessible in every situation, and, regardless of the odds provided by existing social institutions, he was faithful to this will. He sought God's Kingdom in hope and, regardless of seeming frustrations, trusted this promise of God to the end. Against the greatest odds, he maintained full confidence in God's ability to turn to good account all the evils that men might do in their loyalty to false gods. He saw the disciples' treachery, yet he humbly washed their feet, loving them to the end.

By exalting his Servant Jesus, God vindicated this faith, raising from the dead this Son who had thus subjected himself to his earthly superiors. In doing this, God had declared openly the "mind" and the "power" by which any man may receive the same emancipation. This emancipation was designed to demonstrate the reconciliation of all existing authorities to God, to make it possible for them to be united in fulfilling a single purpose, that of the glory of God. The reconciliation is realized when men now serving Satan through these channels become the servants of God through the same channels. The rulers of darkness thus become the servants of Christ Jesus when men over whom they rule use each relationship as an opportunity to become sons of God, worshiping God by walking the road that Jesus took, from that initial temptation in the wilderness to that final temptation in Gethsemane. Thus the sign of the cross becomes the sign of victory over principalities and powers and the means of their reconciliation to God. To illustrate this in greater detail, let us consider again the personal story of Jesus' disciples as they learned to follow, in their halting way, the path of the Messiah.

B. THE CREATION OF A NEW RACE

Jesus had come proclaiming the new age as a gift from God that begins now. He had taught that this gift is apprehended only by those who enter the narrow gate. From his example they had learned that the gate is as narrow as the cross. It is so narrow that men must enter it single file. Only by climbing Golgotha could one see the Promised Land. By the power of the risen Lord, however, there were some who chose to imitate Jesus. It was along that path that they learned how God makes a new community and a new age. Let us try to think with them concerning the entrance into the new order, taking our cue from the teachings of Jesus which guided their discoveries.

We may begin with Jesus' demand that only the wholly repentant man may see the Kingdom of God. This seems at first thought to be an exclusively individual matter. Only the individual as an individual before God can fulfill the demand to repent. If he is dependent upon social pressures, his repentance is not fully genuine. To follow Jesus required the renunciation of all attachments to the communities of the old age, but those who broke out of the chain of these attachments discovered something else. In the act of penitence they discovered that all previous walls among men were leveled by this frank recognition of their solidarity in sin with the old age and their mutual responsibility for all men. In and through the very act of being humbled, where every knee bows in the name of Jesus, the shared experience of meekness created a new fellowship among the strangest assortment of people, bringing Jew and Greek more closely together than any previous prejudice had ever held them apart. The community of the new age was thus born at the sign of the bent knee.

Or one may recall Jesus' demand for expectancy and his whole-hearted alertness for receiving the gift of life. In seeking first the Kingdom of this Messiah, every man becomes a displaced person, a pilgrim, who refuses to look behind him at entangling alliances with kinsfolk or friends who are seeking other things first. But in his very aloneness as a pilgrim, this exile finds himself in company with others who with him form " a colony of heaven." Because they are all heirs of a common hope and inheritance, they are willing to pool all their resources and to give to each according to his need. The future age, sought with complete trust, welds a fellowship stronger than all the cohesion provided by lords and rulers of the old age.

Consider the stringent requirement of mercy which was so central in Jesus' message. The command to forgive is always addressed to an individual: " *You* must forgive *your* enemies. You alone *can* forgive

your enemies. And if you do not forgive, no community can force you
to forgive or can offer forgiveness in your stead." And judged by the
cross, the old age is characterized by its incapacity for radical forgiveness. But when a man forgives his enemy, he unites two into one, and
when the two forgive others, the circle of fellowship spreads. Because
this act of forgiveness represents God's forgiveness of a particular man,
embodied in his forgiveness of his enemy, a community of the forgiven
is formed, bound together by the ties of a common debt and a common
eagerness to forget self in ministry to others. The dynamic intention of
this community is to include all men within the same circle of the forgiven and forgiving.

Jesus had taught that no man can serve two masters, and he had exemplified what it means to serve one alone. But it was only through
the inalienable freedom of his own choice that Jesus became a slave of
one master. Through his voluntary sacrifice on the cross he communicated this same freedom to his disciples, so that the schism in their
mind and heart could be healed through their becoming slaves in the
same household. To be sure, the gods of the old age promise freedom
and fellowship to their adherents. And they support this promise with
all sorts of external and persuasive pressures. To the extent that they
succeed, they succeed by making every man afraid to be at odds with
his society, or with certain segments of it. But Satan is never wholly successful. Such freedom and fellowship as he permits are only partial, because he is the father of lies, and because the result of obeying him is at
once a divided heart and a divided world.

The disciples of Christ found true freedom and true fellowship
among those who said, "We must obey God rather than men." A common Master, followed by those who in the secrecy of their own hearts
had climbed Golgotha, thus became the first-born brother of a new
family: "Whoever does the will of God is my brother, and sister, and
mother" (Mark 3:35). The two ages are constituted by their rulers,
but only the true ruler can create true unity and peace and joy.

We may remember again Jesus' emphasis upon unconditional trust in
the powerful goodness of the Father. It is only in his most solitary hour,
when all earthly securities evaporate, that man's ultimate confidence is
manifested. Will he trust God when none other seems to trust him, and
when all history seems to show the folly of such trust? The cross again
is the test of the individual; but through him it is constitutive of com-

munity, for through faith in the Crucified One the individual can trust God as working everywhere and in all people. "Love . . . believes all things, hopes all things, endures all things" (I Cor. 13:7). Confidence of this sort has no limits; it refuses to despair of either God or man, refusing to relinquish to Satan any final power over any segment of human history. Henceforth the disciple says,

> "None of us lives to himself, and none of us dies to himself.
> If we live, we live to the Lord,
> And if we die, we die to the Lord;
> So then, whether we live or whether we die, we are the Lord's.
> For to this end Christ died and lived again,
> That he might be Lord both of the dead and of the living"
> (Rom. 14:7-9).

One recalls that to Jesus integrity of will is the counterpart of complete unawareness of one's own goodness. "No one is good but God alone" (Mark 10:18). Unconscious goodness of this sort is obviously an individual affair which is destroyed immediately by comparative judgments. The old age lives by its reliance on comparative judgments, by the holier-than-thou assumptions of persons, families, races, civilizations. But in the dying to that self which lives by comparative judgments, the basis of community is transfigured. If I cannot consider myself better than any other man, then the barriers are indeed broken down and the pharisaic tendency in all institutions is sterilized. I find myself in a community where self-esteem can never serve as the basis of classification, where self-forgetting love eliminates the desire to love myself by loving my kind.

All these teachings are facets of the total meekness and self-denial that the Messiah had commanded and exemplified. In each of them it is clear that only in terms of his own free choice as a person before God can a man make the sacrifice required. Disciples cannot make sacrifices in another's name or evade the demand for self-denial by resting in the shade of martyrs' tombs. Yet if they are willing to renounce everything for the sake of Christ, they find themselves in a community where each member suffers when another suffers, and each rejoices in another's joy. The law of vicarious redemption is fulfilled here, but only because each member has entered by the narrow gate. If the apostles suffer, it is for the glory of others. If they suffer for the faith, it strengthens the fabric of the whole Church.

In all these ways, then, the birth of the new man is inseparable from the inception of the new age. When a man dies with Christ, he dies to all the social groupings of the old age and is raised as a member of the body of Christ. Unless he is willing to stand alone against the world, he is not worthy to be a follower of Jesus. If he is willing, he is incorporated into the new fellowship and the new family. Israel is reborn in the rebirth of the individual. The Church comes into existence in the same event as does the new man. In the obedience of Jesus, the new race is constituted, with the cross becoming its covenant.

This new age is defined by man's reorientation to God in Christ. It is manifested wherever the mind of Christ rules, wherever his love continues to edify, wherever his authority is obeyed by his servants, wherever his power over the demonic rulers of the old age is tested, wherever his Spirit communicates his presence, wherever he is judging and forgiving sinners, wherever a knee bows and a tongue confesses that Jesus is Lord.

His "little flock" lives from the coming age into the dying age, witnessing to the transition by each successive act of faith. Each today is subjected to the power of God's Tomorrow, and all contemporary circumstances are irradiated by light from the dawning Day. The sons of the Day live now by a hope that will not be put to shame. Their work is to continue the work of their king, proclaiming the divine mystery to principalities and powers and reconciling conflicts among men according to the pattern by which their own conflicts have been reconciled, the pattern of humiliation-exaltation. In this work they know that everything belongs to them, "the world or life or death or the present or the future." But they have come to know this only through knowing that now they belong to Christ and that Christ belongs to God (I Cor. 3:22, 23).

C. The Shift in the Balance of Power

Looking back over our discussion of the means by which God wins his victory over Satan and graciously invites men to share that triumph, we can perhaps summarize the contrast between the two ages. Of the present age, defined by its contrast with the new age, two things must be kept constantly in mind: (1) In no historical situation are men left without witness to God, without evidence of his sovereignty and mercy. They are therefore "without excuse." (2) Before faith comes, God's witness has been unable to communicate power to fulfill God's commands. Men are without a Lord who gives his servants power to rout the lords of this age. The sovereignty of the " many ' gods ' and many ' lords ' " has not been broken. The witness of God is thus a mark of death and condemnation, a measure of the alienation of the age, of the oneness of the body of sin and death. The old Israel does not know the power of the resurrection, for the power and work of the Lamb has been " hidden since the foundation of the world."

In the living Christ, God has taken adequate means to communicate that power. Members of the Messiah's body throw off the sovereignty of " many ' gods ' and many ' lords.' " They participate by faith in Christ's victory, in his body of life and righteousness. The new Day brings peace and joy to its sons, a fulfillment denied until now to the prophets and kings of the old age. God in his mercy has given them the supreme reward — citizenship in a Kingdom that cannot be shaken. The transformation consists of an actual shift in the balance of power, a shift that manifests itself in the five interlocking areas that constitute the age: i.e., the hopes by which men live, the mind by which they judge, the fruits of their work, their attitudes toward earthly institutions, and their allegiance to invisible lords. There is no situation in the world that can exclude this power. All things *have been subjected to Christ*. Subsequently, history does not present to disciples a tangle of insoluble dilemmas, but a series of occasions for manifesting the power of the Lord over all his enemies.

Perhaps the reader has been suppressing certain very natural objections to this logic. The victory as described above may appear to be limited to too narrow an orbit — the subjective experience of isolated individuals, or at most of a minority religion. These people may have felt released from various tyrannies; they may have been exceedingly joyous over that release; they may even have shown unusual stamina and courage as a result. But that falls far short of demonstrating a victory over all historical and cosmic forces. It does not suffice to explain the entire pageant of public affairs. What does the salvation of scattered individuals have to do with the destiny of great corporate entities, such as races, nations, and civilizations? Surely there must be other meanings in the march of time than the salvaging of sons. What is needed is an over-all design that will assign to each century and civilization its place in the total scheme of things.

This unquenchable desire for a cosmic blueprint is plausible enough, though it may not be so innocent as it appears. It may mask the drive for superior wisdom and power which, when granted, would enable men to exalt themselves above their allotted place. It may set specifications for an answer which God does not see fit to gratify (cf. Job, ch. 38; Isa., ch. 40). Certainly it is a desire which men have sought to satisfy since the beginning of time, in spite of the fact that such a satisfaction has never been granted for long to many people. Just as certainly this inveterate quest for an all-inclusive design detracts a man's thought from the sphere of his immediate responsibilities. And in doing so it betrays a tacit verdict concerning the significance of the individual and his decisions which is the antithesis of God's estimate (Matt. 10:29; 18:10). The ambitious philosopher of history, in seeking first of all to know the rhythms of societies, may despise " one of these little ones," and in so doing forfeit a necessary means for understanding the life of mankind as a whole. An unbeliever may see little connection between the realization of international order and the rebirth of sons, but no follower of Christ may ignore His estimate of priorities.

It must be admitted that non-Christians do think about the balance of world power in ways quite foreign to their ideas of individual fortunes. It is also true that this mental habit is characteristic of many nominal Christians, perhaps because they do not see *how* all things have been subjected to Christ. One mark of this unauthorized divorce between personal and cosmic destiny may be noted in the attitudes toward personal temptation. It is not the habit of the world to assume that private wrestling with inner passions is of primary importance in determining the shape of public affairs. The private struggle is merely a test of a person's wit and will, demonstrating the tenacity of his purpose or the strength of his ideals. Whether a person succeeds or fails does not affect the course of history, that is, unless he is also an important cog in the wheels of a strategic machine.

Not so, according to the logic of the New Testament. Here victory or defeat of the individual involves much more than his own stability and resourcefulness. His decision, on however small a stage, brings into play all the forces that contend for the domination of the world. It determines his allegiance to Christ or to Satan, becoming a crucial weight in the balance of cosmic diplomacy. It marks a triumph of either the old age or the new. If the latter, then a creative act has taken place, an act of freedom that lifts the self with all its affiliations out of the groove of blind recurrence, an act where God exerts his power to redeem the time. A faithless choice, on the other hand, means the continuance of the ball-and-chain routines of sin and its consequences. Freedom is denied both the man and the creation whose rebellion is embodied in his act. The battle with temptation conceals the stakes of life or death for that creation whose solidarity with the individual is realized in his act.

The interpreter of history who cannot deal adequately with the ultimate source of spiritual freedom in a single choice, who cannot discern the cosmic relevance of the experience of life in the midst of death, will detect no momentous power in the birth and death of a Nazarene carpenter. But the disciple who has beheld God embodying himself in ordinary human existence, and who has experienced the transformation of his earthly pilgrimage, will have some basis for understanding the claim that Christ has actually dethroned all other kings.

The understanding of this claim, of course, did not come to the first disciples by mental gymnastics, by the ingenious rearrangement of ideas into a new pattern. It came rather through personal battle with the forces that actually dominate history. When this battle began in a man's first confession of Jesus as Lord, he did not prove himself completely victorious at the outset. His former logic left its imprint on his mind. Before faith came, he had been skeptical over the power of a dead man to challenge the momentum of historical juggernauts like the Roman Empire. How could Jesus, in his weakness on the cross, transform the power structure of ancestral social institutions? Nor did the first steps of faith wholly exorcise this skepticism. The inertia of social customs, the corporate idolatries of the masses, the dogmatic assertiveness of commercial and political leaders — all these presented the disciple with a solid wall of opposition. And the very strength of the tempter lay in the obvious fact that this wall could not be breached by an individual's arrow.

Consider, for example, the difficulties in the way of obeying the Messiah's command to forgive one's enemies. As he continued along the path of humble love, the disciple discovered that this command increased in range and depth. He must forgive not only once or twice, but an unlimited number of times. He must forgive not only his petty foes but his deadliest enemies. And these enemies seemed to become more numerous, more organized, and more deadly. Yet he must forgive them for what they had done in the past, and for what they might do in the future. He must forgive them not only in word or act, but also from the heart, where no trace of self-pity or resentment could be allowed to fester. In dealing with such a command, he found that each act of forgiveness prepared the way for a situation in which there were greater opportunities for reconciliation just because there were greater obstacles to it. Although this made the temptation to despair more acute, it also extended the range of potential victory.

Shall I forgive my enemies? But who can forgive all of them? And what is the use when opposition pyramids itself? And how do I deal with men who are not personally guilty, but who simply channel the guilt of corporate institutions? If I forgive them as persons, what can that accomplish when the real foe is a "mass man," a corporate entity that is by its nature impervious to reconciliation in personal terms? Nations continue their jockeying for primacy with no genuine grace of forgiveness. Wealthy employers and hungry laborers cannot and do not forgive each other, at least when they are representing their group interests. Individual Jews may forgive individual Gentiles, but the clash of race and religion shows no sign of abating. Surely one act of forgiveness (especially if it means death for the one who forgives) is worthless so long as large-scale forgiveness alone can effect reconciliation among nations. How can an individual deflect the policies of nations as they career from one war to another? At best the individual leaves but a tiny scratch on the surface of things; only powerful social institutions can write in indelible ink. What, then, is the significance of a single painful act of self-humiliation?

This is obviously the kind of reasoning that gives temptation its hold over men. This is the rationalization by which men call Jesus "Lord, Lord," but disobey his commands. The New Testament is fully aware of the stubborn facts that seem to justify such rationalizations. It recognizes the glacierlike stubbornness and weight of corporate organizations. It appreciates the power of the multitudes over the individual, and candidly calls it slavery. It is quite aware that no person can emancipate himself, that only divine sovereignty can set limits to the aggressions of massed power. But this, it says, is just what has happened. Against Jesus the pressure of historical magnitudes reached its zenith. As one man alone against a hostile world he was commanded to forgive

his enemies, in a setting which seemed to make such forgiveness absolutely futile. He conquered the tempter. Because this tempter is the
hidden power behind all entrenched evils, this work of forgiveness by
a solitary man on his cross actually represented a cosmic victory. Subdue the ruler of a kingdom, and you win his kingdom as well.

This is the victory that is shared whenever men follow Jesus' Way of
humble reconciliation. His follower, whether in obedience or disobedience to his earthly superiors, does everything in self-forgetting love.
This means that a revolution has taken place, not first of all in the external associations of men, but in their inward motivations and their
ultimate allegiances. The man who loves as Jesus loved has but one
Master and one mind. He wills but one thing. This enables him to say
with Paul:

> "There are many 'gods' and many 'lords' — yet for us there is one
> God, the Father, from whom are all things and for whom we exist, and
> one Lord, Jesus Christ, through whom are all things and through whom
> we exist" (I Cor. 8:5, 6).

The old age, according to this testimony, is ruled by many lords; the
new is ruled by one. Citizens of the old may verbally deny the existence
of their lords, yet by their acts testify to that existence. Citizens of
the new age may verbally affirm the existence of Satan's retinue,
yet by their free obedience to God testify to the termination of Satan's rule. In either age the actual power of Satan is dependent upon
the response of men to God's will and the corresponding resistance
they offer to the tempter's snares. Wherever they are induced to
accept the power of social institutions or their human agents as absolute, they participate in the worship of no-gods (whatever may
be said or thought of their existence). But in all such idolatry, whether
its occasion be provided by the family, the state, or the religion, the sin
lies not in the institution but in the human servant and the heavenly
ruler who by depending on each other rob God of his rightful glory.
On the other hand, when a man learns the principle by which Satan
establishes his regime, when he learns by difficult experience the power
of meekness, he makes every social institution the instrument for serving God, and finds in so doing that the institution becomes again what
it was meant to be: the servant of man. Having learned the secret of
Satan's power, he joins the exodus of God's people from the land of

slavery, using as a door the cross. For it was in the cross that Jesus demonstrated the illusory and temporary character of Satan's power, here that he opened a new road to freedom which can never be closed (I John 3:10–18; 5:19; Heb. 2:14, 15).

For freedom Christ sets men free. Those who receive this gift know that it involves much more than a private, subjective feeling of release, induced by emotional or intellectual activity alone. They know this because the God who has freed them is the ruler of all creation, because the Messiah is a carpenter of Nazareth whose freedom was actually won in concrete decisions, and because their own relationships to empirical situations have been radically changed. They know it because they have passed through the fires of a final judgment, fires that continue to burn wherever the battle with sin is undertaken. Emancipation is always, for the early Christian, a close companion of this judgment. He is freed when he recognizes in God the sole right to judge his creation, and when he accepts this judgment upon himself. The operation of judgment takes many different and always unexpected forms, but it is always nearer to the sinner than he supposes. God adapts the form and time of judgment to a particular sinner and his particular idolatry.[12] In some cases, God allows Satan's promises and men's desires to be fulfilled, but he makes the fulfillment hollow. Lusts become sated. Greed produces wealth, but not security or contentment. Political and military activity produce temporary power, but not peace. Religious zeal yields a harvest of self-righteousness that does not succeed in subduing a deeper sense of guilt.

In other cases, God frustrates Satan's offers and men's hopes. Wealth is suddenly taken by a thief; luxurious clothes are eaten by moths; the farmer's barns are full, but his soul is required of him. An economy built on profit becomes inflated until the profits are worthless; a nation that trusts in its battlewagons is crushed; earthly wisdom is shown to be folly by contrast with the wisdom of what it considered to be folly. God destroys accepted standards of honor by giving honor to outcasts. The nation that looks for a Messiah does not recognize him when he comes. A world seeking happiness finds boredom. Men who conquered mountains cry for the mountains to fall on them. They sought life but now crave death, without, however, being able to find it.

When the sinful pretensions of individuals and groups reach their pinnacle, when their many lords seem to flourish most effectively, that is the time when the abyss is revealed by God's judgment. His verdict comes as suddenly as lightning, as silently as the thief, as catastrophically as the flood. The disciple remembers the hour of darkness at Jesus' crucifixion, the hour of temptation when Peter heard the cock crow, the hour when Paul was struck blind on the road to Damascus. He knows that the night is darkest just when the morning star rises.

In other words, for him the hour of judgment is also the hour of forgiveness. In showing him the character and wages of sin, God shows him the character and fruits of righteousness. In unveiling the source of Satan's power, he frees man from that power. Because Satan extends his tyranny by claiming final authority over men, God allows him to wield that authority over his Son, and in doing so discloses that the claim is fraudulent. Since Satan lives upon men's fears, it is in the heart of man only that his kingdom can be vanquished. By his free act of obedience, undaunted by all the powers of darkness, Jesus defeated them at the only point where they are vulnerable. And his victory, when received by others as a final victory, frees them from the same tyrant and brings them to glory as sons of God.

Thus the creation of sons through faith presages the termination of Satan's sovereignty over mankind. Jesus humbled himself beneath all human superiors, following the path of descent until he was last of all and least of all in earthly authority and power. He refused to follow the standards of security and superiority by which the rulers of the Gentiles lorded it over them. This was the only road to freedom that had not been tried in men's efforts to gain their own freedom from earthly masters. And it was the only road by which exodus from Egypt is possible. His example enabled his servants to take the same road to the same goal. More than this, through Jesus' obedience Satan was cast out of his throne in heaven so that his demons could be cast out of men on earth. And this expulsion is the sign of Satan's coming banishment when God's Kingdom comes in its fullness.

To be sure, this end of Satan's rule is hidden from the eyes that are still blinded by Satan's own stratagems, from those men who still worship the invisible powers that lurk behind social organizations. The world continues on its way oblivious to this revolution in the balance of power. It supposes that victory on these terms and with these fruits is no true victory over the gigantic evils entrenched in historical processes. But Satan recognizes what his slaves do not; he sees that his empire will crumble unless he can keep his servants from hearing or obeying the emancipation proclamation. The sign of this recognition is the bitterness and subtlety with which he attacks those who, in the freedom that Christ gives, continue to exorcise demons and to announce that Satan has been ejected from heaven by a stronger lord.

7

THE PROMISE OF THE GOSPEL

THE Day whose beginning the gospel proclaimed also had an end, and just as the story of Jesus Christ revealed the character of this beginning, so also did it reveal the character of the end. The beginning determined the disciple's retrospect; the end determined his prospect. The inauguration of Christ as king constituted the most decisive pivot in history — the history of the believer and the history of creation. So, too, the coming manifestation of Christ in power would mark the fulfillment of the disciple's mission and the fruition of the whole creative process. In turning to obey the living and true God, men began "to wait for his Son from heaven, . . . Jesus who delivers us from the wrath to come" (I Thess. 1:8–10). In sharing the humiliation and exaltation of Jesus, they received a share in his coming inheritance. Both the initial and the ultimate acts represented the gracious gift of God; both set before man the tasks of faith; both released in his heart the gratitude and energy that enabled him to serve this Master and to receive from him the crown of life. In the preceding section, the significance of the new beginning was assessed; in this section we must explore the ways in which this new expectation exerted its gravitational pull over life in the new age.

No aspect of Biblical thought, however, is more difficult for the modern man to comprehend than this dependence upon God's promise. It is of course clear that the early Christian lived by this hope for the return of Christ. But it is difficult to grasp the essential meaning and power of this hope. Two of the greatest obstacles to such an understanding are these: a faulty orientation toward the place of promise in the experience of salvation as a whole; a faulty set of mental habits in interpreting specific predictions. Let us, then, deal with these two obstacles before attempting to interpret the ways in which the gospel proclaimed a new end and a new hope.

A. SALVATION AS PROMISE [15]

We have already noted that to men of the Bible God is the only source of true salvation. He sends messengers to announce that his salvation has already gone forth. He determines the day of salvation and brings it near to men. He opens the long-obstructed road to salvation, exalting the valleys and bringing low the mountains. He intends to establish his will in the land, and graciously includes men within this goal. His current activity is a direct manifestation of his holiness, righteousness, and love. The word " salvation " thus refers to the manward aspect of God's activity. Consequently, each separate message of salvation derives its primary meaning from God's purpose at work in that particular historical situation.

Equally central, however, is the thought of salvation as the Godward aspect of man's activity. It is a goal to which man must give priority above every other hope. If a man classes this promise as one among many promises of life, he fails to understand it. If he rates this motive along with other motives that impel men forward, he is essentially faithless. The purpose that God announces must establish a total claim on man's allegiance. Yet, although God's promised deliverance transcends infinitely all the lesser goods which men may crave, it is mediated to men within their allotted time and place. It comes within range of their choices here and now. To yield priority to God's purpose brings integrity to man's heart and unity of direction to his multifarious interests. It confers upon man the strength to stand, so that his foot will not be moved. In responding to God's word with his whole strength man learns that he can be obedient to a final hope in the midst of the fluctuating possibilities of a fluid situation.

The promise of ultimate deliverance is as near to him as his own lips or heart (Rom. 10:8). It is this message that calls on him to work out his own salvation with fear and trembling. And this will and this work are themselves a sign of God's deliverance (Phil. 2:12, 13). The message of salvation thus points to an experienced synthesis between the manward aspect of God's activity and the Godward aspect of man's activity.

But man does not through his own wisdom and goodness establish this synthesis. He seeks God's Kingdom with a fragment of his energy within a chosen segment of his human associations. In actual life he continues to treat this hope as secondary in importance and value to competing human goals, and as dependent upon them. When the going gets difficult, when the choice of the good requires self-denial, then it is easy to deny God's promise because it is the least tangible of the goals in a given situation. But to repudiate God's purpose in this situation corrupts all other desires, including those which man has exalted as most meaningful and sacred.

In this impasse God alone can restore his total sovereignty over man's existence. God has created him according to his own purposes and these purposes define man's true end. He wills to be all in all. He creates all things as signs of his eternal power and love. This invisible pull of God's future determines the potential meaning of every other prospect open to men, an order of priorities that the world would reverse.

Finding in his community a momentum in men's behavior that is basically " theofugal," the messenger from God proclaims the nearness of a day of wrath. But each threat of condemnation is also an invitation for the restoration of the true axis of man's life. This word becomes " the power of God for salvation " to everyone who believes. Salvation is communicated at the point where God's faithfulness and man's faith meet, the point where the line of God's promise meets the line of man's hope. The career of Jesus had underscored the divergence of these lines, and the radical character of the divergence. Because of this divergence, the initial step in the fulfillment of God's promise can be taken only when God turns toward man in judgment and forgiveness and when man turns toward God in repentance and faith. The covenant between God and man must be revealed as a broken covenant before it can be restored.

The metaphor of the road is used as a spatial image for charting the dynamics of this spiritual situation. In applying this image, God's spokesman reduces the multiple possibilities in human movement to the choice between two roads. One is the road to destruction; he who walks in it goes farther and farther from God and life. The other is the road to salvation; he who takes it moves toward fellowship with God and life. The Messiah found men walking the former path. Travel here is easy and the traffic is heavy, but the path leads to a dead end. The Messiah announces God's intention to open a new way: " The kingdom of God is at hand." The gate is narrow and the pitch is steep, but every effort to follow is blessed with God's help. God steps toward man with his threat of doom, his offer of pardon, his assurance of life; man steps toward God with his repudiation of sin, his desire for succor, his trust in God's promise. It should be obvious that this use of the term " road " is qualitative and imaginative. Externally considered, three men may take the same road from Jerusalem to Jericho on the same day, but for only one of them is this the road to life. Or, as Jesus put it, two women may be grinding at the same mill; one will be taken and the other left (Luke 17:35).

The divergence and convergence of personal wills is also projected into temporal as well as spatial images. The manward aspect of God's activity takes the form of ushering in a new day, a new year, or a new age — a period of time that is qualitatively different from man's present plight. At the outset of his ministry the Messiah detected signs of the dawn and pointed them out to his hearers. Repentance is accordingly visualized as awaking from sleep, alert and patient watching for the " morning star," walking now by the light of the rising sun.

Some, of course, prefer to sleep, relying on their own ability to tell the difference between night and day. They anticipate the future in terms of their own designs and their own estimates of earthly probabilities. They predict " the shape of things to come " by projecting into the future a curve that is based upon events they have observed in the past and present. They assume that the proportion of weal or woe tomorrow will depend upon today's alignment of earthly powers. They fear that the morrow will produce no new thing, yet they hope for an improvement in their own status. Their fears are fulfilled and their hopes denied because tomorrow turns out to be a continuation of today so long as the world's promises take precedence over God's. Darkness continues so long as men trust in these false " futures " of the dying age.

The approach of God's Day confronts men with a new future, a future that is spiritually opposed to the illusory tomorrows of men's dreams. God's judgment and man's sin render this Day qualitatively distinct from the night. God's forgiveness and man's repentance accomplish a transition from the realm of darkness to that of light. The assurance of forgiveness thus presents to man a genuinely new possibility, but one that requires an extreme dislocation in his attitude to time. The new Day with this new opportunity is not simply the third factor in the succession of tenses — past, present, future. It is a new creation which permeates and interrupts the apparently self-perpetuating series of days. The new Day is a projection of God's purpose from the future into the present; it is a heavenly future that judges and redeems whatever the earthly future may hold. Likewise, man's hope by which he apprehends this miraculous opportunity transcends all other hopes by its immunity to their transiency. It can never become wholly domesticated within the mundane accomplishments of men. Yet men can live by it, and to live by it redeems all other desires from emptiness.

So long as he walks by faith, man's life becomes continuous with the new Day. He has been saved, is being saved, and will be saved. In other words, the term " salvation " embraces all phases of life in the new age. This age has its own time span and imparts its own sense of duration. It is punctuated by those acts of power whereby God extends his sovereignty and by those experiences whereby man's faith is tested and strengthened. For the believer, the real sense of progression stems from knowledge of what God has done, is doing, and is about to do. This outlook reduces to secondary importance the prefaith calculations of what may happen tomorrow. The significance of coming days is now measured by reference to God's purpose rather than to man's calendar.

Even within the span of God's Day there remains an important distinction between the present and the future. The two are, of course, very closely related. The victory of faith now brings confidence of victory then; the victory then is the completion and ratification of the victory won now. Yet the existence of a span between these two victories is essential to God's intention. He can either shorten or lengthen the interim in accordance with his love and long-suffering. Sons must be disciplined in both expectancy and patience. They must be trained as servants toward the goal of perfect obedience and humility. The leaven must have time to work, the seed to produce its harvest. Love must prove its power to endure to the end. Thus, for the sake of his sons, God sets before them " a little while " as Lebensraum for their faith. This theme will be expanded in the following chapter.

The promise of a glorious consummation is a mystery that is conveyed only to those who through faith are being saved. Just as the joys of the new road are accessible only to those who enter it, so too the preview of its end is made intelligible only to them. Knowledge of their inheritance remains a miraculous gift, the source of awe and gratitude. They realize that this knowledge is partial and fragmentary, but they are content with its adequacy for their needs. They are less impatient to discern the full outline of coming events than are their associates in the world, for they have a task that requires all their energies. Their knowledge of what lies ahead is not sufficient to make them immune to temptation, but it is adequate to the needs of their work as stewards. Engaged in this work, they know that they are known and are willing to trust in the power of their Lord to redeem his pledge (II Cor. 4:1–12; II Tim. 1:8–12).

God's redemptive activity thus includes within a single span the whole of the new road, from its beginning in the first act of obedience to the end when obedience is made perfect. It connotes the whole of the new Day (or alternately, the age), from its inauguration in God's word and man's response, to the redemption of all creation. Just as the incarnation of God's purpose in Jesus embraced the whole course of his ministry, so too the eternal life incorporates into a single unity the entire road of the disciple, thus bringing the whole time of his pilgrimage under the promise of blessedness. This blessedness is a good that transcends all other goods and hopes, yet it is capable of being realized wherever, in his immediate situation, the disciple moves forward in meekness and mercy. The athletes who run their race with abandon discover the joy in running and know that this joy is a foretaste of the prize. Complete knowledge of what this crown will mean awaits the victory in running. Toward that victory the runner is " straining forward " (Phil. 3:2–15), and as he runs, his knowledge of the promise is enhanced.

This estimate of the place of promise in salvation is strikingly different from a perspective that has frequently been falsely attributed to the Bible. Many people assume that the chief attraction in God's promise is the assurance of life after death. They are haunted by the uncertainties of existence beyond the grave, and they seek to stifle their dread by accepting pious doctrines and practices. They want a place in heaven, and they are afraid of a place in hell. This dread is nourished by ignorance. Men have not yet experienced death, nor are they able to communicate with those who have. Considering a future life to be the highest good, yet unable to penetrate behind the curtain, they speculate about its terrain. Dubious of the dependability of such guesses, they turn to the Bible for a preview in which they may place confidence.

But let us observe the controlling attitudes underlying this concern with Biblical predictions. A person in this case assumes that he knows what death is and that he can measure its approach and arrival. He assumes that his eternal destiny is determined by his relationship to this fortuitous event, rather than by his relationship to God in earlier events. He assumes that he already knows what life is, and what is necessary for its desirable continuance. He wants above all else that his own cherished values may survive, and he measures their survival in terms of the continuance of the same time line that has prevailed during his earthly life. It is by reference to this objective time quotient that he distinguishes life before death from life after death. Thus the axis of his life turns on his relation to impersonal factors, not on his relation to God. His treasures and his heart are not really laid up in heaven, i.e., with God.

The disclosure of God's saving righteousness in Jesus Christ produced a very different complex of attitudes. In the New Testament death's reality is taken for granted: " All flesh is like grass "; yet death's meaning derives from the character of man's relationship to God. The only death that men may fear is that which comes through sin, through man's own choice and through God's righteous judgment. Because all men have sinned and all stand under judgment, death has spread through all (Rom. 5:12–14). Men have become enslaved to fear of these two enemies: sin and death. God takes the initiative in releasing them from this slavery by taking captivity captive. "For our sake he made him to be sin who knew no sin " (II Cor. 5:21). For our sake also he died, being " made like his brethren in every respect " (Heb. 2:17). The cross underscores the reality of death for all men, and at the same time the miraculous possibility of victory over death. This victory was made possible only because in dying Jesus was expressing his perfect obedience to God. He was dying to sin and for sin; he was dying for men " while we were . . . helpless . . . sinners . . . enemies " of God (Rom. 5:6–11). His death marked the full realization of God's power and love. Therefore God exalted his servant, designating him " Son of God in power according to the Spirit of holiness by his resurrection from the dead " (ch. 1:3, 4).

This is the true beginning of the new Day for his disciples, for Jesus is the first-born of many brethren. In the moment of their repentance and faith, they are reborn as children of God, becoming something that they had not been before. The decisive turning point from death to life is determined, not by what happens in the grave, but by what happens now. Today men are called upon to die with Christ, to die to self, to the law, to flesh, to sin. *This* death is the victory, for here God makes them alive with Christ (ch. 6; Eph., ch. 2). " If Christ is in you, although your bodies are dead because of sin, your spirits are alive because of righteousness " (Rom. 8:10). It is through Christ that salvation is begun. Here God's love manward elicits man's faith Godward. " In Christ " men share the mind of Christ, obey his purposes, carry on his ministry of reconciliation. " In Christ " God elects men to share in his heavenly inheritance of life and joy. Faith is the victory that overcomes the world because it enables God to make us one with Christ, who already has overcome the world by his faith. The redemption that Jesus brings is thus a source of power by which men now may overcome the world, but it is a power that is made available only through a trust in God's promise. For what does the faith of Jesus Christ signify if it does not refer to his eagerness to live by the promise of the coming Kingdom? To share with him in that promise, therefore, requires that the disciple emulate his faith with regard to the way in which he interprets God's promise. In renouncing the old age, the disciple renounces as well the world's way of appraising the future. Let us turn, then, to a discussion of the method by which the believer interprets the assurances of God and turns his steps toward their fulfillment.

B. Interpreting the Promise

At the outset it is clear that the believer must react to the message of coming events with the assumption that this threat-and-promise is addressed to him.[16] The unbeliever may toy with the same message as something intended for others; should he speculate on the possibility that it might refer to him, he gets no farther than that. Moreover, the believer understands that it is addressed to him in the midst of today's immediate dilemmas. It involves the whole web of his relationships — to persons, groups, institutions — by bringing those relationships under the scrutiny of a final judgment. In the context of these particular associations he is confronted with an opportunity and a choice that have a decisive bearing upon his destiny.

Furthermore, the believer understands that the message is directed primarily at the invisible bond that links him to God, a bond that is embodied in the same web of relationships. God makes a perfect diagnosis of his illness and adjusts his prescription to that diagnosis. God knows in what his present deafness consists, what his most subtle temptations are at this particular stage of his pilgrimage. The prediction of coming wrath is aimed at his lack of faith, seeking to replace one set of competing hopes by a single-minded loyalty to God. The chasm between the coming redemption and the present moment is as wide or narrow as God's purpose and man's response make it.

In responding to God's promise, the believer knows that the whole purpose of God is behind each expression of his desire for man. The word that comes to him today may be couched in limited and nonrecurring terms; for instance, it may assure him simply of bread for the morrow. Tomorrow God may express his promise in different terms. Yet however limited and nonrecurrent the scope of a particular prediction, the faithful listener recognizes that this prediction is an intrinsic part of God's design. Today's dialogue, in whatever terms it may be couched, is initiated by One who from the beginning knows the end. Each promise to a particular disciple or community is a step in a far-flung plan. This deeper intention lies hidden, since it embraces new things to which men's eyes and ears are not yet adjusted, but each expressed promise, so far as it comes from God, discloses the direction toward which man must press to receive the invisible inheritance.

Therefore, the disciple is humble in estimating his power to understand fully the future which is opened to him by God's word. He remembers that his response to former promises has often been inadequate and stumbling. And he traces this previous resistance to his earlier confidence that he was quite capable of knowing what the situation required. Before faith came, he had believed that he could estimate the future in terms of his own conception of historical possibilities. But this assumption had been based upon a distorted sense of what he wanted and a faulty analysis of the social changes necessary before he could get what he wanted. He had made the fulfillment of his desires conditional upon a time schedule that was based on a pragmatic estimate of earthly conditions. He had said to himself: " Before this hope can be realized, this must happen, and that, and that. This step will require so many days, this step so many months. Only after these steps have been taken, will I be able to say, 'Lo, here it is!', and find the object of my desire." But in faith the same man recognizes that such calculations envisage a goal that is essentially earthly, a goal that depends on ordinary human resources. If they succeed, these efforts usher in a day of fulfillment that will not be qualitatively different from the other days of personal history.

God challenges such appraisals by his urgent word that his "Day" is at hand. His Kingdom is not merely one day among others, coming in sequence with others at their end. His is an eternal Day, which redeems the evil time and makes it fruitful. Power over the new Day rests with God, not with men. This Day does not wait until various human specifications are met, because it is not a projection into the future of man's present desires (based on past frustrations). Rather, God hastens his Day by advancing his future into the present, as a means of revising the current alignment of man's heart. This Day cuts across the time-consciousness of men, forcing them to choose now the age in which they shall live. The believer thus learns to listen with humility to any new promise from God.

From his earlier experiences the disciple has learned also to expect God's word on the lips of a very human messenger. He is therefore alert to the need for recognizing a prophet, even though he appear in an unusual garb without the expected credentials. He knows that the true prophet himself is a sign of the times, for he stands at the point where God's Day is dawning. He knows that the prophet is sent from the future into the present to relay his understanding of the requirements of life in that Day. To interpret the prophet's word correctly, then, he must stand with the prophet at the same intersection of the times. He must look forward from the prophet's point of standing, facing the new future that is opened by God's invitation. The Spirit, which speaks through the prophet, must enter the listener's heart if he is to hear, to obey, and to interpret that message for others. Thus does the Holy Spirit, herald of the dawn, extend his outreach through the prophet to the people addressed.

Nor does the Holy Spirit stop there. God is about his business of calling into being a people who are not now his people, so that they in turn may carry on that same work. The prophet is God's instrument in this enterprise; to share his point of view, therefore, the interpreter must accept for himself the prophet's task. When he heeds the prophetic warning, he finds himself called to a particular task in the life of the community; if he accepts the call, he will be given through the Holy Spirit the endowment needed to accomplish that task. Thus is created a peculiar fellowship in the coming Day, a fellowship with those through whom he hears the message and with those to whom he is in turn sent. Speakers and listeners move forward together as pilgrims to the enduring City, thereby indicating their citizenship in it.

Having thus glanced at the perspective within which the faithful disciple listens to God's promises, let us recall some of the specific predictions through which Jesus shared his mission with those who followed him. The whole range of promises is well summarized in the tenth chapter of Matthew. Here may be found predictions addressed to all servants side by side with others addressed to a particular group — predictions that constantly recur in many situations along with those that are apparently limited to a single situation. The passage is thus something of a test of the reader's ability to select those which are addressed to him in his own place and time. There are those, of course, who interpret all these promises on the same level. All of them, one group believes, were applicable only to a situation that does not recur. All of them, in the view of another group, are addressed to all men in all situations. The interpretation of this passage is thus a test of the reader's powers of discrimination, and by no means an easy test.

As reported to us in the Gospel of Matthew (and we are now primarily concerned with the meaning in this context), this message of Jesus represents his first commissioning of reapers to help in gathering the harvest. Heretofore in the Gospel, the Master had been the only harvester, granting the grace of eternal life to sinners according to their faith. But the harvest is too vast for him to reap alone; he must call others who will fill the granary (Matt., chs. 8; 9).

To guide them in their work he discloses to them the conditions of employment and the rewards open to them and to their auditors. The basic, all-inclusive promise is one which they themselves have been seeking: "The kingdom of heaven is at hand" (ch. 10:7). This they are to proclaim to the lost sheep of Israel. Like their leader, they are empowered to forgive sinners, to cleanse lepers, to cast out demons. Like him they are to interpret these deeds as signs of the promised age.

In their work as harvesters, God's Kingdom draws near to men for their acceptance or rejection. There is a decisive finality about both the promise and the response to it.

Those who reject it are assured of eternal judgment: " It shall be more tolerable on the day of judgment for the land of Sodom and Gomorrah " (v. 15). Those, on the other hand, who are hospitable will share the reward (vs. 40 f.). What, then, is this reward? The disciple who loses his life will find it (v. 39). If, when he is summoned before governors, he acknowledges the Master, then the Master will acknowledge him before God (v. 32). He that endures to the end, though that end be earthly disgrace and death, will be saved (v. 22).

These assurances are integral to the disciples' faith and work. Moreover, they are integral to the whole message of Jesus and are repeated in various forms on many different occasions during his ministry. All of them have reference to immediate decisions demanded of men within their actual environment, but the reward and punishment far transcend the observable results in terms of mundane fortunes. This life, this inheritance of the new age, is such that " even the hairs of your head are all numbered " (v. 30). Such promises are not limited to the day when they were first uttered, at least in the opinion of the Gospel editor. He is writing for a Church at least half a century later than the initial utterance. He has in mind the needs of disciples during his own day, although he is quite aware that decade after decade these words had mediated God's purpose to different disciples in many different conditions. He was convinced that wherever and whenever followers of Jesus share the mission of the first harvesters, their work is oriented around these same promises, and is supported by them.

The fulfillment of these promises cannot be tested by ordinary criteria; the fulfillment is disclosed only from faith to faith. Unless one loses his life he will hardly know what it means to find it (v. 39). The work of witnessing to the new age consists of trusting in the hidden and secret presence of God's power. And this trust rests upon the assurance that " nothing is covered that will not be revealed " (v. 26). The messengers have a part in this unveiling of secret things, but ultimately it is God who will make every hidden reality known to all. This is another promise integral to their mission.

Woven together with these promises are others that refer more explicitly to observable happenings, predictions that are more limited in scope. By that very token they seem to be less adaptable to recurring situations and more open to the usual tests of accuracy. For example, the messengers are forewarned that they will be delivered up to councils, flogged in the synagogues, dragged before kings. Hated everywhere because of their loyalty to Jesus, they will be betrayed by their own kinsfolk. As they pursue their task from town to town, they will be followed and persecuted. An alarming prospect indeed. To still their hearts a specific assurance is given: " When you are summoned to stand trial before hostile courts, ' what you are to say will be given you in that hour; for it is not you who speak, but the Spirit of your Father speaking through you ' " (vs. 19 f.). The prospect of the eternal Tomorrow involves this very tangible prospect in the earthly tomorrows. The underlying basis for both prospects is this:

> " A disciple is not above his teacher,
>   nor a servant above his master;
>   It is enough for the disciple to be like his teacher,
>   and the servant like his master " (vs. 24, 25).

The message of teacher and disciple is the same; so are the task and its hazards, the resources and the rewards. How are these predictions to be assessed when one considers some of the more obvious facts of history? The historian is forced to observe that these events did not take place during that particular journey of Jesus' disciples; they were not dragged before kings during the ministry of Jesus — that is, if other records are to be trusted. Nor did the predictions come true for many disciples between Jesus' day and the date of the Gospel of Matthew; for some, indeed, but not for all. At this latter date, the Church was facing sporadic outbursts of official persecution, and the teacher who wrote the Gospel may have been preparing his audience for that contingency. In any case, it is probable that the sayings of Jesus were amended during the intervening period so as to apply more directly to conditions that did not pertain to the initial setting. Even so, it is doubtful if this prediction was ever literally fulfilled for all disciples at any given epoch in the Church's history. When have all disciples been hated by all for his name's sake (v. 22)?

How, then, are disciples to listen to these words when it is unlikely that they themselves will ever be flogged in synagogues or delivered over to the Sanhedrin? They may conclude that the predictions do not apply to them; they may return them, however reluctantly, to the musty archives of the past, assuming that their function has been accomplished. They may defend their literal truth but maintain that they refer to events still pending. Whether they defend the truth as something that has been demonstrated or as something yet to be demonstrated, the words appear to have little immediate bearing upon the decisions of contemporary disciples. Perhaps we should leave the matter there, but neither the editor of Matthew nor his successors in the Church have been content with that. They have been convinced that the Messiah continues to speak to his servants through these promises.

One possible reason for this conviction may be noted here. Let us remember the wider principles that cover these more detailed expectations. "Whoever would save his life will lose it" (ch. 16:25). "A disciple is not above his teacher" (ch. 10:24). These proclaim that every disciple must, as a disciple, share in one way or another the teacher's self-denial and his sufferings. Now the sufferings of Jesus are not comprised only or even mainly by the bodily anguish on the cross. When the disciple takes up the cross, he does not die in the same way that Jesus did, but still he dies. His task alone requires that he leave the old age and seek the new. And what does that mean? To answer this question we need to recall the points at which the two ages are in conflict. The disciple stands at the place of tension between the desires and fears, the mind and heart, the hidden sovereignties of the two ages. He is not a true disciple unless he stands here, unless he witnesses to the new age in a form that aggravates these tensions with the old, unless he gladly and humbly accepts the growing cost of these tensions, out of gratitude to his Master and for love of men. Whether the form in which he pays this cost is that of trial before the Sanhedrin or family dissension or social ostracism or the indifference of men to the word of peace, the cost is exchanged into the common currency of an inner agony of spirit, where fellowship with the Messiah's sufferings is actually consummated. The prediction, "You will be dragged before governors" (ch. 10:18), may not apply to him, for the world's hostility is not expressed in exactly the same way twice. But that it will be expressed in ways appropriate to each disciple is one of the basic promises of the New Testament.

There is yet one more prediction to be dealt with, one that is perhaps most troublesome of all. As the disciples of Jesus started on their first assignment, Jesus is reported to have said to them: "You will not have gone through all the towns of Israel, before the Son of Man comes" (v. 23). Few predictions of the Gospels are more difficult to interpret than this one, and its opaqueness is indicated by the diversity of conflicting interpretations. It is not hard to locate the core of the difficulties. The hearers addressed by the Master are very clearly identified and the terms of the promise made entirely definite. The disciples of Jesus — those who heard him on a given occasion — will not have finished this particular trip through the towns of Israel before the Son of Man comes. We cannot doubt the place or the time or by some feat of legerdemain substitute another setting. Jesus assures them that within the limits of this setting the Son of Man will come to them. It may be noted that by the time the Gospel was written this setting was already obsolete. The disciples had gone far beyond the towns of Israel. And yet the prediction was preserved in spite of its obsolescence.

Must one not concede that the prediction was not fulfilled? The Son of Man did not come when promised; nor had he come when The Gospel According to Matthew was written; nor has he come since. Must we not, then, either relegate the prediction to the class of mistaken guesses or join the ranks of those who embarrass the Church with their literalism and millennialism? Perhaps. But it may be wise to pause, not because we are afraid to concede the presence of such errors in the sacred Writ, but out of curiosity, if nothing else. Why is such a prediction preserved by Matthew and by others who recognize candidly this very difficulty?

Let us remember that the Day of the Son of Man is other than the days of man's calendar. And let us also remember that this Day does not dawn for all men at the same instant by the objective clocks of the world. The term "day," as we have seen, is a qualitative image which articulates the dynamic momentum of divine-human relationships. It is closely parallel to the expression "year of the Lord" and to the new age. It is virtually equivalent to the fullness of eternal life, which is the overarching meaning of salvation.[17] Much of the confusion in interpreting this passage stems from the assumption of the interpreter that the coming of the Son of Man is everywhere treated in the New Testament as a single objective event, like the coming of a train, and that its coming can be scheduled accordingly. We have already, perhaps, described sufficiently the qualitative constituents of the new age. And we could amass much New Testament evidence to show that, with one important qualification to be made later, the Son of Man does not come to all men and all places at precisely the same instant or in the same fashion. The parables of Jesus, for example, picture the future judgment as coming at different times to different people, in accordance with their watchfulness. In The Revelation of John, the Son of Man's coming is determined in part by people's response to his knocking (Rev. 2:5, 6, 25; 3:11, 20; 22:7, 12, 17, 20). The time of his coming to the martyrs, whose faithfulness has already been tested to the uttermost, is not the same as the time of his coming to those whose work is not yet done (chs. 6; 7).[18]

When once one has realized this flexibility in the "image" of the Messiah's coming, the way is open to fruitful exegesis of the prediction. Into such exegesis we cannot go fully, but a tentative suggestion, at least, should be made. The author does not intend to rest the argument of the chapter upon this interpretation, which may or may not commend itself to the reader. But it is worth-while to look occasionally at the tougher riddles with which the Gospels supply us.

Let the reader, then, apply the principles of interpretation which we have been sketching. Let him remember that according to the Gospel of Matthew this promise belongs with the others that we have reviewed and is not wholly incompatible with them. Like them, it articulates a hidden, spiritual relationship between the visible work of the emissaries and the invisible fruit of that work. It relates a specific task (i.e., going through the cities of Israel) to an eternal judgment, pointing forward to the time when everything hidden will be made manifest (i.e., the coming of the Son of Man). Let us not forget the other things that will happen to the disciples as they seek to fulfill their commission (Matt. 10:6 f.). Some of them will be killed in line of duty. All of them, to the extent that they exercise Jesus' power, will face infamy and persecution. In advance, therefore, Jesus assures them that *their* road to *their* cross is the place where the Son of Man will meet *them.* They must rely completely on him, matching his confidence and fearlessness. Tempted to resentment and violence by the world's hatred, they must persevere in meekness and mercy. When their faith reaches its maximum strength in the struggle with maximum trials; when, that is, their humble obedience has, like his, been made perfect in suffering, then will they experience, not only the presence of the

Holy Spirit (v. 20) and the assurance of God's love (v. 30), but also the " Well done " of the Son of Man, to whom has been given the final right of judging their loyalty. This coming of the Son of Man will represent the fulfillment of the promise which sustains them, the disclosure of the glory which now lies hidden in their penitent obedience. As they pursue their task, this promised advent is near enough to require haste and instant alertness, but remote enough to require diligence and patient endurance. The accent does not fall upon the prearranged timetable, but upon the disciples' participation in the mission of the Messiah in all its aspects, and upon their reunion in the fulfillment of that mission. The pledge of reunion does not enable them to foretell the day of the Lord's coming, but it demands a career of self-denying love according to the pattern of the Master in his humiliation (compare Matt. 16:24-28; 19:28-30; 20:20-28; chs. 24:45 to 25:46).

The promise of this end to their mission constitutes also a threat to those who reject them and their message. The events that mark their final faithfulness will exert a final judgment upon those who put them to death, a judgment less tolerable than the fire and brimstone which obliterated the Cities of the Plain (ch. 10:15, 40 f.). Their death, like Jesus', will represent the night's rejection of the Day. Their obedience and perfect humility will serve to manifest the scope and character of God's judgment on the old age. Their suffering, since it is like that of the Son of Man, will in its way mediate the exaltation of the Son of Man as Judge and Forgiver. Their meekness in the midst of hatred will ultimately proclaim God's design, just as Golgotha was the pulpit from which God proclaimed his redemption of the world. Wherever this proclamation, embodied in sacrificial love, is heard in its decisive form, there again the Son of Man comes among men, revealing the power of the new Day to overcome the powers of darkness. (A good commentary on the prediction of ch. 10:23 may be found in ch. 23:34-39; cf. also chs. 11:20-30; 12:38-42.)

Embedded in all these predictions is a twofold conception of God's promise as expressing the true end for both Master and disciple. This conception is visualized in terms of two victories of the Son of Man. " The Son of man has come . . ."; that victory constitutes the beginning of the new age. " The Son of man is coming "; that victory constitutes the end. These two victories are often designated by the phrases "the First Coming" and "the Second Coming," but these designations are not wholly adequate. They imply that both these comings can be dated and the interim between them measured in weeks or years. A better distinction is between the coming of God's servant in humiliation and his coming in exaltation, or between the coming of the Kingdom in hidden form and the coming in revealed form. Expressive of the first is the promise, "He who humbles himself will be exalted." Expressive of the second, "nothing is . . . hidden that will not be known." The appearance of the Messiah in the form of a servant had hidden his true glory, just as the signs of the Kingdom had kept its presence a secret. But faith knows that in this form and in these signs are latent the power that will transform the world. And faith hears Jesus utter the conditions for that transformation. The word and work of the faithful disciples are cloaked in the same humiliation; the response to their mission indicates that the secret is still hidden from the world. But the risen Lord is the guarantor of a pledge concerning the outcome of their service. He will come to them and share with them that final glory which is his to give.

Thus the very concreteness of setting for this prediction, far from making the prediction obsolete, may constitute its abiding truth. Jesus' assignment to every witness is always in terms of a specific time and place. The Kingdom must come, in the first instance, in the midst of the ordinary visible activity of ordinary men. It must come masked in humility, in the towns which each witness visits. His task may involve the death of the witness or it may not, but it must manifest a sharp judgment on the world and a humble effort to heal the world. In any case, this mission is always the prelude to the final victory — the only sort of prelude offered to men. Implicit in the prelude is Jesus' promise concerning the end of the ministry of reconciliation: i.e., he will come again. Because he comes to some whose lives are lost for his sake, his coming to them will be hidden from all except the eyes of faith. They receive a divine transfiguration that is like that of their Lord, an exaltation to be with him in the heavenly mansions. Such a consummation cannot, as we have said, be simply identified on the calendar at a single instant, an instant that is the same for all men in all places.

The single important qualification to this statement, previously mentioned, is this: The first point of reference of all the promises is to the accomplishment of God's design, the fulfillment of salvation for his whole creation. The coming of God's Kingdom in power represents the consummation of his eternal purpose. The coming manifestation of the Son of Man will signal the consummation of his mission. The coming of the same Son of Man signals the completion of the task of the Church, and the tasks of all members of that body. Because this one eternal purpose, shared thus by God and his sons, is content with nothing less than reconciling the whole of creation through the power of love, the task of none of the sons, whether of the first-born or of those who are created in his image, is wholly complete until the Son of Man is revealed to all and through all. In this sense his coming is awaited by the early Christians at one time for all men in all places. The one purpose will have but one end. When the Messiah returns with his saints, the Holy City will descend from heaven to earth and time itself shall be no more (Rev., ch. 21). The promise *that* he will come again is implicit in every call that Jesus gives to his servants. The knowledge of *how* he will come remains a mystery into which even the chief apostle sees but darkly. But he sees enough to affirm with confidence that:

> " in Christ shall all be made alive. But each in his own order: Christ the first fruits, then at his coming those who belong to Christ. Then comes the end, when he delivers the kingdom to God the Father after destroying every rule and every authority and power " (I Cor. 15:22-24).

The first fruits of the harvest have already been gathered, the life of Christ as victor over death. Jesus is now seated at the right hand of God until God has made all his enemies a footstool for his feet. He now reigns and will reign until the last enemy is destroyed. The disciples will become fruits of the same harvest when the seed sown in their lives is reaped at the end of their several missions. When they have been made perfect through humble obedience, they will " bear the image of the man of heaven," just as now they " have borne the image of the man of dust " (I Cor. 15:49). They are now, during their earthly pilgrimage, being transformed " from one degree of glory to another," each momentary affliction yielding its eternal weight of glory (II Cor. 3:18). This process of sowing and reaping will continue until the final harvest includes all creation. Then Christ's power and love will be manifested everywhere; then he will come " on the clouds of heaven," so that every eye will behold him. Then will his Kingdom, being recognized by every enemy as the truth, be submitted to God, so that he may be " all things to all men " and so that he may " fill all creation with his fullness."

In the preceding paragraphs we have moved beyond the original purpose of this chapter, which was to remove two obstacles to understanding the Scriptural attitudes toward the future. The first is removed when we grasp the centrality of God's promise in his total plan. The second is removed when we learn how to orient ourselves to the specific predictions imbedded in the tradition. Now we must look more in detail at the way in which the promises determine the immediate prospect for each disciple and then at the way in which all historical processes will find their consummation in the coming victory of Christ.

8

THE PROSPECT OF THE DISCIPLE

FAITH in Christ involved two basic axioms. In the first place, it affirmed the coalescence of the story of Jesus with the beginning of new life for the disciple and the age. In the second place, it affirmed the coalescence of the story of Jesus with the end of the disciple's course and the consummation of all ages. This solidarity with the coming fulfillment is created when Jesus' promise becomes the basis of the disciple's hope. The basis for this fusion of destinies is the fusion of wills, both expressed in the principle " like master, like servant " (Matt. 10:24, 25). In the previous chapter the initial implications of this axiom were sketched. Now we need to look more closely at the specific ways in which Jesus' promise determined the prospect of the disciple. In keeping with the above axiom, we shall look first at Jesus' responses to God's promise and then at the way in which the responses of the disciple paralleled those of Jesus.

A. THE EXAMPLE OF JESUS

The beginning and end of Jesus' race had been very closely related to each other, since they represented a single divine purpose and vocation. When Jesus said, " I have a baptism to be baptized with " (Luke 12:50), he pointed back to the initial act of repentance and forward to the coming trial in which that repentance would be supremely tested. The Spirit of the new age linked every intervening decision to the moment of anointing, an anointing that accompanied the Father's call and the Son's response. But the Spirit also linked every intervening decision to the final anointing when God approved the Crucified as his Son. The interval between the two anointings was short: measured in time, a few months; measured in space, a few miles. And it was also brief when measured in terms of the keen anticipation of Jesus; from the beginning he looked forward to the fulfillment in "a little while." Each day's decision, taken in faith, was a repetition of the initial obedience and a preparation for the final obedience. The effectiveness of this memory and this hope in determining the present resulted in the irradiation of each day by the light of the coming Day.

Considering the career of Jesus in retrospect, his followers traced the beginning of his mission to his baptism. That event had marked at least four changes for Jesus: repentance in preparation for the coming wrath; the descent of the Spirit with power; the call of God to begin his work of preaching and teaching; and the initial battle with Satan. From the time of his baptism, Jesus believed in the good news that the powers of the Kingdom were already leavening the present age. In patience he served God and him only, waiting for "the hour" when his mission would be completed. He learned to be a son through accepting in meekness the chastisement of a son. The upsurge of hostility did not shake his gentleness or make him weary and fainthearted. Rather, it was "for the joy that was set before him" that he endured the suffering and despised the shame (Heb. 12:2–6).

Jesus lived by an unfaltering trust in God's promise and by humble acceptance of the limitations and conditions of his earthly lot. In fact, what others considered limitations he treated as occasions of grace. Living by complete dependence upon God, he moved quietly through the turbulent throngs and the haunts of lepers. The Spirit rested on him, giving him power over Satan and words of authority to forgive sinners and to announce the fulfillment of the Law. To him one might apply the statement later made of a disciple: He commended himself as a servant of God

"through great endurance, in afflictions, hardships, calamities, beatings, imprisonments, tumults, labors, watching, hunger;

"by purity, knowledge, forbearance, kindness, the Holy Spirit, genuine love, truthful speech, and the power of God;

"with the weapons of righteousness for the right hand and for the left; in honor and dishonor, in ill repute and good repute" (II Cor. 6:4–8).

Here was the Runner who ran his race with perfect devotion. The end of this race was the cross — and life. The pioneer of salvation was made perfect through suffering (Heb. 2:10). This event represented the fulfillment of God's promise to him, and the manifestation through him of life for the world. Because a single purpose integrated his career, the authors of the New Testament could speak of that career as a single divine deed, an act that began with his initial obedience and ended with his final obedience.

> "Thou didst make him for a little while lower than the angels, thou hast crowned him with glory and honor, putting everything in subjection under his feet" (vs. 7, 8).

From the perspective of the Christian runner, however, the event which was for Jesus the end becomes for the disciple the beginning. During the lifetime of Jesus the baptism of the disciples had been incomplete. (It is in fact not mentioned.) If they had been baptized with water, it was not yet a baptism with the Spirit, for they had denied him in Gethsemane. Their baptism with the Spirit came after his death, when they confessed his glorification.

They saw, however, in this latter baptism certain parallels between his experience and theirs. Like his, their baptism indicated four changes: repentance as a "dying" to the old age in preparation for the new; the descent of the Spirit with power; their commissioning as stewards of his mystery; and the initial counterattacks from the dispossessed ruler, Satan. In the light of his baptism, theirs became a very significant pivot in their memories. In the light of his death, baptism was seen to be the most decisive change that can happen to a man. For in baptism they were not only initiated into a career like that of Jesus; they were baptized into his death and raised with him to new life. This meant that as brothers of Christ they had a home in heavenly places. It meant that in dying with him they were actually passing out of the dominion of death. The specter of death could no longer terrorize them; they could now call it a sleep. Their baptism meant also that they had "died to sin," freed from it and all the other "beggarly elemental spirits" of creation. As long as they remained "in Christ Jesus" their victory over all such bogies was assured.

"As long as"—but how long is that? "Bogies"—but do these things, sin and death and the like, remain bogies? Along the way there was ample opportunity for them to stumble. There were times when the promise became dim and their faith wavered. They could speak about conquering sin and death, but had they? Their baptism was not only a signal of their dedication; it was the signal for Satan to attack them. And his attacks proved that their repentance, their forgiveness, their self-denial was far from total. Disciples learned that each act of penitence, which at the time seemed to be complete, must be followed by another act on a deeper level. Each day they must die. "As long as it is called 'today'" they must humble themselves in love. Faith lives only in the immediate tussle with lack of faith. And it was in the midst of this tussle, that they learned the need for "looking to Jesus." At each step of the difficult marathon they considered how Jesus had run that same race.

Nor were they unable to recall "snapshots" of the pioneer. The tradition was replete with pictures of Jesus en route, episodes when he met successive temptations by finding the power of God available in every situation. This is why they retained with such care the memories of Jesus, and why those memories, now preserved in written Gospels, became so central to the life of the Church. The stories about Jesus were able to provide a continuing dialogue between the Lord and his servants. With Jesus himself as an example, these stories indicated how the promise of God can become the basis of present struggle with temptation. Jesus had lived each day in a single allegiance to God's Tomorrow, and in so doing had been able to redeem the "present evil age." In the stories about Jesus they now see that a man *can* act on the premise that "the time is fulfilled, and the kingdom of God is at hand." In him they see how the buoyancy of hope overcomes the fatigue of despair. In him they see a man who had put his hand to the plow without looking backward. In him they see the trader who had glimpsed a pearl and had sold everything else in order to buy it. In him they see the joy of the bridegroom's friend who trusts the announcement that the wedding feast is now ready. Here was a steward who, when his master had seemed to be far away, had faithfully performed his duties as if the master were expected to return during the next hour. In other words, here was a man who had lived wholly from the future age into the present.

The same stories, however, which accent Jesus' joy and hope, make it clear that this joy was a mysterious companion of strife. The Kingdom that brought joy brought suffering as well. To Jesus baptism was a fire "already kindled"; why, then, should a disciple resent the fire?

For Jesus, the future was a sword that divides human families; why should the disciple be disturbed if that becomes true of his family? In the case of Jesus, Satan had turned the whole world against God's servant; why should not the disciple rejoice if he finds that Satan has begun to torment him through the same means? "The Son of man has nowhere to lay his head"; why then should his disciple worry about future lodging? All these stories point to the Master's race as one that inclined downward toward the lowest humbling of the servant, and thereby toward the increase of love and joy.

The apostle Paul was one who saw these implications in Jesus' mission most clearly. It is because of the Messiah's victory in his death that the apostle is content to be "in peril" every hour. From Jesus he had learned that the power of God is made available in weakness. The light that shone out of the darkness of Jesus' death could thus illumine Paul's heart when he was facing death for the Master's sake. And this light was not simply a reflection from a past event; it was also the light of the dawning Day.

> "We are afflicted in every way, but not crushed; perplexed, but not driven to despair; persecuted, but not forsaken; struck down, but not destroyed; always carrying in the body the death of Jesus, so that the life of Jesus may also be manifested in our bodies. For while we live we are always being given up to death for Jesus' sake, so that the life of Jesus may be manifested in our mortal flesh" (II Cor. 4:8-11).

Nor should the apostle's testimony be considered to apply only to himself or to the small band of Christian leaders. The "we" in the above passage includes all who have been truly baptized into Jesus' death. Wherever Paul finds believers who feel themselves exempt from this rule, he protests their treasonable return to former slaveries. He who knows the power of Christ's resurrection will "share his sufferings, becoming like him in his death" in order to "attain the resurrection from the dead." All those who are mature will have this same mind (Phil. 3:10-16). When death is at work in one of them, it brings life and glory to others (II Cor. 4:12; Eph. 3:13).

Paul, of course, is not pleading for everyone to commit suicide, or to antagonize the authorities needlessly in order to hasten martyrdom. He is not speaking of physical death when he says, "I die every day." Rather is he speaking of becoming like Jesus "in his death." To become like Jesus requires something more difficult than bravado, the exhibitionism of a daredevil, the hidden pride of masochism. Rather, it requires the faith, hope, and love of a man who is wholly controlled by the promise of God's coming Kingdom. This is the mind of Jesus which the mature disciple will have. And it is this mind that comes through a daily dying. One can have true fellowship with Jesus only by standing with him on the margin between the two ages, sharing his obedience, joy, humility, and glory (cf. pp. 89 f., 101-106). Only here is the fellowship of the Holy Spirit actualized, for the work of the Spirit is to create and preserve this inner connection between Jesus' choice and the disciple's. This fellowship of the Holy Spirit is realized in the community of those who bear the marks of the Lord Jesus.

"The cup of blessing which we bless, is it not a participation in the blood of Christ? The bread which we break, is it not a participation in the body of Christ?" (I Cor. 10:16).

Thus does the disciple from day to day give witness to the contemporaneous power of Jesus' example. It is for him no glib generalization to say that in the death of Jesus "all have died." Nor is it idle sentimentality to underscore the motive for this dying: "that those who live might live no longer for themselves but for him who for their sake died and was raised" (II Cor. 5:15). For the Christian, this epic of dying and rising is repeated in each Eucharist, when the members of the community "proclaim the Lord's death until he comes" (I Cor. 11:26). One sign of the sanctity of this covenant is the threat that accompanies thoughtless or indifferent observance. By frivolity the one who eats can turn the table of the Lord into a table of demons (ch. 10:14-22). If he profanes the body and blood of the Lord, he "eats and drinks judgment upon himself" (ch. 11:29). Likewise, if a man does not allow his baptism to determine his daily behavior, he is "destroyed by the Destroyer" (ch. 10:1-13).

The portrait of Jesus, given both in episodes of his active work and in his sacrifice on the cross, thus confronts the disciple at every step with a warning and an invitation. By ignoring the demand to die daily, the disciple accepts the curse of those who fight against God. By accepting the demand, he receives the power and life of the risen Lord. In his own consciousness, then, his conversion and baptism, which may have taken place years before, remain as contemporaneous as this threat and promise, as present as today's decision.

B. The Power of a Sure Hope

It is important to note as we have done how the story of Jesus furnishes the starting point of the believer's race, the pattern of his running, and the power by which he forgets what is past and anticipates what lies ahead. It is important to remember the bond of contemporaneity, first, between Jesus' death and the disciple's baptism, and second, between the latter's conversion and each successive testing of faith. Such contemporaneity indicates what a radical change has taken place in the time consciousness of those who stand on the boundary of the new age.

The same telescoping of time appears in the disciple's anticipation of the future. The end of his race is foreknown as being, in some mysterious way, the same as the end of his Master's race. He will receive as a crown the same life that God has given to Jesus. This hope binds each day's decision into a real solidarity with that prize which he seeks. He does not estimate the days and years that separate the present from God's Tomorrow, but runs with eyes fixed on the joy of his Lord.

Various disciples described this glory in various ways, but through their descriptions runs a common motif. Soon the Lord will return. Then he will be manifested as Lord, and in this manifestation everything that is now hidden will be declared openly. Then he will fulfill his promises to his servants. Servant and Master will be reunited, sharing the same glory as citizens of the heavenly city. Then the disciple will know as all along he has been known. The servant will become like Jesus, for he will see him as he is. He

" will change our lowly body to be like his glorious body, by the power which enables him even to subject all things to himself " (Phil. 3:21).

Then will be fulfilled the mission for which " Christ Jesus has made me his own " (Phil. 3:12). But so long as this mission is incomplete, all energies must be devoted to its completion. Yielding himself to this work, the servant finds that his hope shortens the time span that separates the present step from the end of the road. Christ's promise and his alertness serve to bring the Kingdom very near. One expression of this eager yet patient expectancy is the phrase " a little while." It is well to explore the flexibility with which this phrase is used in various parts of the New Testament.

In Hebrews this phrase is applied both to Jesus and to the disciples. God made Jesus "for a little while lower than the angels" (Heb. 2:7, 9). This "little while" represents Jesus' earthly pilgrimage, the period of his weakness, his subjection, his sharing of human ignorance, sin, suffering, and death. This was the necessary period for "chastising" the son, for testing his confidence and endurance. Only because Jesus was faithful unto death was he shown to be worthy of being placed over God's house as a son. By making himself "perfect through suffering" during his "little while," he enabled many sons to become sanctified through a similar suffering. Consequently, their "little while" is the period in which they must live by faith, without any shrinking back (ch. 10:37, 38). In fact, it is this confident expectancy, this reliance on God's promises, which constitutes faith, as a long chain of pioneers makes clear (ch. 11).

These general attitudes are personalized vividly in the Fourth Gospel. Jesus waits for his hour to come as does the player in the symphony who counts the measures until his instrument is needed. In the early months of his work Jesus knows that his hour is not yet. Later, during the Passover season, he recognizes that the hour has come. Now he knows that glorification awaits the little while until the grain falls into the earth (John 12:23, 24), until he is "lifted up" (vs. 31, 32), until he has "loved his own who were in the world . . . to the end" (ch. 13:1), until the world will see him no more (ch. 14:19).

The phrase "a little while," however, baffles the disciples. Jesus tries to tell them why this phrase applies also to them, yet they are unable to understand it until after his death. They are not yet ready to hate their life or to serve him by following him (ch. 12:25, 26). They do not understand the power and victory of the cross (v. 32). They are unwilling to have him wash their feet (ch. 13:8). They cannot go with him yet because they do not yet love one another perfectly and because they are not yet willing to lay down their lives for him (vs. 33–38). They cannot yet rejoice over his death as the triumph over the world (ch. 14:28), nor share in his full joy (ch. 15:11).

The "little while" in their case is a sign that their vocation has not yet been completed. It is also a promise of what lies ahead when they will see him and live in him (ch. 14:18); when they will know him, obey him, and love him (vs. 20, 21). The Holy Spirit will come to stir their memories, to provide peace, joy, confidence (vs. 26, 27). Through

the Holy Spirit their witness to a hateful world will be an effective witness of the Father to the Son. Their word and work will, validate and
continue the word and work of Jesus (ch. 15:26, 27). Through them
the Spirit must convince the world " of sin and of righteousness and
of judgment " (ch. 16:8). The little time until they see him is described most sharply by the following prediction:

> " You will weep and lament, but the world will rejoice;
> You will be sorrowful, but your sorrow will turn into joy. . . .
> I will see you again and your hearts will rejoice,
> And no one will take your joy from you " (John 16:20-22).

The indication of the date when this prediction will be fulfilled is
ambiguous. Does it come when the risen Lord appears to his disciples
and their unbelief turns to faith, when he breathes on them the Holy
Spirit? Yes (ch. 20:19-23). But even after this event, there remains " a
little while " (ch. 21:15-53). In this interval the love and obedience of
each disciple must be evidenced by his feeding the sheep, and waiting
in patience until his mission is fulfilled according to Christ's intention.
The date of this fulfillment in Peter's case is not the same as in the case
of the beloved disciple. Yet the goal and the requirements are the same
for both, and woe to him who worries overmuch about who will be
first, himself or his colleague (vs. 18-23).

The prophecies of Revelation serve to bring all creation under the
threat and promise of " a little while." The exalted Christ promises his
followers that he is coming soon. He has won the authority for making
this promise by being " the faithful witness, the first-born of the dead "
(Rev. 1:5). The Spirit carries his assurances to those who as faithful
witnesses share his endurance and suffering. They already have " a
lamp in heaven," but they have not yet conquered as he conquered
(ch. 3:20, 21). The examples of the martyrs make clear what lies
ahead of them. To those whose faith has not yet been wholly refined
the injunction is given: " Be faithful unto death, and I will give you
the crown of life " (ch. 2:10). Others, however, have already obeyed
this command (v. 13).

The reward of Jesus to servants as faithful as Antipas is the " pearl
of great price." They eat of the hidden manna, the fruit of the tree of
life. They receive power over the nations, " as I myself have received
power from my Father " (vs. 26, 27). Their new names are written in

heaven, where clad in white garments they cease not singing hymns of adoration and thanksgiving. They are permanently set as pillars in the temple·in God's city, the new Jerusalem (ch. 3:12). In their very chastening, a mark of Jesus' love, Jesus comes to them, eats with them, and gives them a place on his throne (vs. 19–21). They serve God day and night in his temple, while he shelters them from hunger, thirst, heat, and fatigue. Their shepherd guides them to fountains of living water (ch. 7:15–17). Because of the purity of their lives and the integrity of their witness, they " have been redeemed from mankind as first fruits for God and the Lamb " (ch. 14:4). They rest from their labors, " for their deeds follow them! " (v. 13). Because " they loved not their lives even unto death," their blood has been the Lamb's blood and their word has been his word. By his power they have conquered their accuser, and this victory means that the salvation and power of God's Kingdom has come *to* them and *through* them to others (ch. 12:10–12).

There remains, however, a temporal distinction between the end of the disciples' course (in the case of those already martyred) and the completion of the Messiah's work. The full harvest has yet to be gathered. The sovereignty of Christ has yet to be established on earth over all men. Cast down from his throne of authority over these witnesses, the devil's time is short; he pursues more violently the kinfolk of the martyrs, testing their loyalty and accusing them before God as he had accused Job (vs. 10–17). The martyrs rest beneath the altar until the number of their brethren is complete, and until their blood is avenged (ch. 6:10, 11). During this period, however, the martyrs, having been killed and exalted to heaven for their obedience, reign with Christ. " Over such the second death has no power."

These descriptions of the coming goal are cryptic and picturesque. The imagery keeps shifting in a mystifying manner, but underneath the profusion of symbols lies a single tough hope: " Be faithful unto death, and I will give you the crown of life." He who promises is the Lamb who was slain, and by his death has redeemed men. To the man facing martyrdom today, the " little while " has become as short as his answer to his accuser. Jesus, the king of the future, stands at the door and knocks (chs. 3:20; 22:20). So near does the future approach the present in the hour of decision; as near as his crown was to Jesus in Gethsemane and as near as the glory of God was to Stephen at his stoning (Acts 7:54–60).

The category " a little while " also describes the disciple's orientation as presented in many parables of Jesus. We have already noted how for Jesus the future Kingdom, while remaining future, fully conditioned and controlled the present. As his disciples retold and pondered them after his death, these parables gained added meaning in the light of each new situation. Jesus had told stories of the startling suddenness with which the absent lord returns to his servants, to find them either sleeping or watching. In retelling these narratives, it is natural that the disciples should have applied them directly to later predicaments. To them the returning lord is none other than the slain Lamb, and the servants are none other than Christian witnesses. These modifications in the parables have confused later generations by making it difficult to disentangle the original version from subsequent revisions. On discovering the evidence of changes in the tradition, scholars have been inclined to discount the revisions and even to doubt whether the original version goes back to Jesus. What supports the authenticity of the message underlying the stories, however, is not the absence of later revisions, but the genuine correspondence between Jesus' situation and the situations of his followers, between his faith in the future and theirs; yes, between his blood and theirs. His teaching and example through these parables became the pattern of their teaching and example.

Let us look at a few of these parables.

"Let your loins be girded and your lamps burning, and be like men who are waiting for their master to come home from the marriage feast, so that they may open to him at once when he comes and knocks. Blessed are those servants whom the master finds awake when he comes; truly, I say to you, he will gird himself and have them sit at table and come and serve them " (Luke 12:35-37).

This picture tells what it means to seek first the Kingdom of God. The servants cannot tell the hour of its coming, for it comes when the lord of the kingdom comes from his marriage feast. When he knocks, they must immediately open (cf. Rev. 3:20), so they must be ready at every moment. If they are ready when he comes, he himself will serve them (cf. John, ch. 13).

A slight variation in detail may be noted in the story of Mark (ch. 13:33-37). In this case the lord is head of a large household. His servants during his absence have differing assignments and the authority necessary for doing their respective duties in the household. The requirement for them all is to watch for the master's return by being faithful to these assignments.

As developed in later versions, this story makes clear the alternative awards. The servant who patiently and self-forgetfully feeds the "sheep" will be given a share of the master's authority when he returns (Luke 12:42, 43). But the servant who supposes that the lord's return is delayed begins to mistreat the sheep and to place first his own earthly security. Two things are assured for him — the lord will come in an hour when he is unprepared and will eject him from the faithful household. He who expects the lord's return hourly will be faithful hourly; he who ceases to expect the lord's return in "a little while" ceases to obey him. Expectation of the future return and obedience in the present moment are interdependent.

In the book of Revelation, the servants are commanded to procure white clothing that has been purified by suffering; in Matthew the guests at the wedding feast must have on their wedding garments (Matt. 22:11-14). In Revelation the lamps of faithless servants are removed from their heavenly location; in Matthew the slothful virgins allow their lamps to go out and are unable to replenish them in time for the bridegroom's arrival (Matt. 25:1-13). The faithful servant cannot rely on previous efforts, but must continue to trade with his lord's talents (vs. 14-30). Otherwise he is unprofitable to the lord and unworthy of a place in his estate. He must continue to feed the sheep, to show his love for the master by caring for "one of the least of these." Only in performing this daily service does he receive future approval (vs. 31-46).

The New Testament teems with such images, for the experience of faith had freed the minds of men from prosaic dullness, but underneath the prolix metaphors lies the stark reality of a single choice facing each disciple. He who is content to wait a little while, loving his absent lord by patient, sober work, demonstrates the lord's power and receives the lord's praise when he returns. He who becomes discontented with the conditions of his service will protest the delay or postpone it, will act not in accordance with the lord's will but with his own, and by that act bring upon himself the speedy return of his lord in wrath. He makes himself homeless and helpless, estranged from the communion of saints and exiled from the Kingdom of God.

To sum up, let us point again to the way in which life in the new age affects the believer's consciousness of time. By faith the experience of rebirth remains a dominating memory that constrains the disciple each day; it is as near as the act by which he dies daily, as near as the effective operation of the Spirit that was in Jesus. By the same faith, the return of Jesus looms before him as a certain expectation, to be realized in a little while. The true slave serves his master as if this hour were at hand, yet gives to his master the right to conceal the hour until he has been tested as Jesus was tested. His connection with the future is as close as that because the Spirit speaks to him constantly of the coming age. In his consciousness the span between rebirth and glorification becomes very short, although the lord may decide to tarry for many years. However short or long the span may prove to be in years, the disciple knows that the two events are the beginning and end of a single purpose, for they are the repetition in his life of the path of his lord. To view every decision as subject to the momentum of this purpose is the mystery of faith, the faith that overcomes the world.

From one standpoint the interpreter may say that for the early Christian there are two victories rather than one, just as there are two comings of the Messiah. The one victory and advent has taken place; the other victory and advent are awaited at the end of his course. (This splitting of the goal of history into two victories distinguishes the Christian outlook from that of Judaism and of non-Biblical utopias.) [19] From another standpoint, there are not two victories but one, the victory of Jesus Christ, to which triumph every act of faith belongs. From this latter standpoint the past and future triumphs are inseparable from one another, even though the mission of the Messiah is being executed in the interval between them. For wherever that mission is being carried on by members of his body, the prospect and the retrospect fuse into a single will, the coming of God's Kingdom on earth.

Jesus' disciple can have no doubt concerning the main thrust of Jesus' will: he had come to seek and to save the lost, dying for them while they were still enemies of God. The future return of the Lord will therefore ratify the triumph of his purpose over the whole world to which he was sent. Accepting this same purpose, the disciple must seek the redemption of those to whom he is, in turn, sent. When his obedience has been perfected, it will become, like his Lord's, an instrument for God's gracious salvation of the world. Although, because of his humility and love, the disciple refrains from condemning the world during his lifetime, the fulfillment of his mission makes him like Jesus a judge of the world, his humble faith being the standard by which the world sees its own sin and vanity. For the disciple is sure that every work of love continues to bear fruit, even after his death. Because his knee has been bent, others will bend. Through his defeat of the power of Satan others will learn the road to freedom. Love's labor is never lost, but continues its reconciling work until all creation is reconciled to God. With his Master the servant who has been faithful unto death will sit in heavenly places until the time when all the kingdoms of the earth have become a single Realm with a single Ruler. The Holy Spirit continues to descend from heaven to earth until the Holy City itself comes down in its purity and wholeness. The end of the disciple's road thus fuses with the end of the Church's task as the body of Christ. And the mission of the Church is nothing less than

" building up the body of Christ, until we all attain to the unity of the faith and of the knowledge of the Son of God, to mature manhood, to the measure of the stature of the fullness of Christ " (Eph. 4:12, 13).

9

THE SUMMING UP OF ALL THINGS

" THE measure of the stature of the fullness of Christ " — this is one way in which the apostle articulated his conception of the end of all creation, when God's eternal purpose will be perfectly realized among men who seek that realization with their whole heart. What is this measure, as the apostle conceives it? The context suggests that it is the measure of mature manhood, the full growth of the Body of Christ in love, the unity of the faith of God's son, and the unity of his knowledge (Eph. 4:13–16). Here is a vision of unity and peace that is utterly unique. It is, in short, the oneness of creation realized in the oneness of the perfect Man. Because this vision of wholeness is so distinctive, we may well begin this chapter by seeking to grasp the character of such dynamics of personal relationships, remembering that God's peace surpasses our understanding even at the moment when we try to draw it within the range of intelligible discourse.

A. The Source of an Integral Life

The ultimate ground of unity is to be found in the God who can say: " I am the Alpha and the Omega, . . . who is and who was and who is to come " (Rev. 1:8). He is the Almighty, whose design embraces everything that happens, from everlasting to everlasting. Moreover, this design is no vast, impersonal, hypothetical construction, but an immediate, personal purpose at work in the story of every creature. His total purpose stands behind each of his words and deeds. Wherever God is present, he is wholly present.

In Christ he has spoken and acted in such a way as to reveal what this total purpose is. To Christ he gives the power to say to his servants, " I am the Alpha and the Omega, the first and the last, the beginning and the end " (ch. 22:13). And this Messiah has given his pledge to the seven churches: " I am coming soon " (vs. 12, 20). At this coming he will make all things new, bringing a new heaven and a new earth, and establishing a holy city where God will dwell with his people (ch. 21:1–5). This city will have no need for sun or moon, because God's glory, shining through the lamp of the Lamb, will provide ample light. By this light " shall the nations walk; and the kings of the earth shall bring their glory into it " (vs. 23–26).

In these images we find ascribed to Jesus Christ the same quality of creative unity that is true of God. Christ is *wholly present* as a person in each of his words and deeds. A single purpose animates all his work, and this purpose reaches from the first to the final act of creation. Nor is this singleness of mind an ideological abstraction, the dream of a dreamer or the construction of a mathematical philosopher, for this singleness of mind had been manifested in the person of Jesus of Nazareth, who had loved God with his whole heart, and his neighbor with the same heart (cf. Chapter 3).

Moreover, his disciples realized that the purpose hidden in the ministry of Jesus had been the birth of a new community wherein the rapport between God and his people will be as perfect as that now realized between God and the Lamb. Every inhabitant of this city will be motivated by the same single intention. This integrity, as we have seen, summed up all the mandates that Jesus presented to the fishermen and tax collectors who first followed him (cf. p. 60). It is an integrity that they failed to achieve during Jesus' days with them, but the powers of the risen Lord reinstated these mandates as the first and the last duties of man. We have noted, too, how progress toward such integrity on the part of the individual is progress in the birth of a new fellowship. The Holy City and the saint receive at the same moment the life and gifts of the Spirit, a fellowship that is one in Christ because the common mind has been newly transformed by the mind of Christ. The " measure of the stature " of the one true man signifies the final integration of this City, when it will be illumined by God's glory and when kings and nations will walk by this light. Where God's glory becomes the one will and work of every citizen, there perfect peace and fellowship will be consummated.

There is yet one more way of appraising this invisible source of wholeness: this is to contrast it with the apparently cohesive forces that dominate the old age. It has been pointed out that rebellious creation has been inveigled into accepting the sovereignty of Satan. Consequently it forms a single body of sin, of law, and of death. The unity of the Holy City may best be grasped by its contrast to the fellowship pervading the old age.

Of that age, the constitutive features have already been diagnosed in terms of the direction of men's desires, the structure of their common mind, the fruits of their labors, the rulers — both visible and invisible — to which they have been subjected. So defined, this age is a cohesive, interdependent sphere, though its boundaries cannot be located by lines of latitude or longitude, by numerical census, or by the century divisions of the calendar. It began in rebellion against God when men succumbed to illusory offers of its serpent. It continues with man's mind being more and more enslaved, his desires more and more hypnotized by his temptations.

How, then, we may ask, does Christ's Kingdom achieve a unity that differs from this solidarity of sin? The answer is that Satan lacks the final power to fulfill his promise of a community or a heart integrated around his commands. Satan is never, like God, wholly present when he is at work. His promises are never unified and can therefore never become the single goal of human action. As a person he would be wholly present in his words and deeds if man ever as a person would wholly yield to his blandishments. But this never happens, for the demon-possessed is always a divided soul; the demon-ridden community is always unable to find the fellowship and peace that it seeks. Satan offers his peace, the peace of the world, but the fruits of his promise are walls of division, because the basis of his appeal is superiority, which is by nature exclusive. The unity of the old age, if there be such, lies in the finality of its disunities. The antagonism of the many gods and many lords makes an undivided self and an undivided fellowship impossible. Satan is the ultimate lord of broken fellowship, the invisible source of irreconcilable rivalries.

When the cross terminated the old age, it broke down, by the power of its gentle and humble love, all walls of division by which Satan erects his temple. It revealed the fact that the world is torn by schisms which it cannot heal on its own terms. In the cross is created a unity which the world has never known, for here the purpose of God and the purpose of Christ are seen to be *one will,* with power to communicate the same will to men. Here the servant of Christ is enabled to accept that one will as his own. To the extent that his penitence and obedience are total, his mind becomes one with that of his Master. Moreover, he discovers that this one will (God, the Lord, the Servant) is supported by one power, that of humble love. This unity of will and of power creates a unity of fellowship. The servant becomes a citizen of the Holy City, a member of the Body of Christ, a son in the household of God. This solidarity is established with the initial act of faith, but it is established as a promise, because in each act of faith-repentance the disciple becomes aware that his obedience has not yet been made perfect. He is not yet worthy of inheritance in the Holy City. When he, like Jesus, is wholly integrated in an act of surrender, then he is wholly incorporated into the fellowship with the Father and the Son.

The old age had begun in an act of rebellion which had created the solidarity of a community in Adam, but this solidarity could never become total since it was doomed to disintegrate. The new age had begun in an act of love which creates the solidarity of a community in the Second Adam. This whole community is present in any single venture of faith — yes, wholly present when faith has been made perfect. In the prayer of Jesus in Gethsemane as in the genuine Eucharist of the body of Christ, the perfect community of the coming Kingdom is present both as promise and as power. Every faith-impelled and love-guided deed of the believer is an act of this community, a step in the growth of the one new man. God thus carries forward his plan for the fullness of the times, "to unite all things in him" (Eph. 1:10). His method is to break down by the powerful gentleness of Jesus the partition walls of hostility so "that he might create in himself one new man in place of the two, so making peace, and might reconcile us both to God in one body through the cross, thereby bringing the hostility to an end" (ch. 2:14-16).

The unity of the one new man is, to be sure, a mystery, but not an enigma that befuddles or disappoints the faithful. Rather, it is a mystery that elicits the deepest awe and gratitude, for the unity in Christ links each present moment to the triumph of the beginning and the end, binding together into one heavenly fellowship the Father and his whole family of sons. When the Church and its members look back to their origins, they discover this one end; when they look ahead to the promise, they are reminded of their origin. And looking in either direction, they see the cross and its crown as the enduring ground for their communion and the adequate energy for present decisions. They tell again the Passion epic, receive again the new covenant, break again the bread that makes them one with Christ. Their worship resounds with the hallelujahs of the resurrection; their teaching re-evokes the tradition received from the Messiah; their humble deeds of mercy advance the struggle against principalities and powers, proclaiming to those invisible lords that their stronghold in men's hearts has been occupied by one stronger than they.

Thus, in its re-enactment of its baptism, the Church follows the pattern of the individual disciple. It repeats the initial response of repentance by which it becomes anew the household of God. Just as the disciple telescopes the temporal span between rebirth and contemporary dilemmas, so too the Church views today as a time when the Holy Spirit may again bestow the power of endless life. The memory of Christ and the present sovereignty of Christ become one. Through remembering Jesus, the congregation chooses again to accept the commission of Jesus and in so doing becomes his Church. It proclaims his message, humbles itself beneath the rulers of this age, endures the same sufferings, obeys the same divine imperatives, and lives by the same love. In fact, the congregation *is* the Church only in the event of remembrance and renewal.[20]

Instead of bridging the intervening years, it is possible (as we have noted in the preceding chapter) for the disciple to magnify the distance from the beginning. But this is a temptation that easily destroys his patience and endurance, because despair always interprets this delay as separating him from the love of God, whereas faith recognizes that no such separation is possible. The same temptation besets the congregation. When it measures its separation from the Lord in terms of years that have elapsed since his death, it becomes vulnerable to doubt concerning Jesus' power over the age and to the desire to evade his commands. Confidence concerning the future Kingdom can be sustained only by living memories of its reality in the past.

There was another way, however, in which the disciple was encouraged to lengthen his past perspectives, to interpret the whole preceding history according to faith's vision. He sees that during the period before his conversion God's Spirit had been at work, though so secretly as to be wrongly interpreted. The disciple had been called from birth; i.e., even while his mind had been blinded by sin, God had been preparing the way. God had permitted sin to reign in order that man might learn the superlative worth of righteousness, had permitted Satan to enslave men so that they might comprehend the dimensions of freedom. Paul knew himself to be a clear instance of this, for even in persecuting the members of the Way he had been drawn within the magnetic field of its power.

The mind of the congregation was subject to the same logic whenever it pondered the meaning of its previous history. From the outset the kingdoms of this world had been unconsciously readied for their true King. Christ had from the first been ruler of the kings on earth, being present in the promise made to creation, although that presence had been hidden. The world's rebellion had been permitted by one who knew the ultimate end of that rebellion. God had made the wrath of men to praise him, not only in the cross but also in the preceding anticipations of the cross. He who had in the beginning said, "Let there be light," had at the end revealed the character of that light by letting it shine in the face of Jesus and in the hearts of his brothers. In accordance with this conviction, the body of Christ must consider itself to be continuous with the true Israel. The Church had been present in the Exodus, the Wilderness, the Exile. It had been at work, though in a hidden form, in the failures as well as the triumphs of Israel, for through all the circumstances of its checkered career God had been preparing his people for that fellowship with each other that comes through fellowship with his Son. Nor does the existence of the Church in other epochs halt at the boundaries of Israel-according-to-the-flesh. The Messiah is the one true man; therefore his congregation constitutes one body for all men. It is present in all human communities, genuinely *there* even though it be hidden in such a fashion that no man may define its contours. When it is revealed, all nations will have a place within its borders. The mission of Christ is the proclamation to all the world of the presence of this Kingdom. When he is lifted up, he will draw all men to him, and through him into his family.

This tendency to "read back" the one true communion into preceding epochs, to find the new age at work everywhere in the midst of the old, is not an expression of self-importance or wish-projection but a corollary of faith, for only a Church that is fulfilling the mission of its Lord can detect this fellowship within and under all human communities. The scope of this task, of course, often leads the Church, tormented by the weight of the mountain to be moved, to protest, " Lord, how long? " When will the peace of God be finally realized? What are the signs that the task is about to be completed? To these questions we must now turn.

B. The Realization of Unity

In our analysis of the disciple's relationship to the coming Day, we noted that faith is expressed in a shortening of the time, and temptation in a lengthening of it. The category of faith is this: " A little while." This category expresses the awareness that the presence of Christ and the expectation of Christ are one. When the Spirit brings the message " I am coming soon," it makes the command of obedience absolute and gives sufficient grace for the needed response. When the disciple begins to measure the temporal distance between the present and the end of his task, then he complains over the Lord's delay and is induced to stumble. The belief that the Lord is *not* at hand justifies his evasion of the Lord's commands by blaming the Lord rather than himself for breaking the covenant. Faith, on the contrary, confesses that the Lord will determine the hour, and that the servant must be ready now. When the hour of temptation arrives, that is the time for the faithful to hear the voice saying, " Behold, I stand at the door and knock." For the disciple's destiny only tomorrow and today are decisive; he must resist the tendency to dream of the day after tomorrow. The night is far spent; the alert sentry spies in the clouds the " bright morning star "; he anticipates the crown of victory tomorrow rather than the day following.

This same foreshortening of the future applies to the congregation of believers, but in a more complex fashion. God gives to each creature its own distinct time, and measures its span according to his purpose. The event of fulfillment comes to " each in its own order." Consider, for example, the different time spans appropriate to this generation and to the rulers of the age of darkness.

The present generation is always separated from the return of Christ in a way analogous to the time span of individuals now living. For any generation that hears the message of the Kingdom, the time of decision is very short. Its response while it is yet today determines its destiny: either it will come under the sway of the Spirit by repentant faith, or it will forfeit its opportunity to enter the new age. To it God's servant proclaims the crisis under which it stands: "This generation will not pass away till all has taken place." Before the message comes, it is "a brood of vipers," but those who bring forth works worthy of repentance are saved from "the crooked and perverse generation." It may be that we should appraise in this sense the baffling prediction of Jesus:

> "There are some standing here who will not taste death before they see the kingdom of God come with power" (Mark 9:1).

Those, however, who fail to recognize the Messiah are accursed. For them Jesus laments. To be sure, they may build monuments to the prophets. They may say, "If we had lived then we would not have been responsible for their blood." But this self-identification with the prophets of a previous generation and this repudiation of guilt for their blood blind them to their present predicament. Assuming their innocence in the past, they assume their innocence in the future. Assuming their ability to recognize earlier prophets, they are complacent about their ability to read the signs of the times. But this false relationship with past and future, corrupted as it is by complacency, places them under present condemnation. They are found persecuting contemporary prophets. They fail to recognize the Messiah when he comes to the Temple. They therefore come under his condemnation: "All this will come upon this generation. . . . You will not see me again until you shall say, 'Blessed be he that comes in the name of the Lord'" (Matt. 23:29-39). The Messiah appears "before the time" he is expected. He comes like a thief and steals the treasure of those who thought themselves righteous and secure.

In other words, this generation (the only generation addressed by disciples is always the present generation) "seeks for a sign, but no sign shall be given to it except the sign of Jonah." This sign is the prophet himself with his warning of doom. By its response to Jonah's preaching, or to the Church's proclamation, this generation determines its destiny. It cannot rely upon its pride in its sacred monuments, its reputation for supporting the Temple, or its hopes for coming generations. Now is the day. Either it passes through the fires of penitence or it accepts for itself the fires of judgment. No other choice is open. When a religious community thus uses its memories or its hopes to shield itself from the demand of humility, it demonstrates that it too belongs to the dying age.

When the Church is rightly related to the two victories of the Messiah, the hidden and the revealed, it will follow tactics opposite to those that the Pharisees exemplified. In building tombs to the prophets, the latter had implicitly said, " If we had lived then, we would have obeyed them." But followers of Christ, kneeling before the cross, are made to confess, " If we had been there, we would have been among Jesus' enemies." The absence of present repentance had made it impossible for the Pharisees to recognize the Messiah, but so long as the Christian congregation dies daily, so long will it be alert to recognize the Messiah when he comes again.

To be sure, the divine judgment on the Pharisees (their alienation from the Messiah in their midst) was not manifested to them or to the world at that hour. Jesus simply left the Temple and went his way (Matt. 24:1). Their punishment, though the verdict was already signalized by this dramatic exit, was not demonstrated externally by a bolt of lightning. Impenitence can never see the true character of its judgment, for the vision is itself a mark of penitence. Yet each generation draws that judgment upon itself by its very reliance upon its ability to measure what constitutes judgment.

To take another example from the book of Revelation: Here both the martyr and his executioner stand under the same final judgment, but the decision is rendered in accordance with their respective positions. The martyr receives his crown in his death, through the way in which his " fear " of God's judgment overcomes his dread of human judgments. The executioner's hour may come later; he has drawn upon himself, by his resistance to God, a final verdict from God, but the realization of the futility of that resistance will come to the surface only in the future. The judgment upon the men of this generation becomes manifest later than the martyr's death, but it is already present now in hidden form (compare the judgment of the world in Jesus' crucifixion). Moreover, the delay in the day when God's judgment will be manifested is motivated by God's intention of bringing the sinner to repentance. When in humility the executioner accepts the message of the martyr as God's judgment upon himself, then he is freed from the curse of his generation. This is why the prophet can speak with such certainty in proclaiming the woes that will soon fall on the merchants and traders, the generals and emperors, of his own generation. Though these woes may come later when measured in years, if they can be so measured at all, they are integrally linked to the judgments of the Messiah which have already been released.

Each generation has its own life span, but the world and the age have a longer time for flourishing. The Church's mission and message are directed to a world that endures as long as the rulers of darkness retain their power to deceive and enslave. Just as the Church had a hidden mission in the period before the coming of the Messiah, so too it has a continuing mission which extends beyond this present generation. To be sure, the congregation becomes the Church only when its work is controlled by the present demands of Christ. Its prayer, " Thy kingdom come," is the same as, " Come, Lord Jesus." If it fails to live by this prayer, fails to do its errand to the men of this generation, its lampstand is removed from heaven. Yet the event that will mark the completion of its mission is in one sense more remote than the promise to the martyr or to the generation. Its mission is ultimately addressed to principalities and powers, whose life span is greater than that of merchants or generals or emperors. It is commanded to continue Christ's work until all these powers have been subjected. The end of its career is when " we all attain . . . to the measure of the stature of the fullness of Christ," when Christ's body is fully developed in love (Eph. 4:13, 16), and when all things know that they belong to Christ. His power will not be fully manifested until he has destroyed every enemy ruler (I Cor. 15:24-27). His judgment and his love will then become all-inclusive and he will be reunited with his own from all generations. Until all things have been thus restored to their true unity, the Church must continue to proclaim its mystery to the rulers of darkness.

As the Early Church looked forward to this event, it recognized that " the end is not yet." The coming of woes upon a given generation does not signify the end of the Church's mission. " The gospel must first be preached to all nations." Satan must be completely deprived of his power to torment men. Sin and death, as fruits of his harvest, must be completely removed from God's world. Until the new heaven and the new earth come, the Lord's word and his work will not cease. Until then, the Church remains patiently pursuing its task, free from the excitement that looks for premature signs that will enable it to say, " Here it is," or, " There it is."

The patience of the Church militant, however, does not mean that it must relinquish its sense of the nearness of the end. Christ has already been made King of Kings. He has already given his crown to the martyrs who now reign with him. The Church has already received the foretaste of the new age, and lives from that future into the present. The final event is under way, and this event communicates a mysterious solidarity between Jesus' victory, the victory of the individual disciple, and the victory of the Church.

Because this unity has already been consummated in the heavenly places, the Church that is on earth must proclaim to each successive generation that its hopes have already proved futile, that the Kingdom of God has already dawned, and that Christ will soon exercise his judgment over this generation. He is the Omega of all history, but that power can be demonstrated only by his power over this segment of history for which we are responsible. The Church's mission is to one generation at a time; the fulfillment of that assignment is the means by which Christ can extend his power over later generations. Only through present faithfulness does future victory become assured. To the Church that carries on its warfare in the name of Christ, the Spirit gives the promise that the future will be unable to separate it from the triumph of God's love.

C. The Fulfillment of the Promise

How will this ultimate promise of unity be consummated? We have already noted that this question is extremely hazardous for the individual disciple. He may pose the question according to the mind of the old age, selecting some proud vantage point such as lofty Olympus or Everest rather than lowly Calvary. He may want more specific information than was permitted to Jesus in his hour of trial. He may require an earthly timetable before he will trust the heavenly design. He may try through his own wisdom to penetrate the veil of the future, and describe according to his own specifications what must happen and when. In so doing he may express his hatred of his enemies, and his self-love rather than Christ's love. He may assume that Christ's foes are the disciple's personal antagonists rather than the principalities which are tricking him into self-love and its implicit despair.

These temptations apply with equal strength to the congregation. It is prone to think of itself more highly than it ought to think, and thereby become anxious over its own security and prestige among competing social institutions. It may be deceived into accepting such weapons as the Gentiles use. It may gauge its own success in terms other than those permitted to followers of the Nazarene, for instance, in terms of its numerical strength or the visible defeat of its competitors. It may accentuate rather than lower the partition walls in society. It may encourage its members to claim for themselves an insurance against suffering and a pride in God's special favor.

Some readers have felt that the writer of the book of The Revelation of John succumbed to such temptations and thus proved himself to be a false prophet. It is not necessary for later friends to maintain the blamelessness of the prisoner John. After all, his faith was subjected to greater strain than that of most of his critics. His book's authority, however, does not rest on his attainment of perfect virtue. It rests rather upon the Word of Christ, the Head of the Church, where that Word is productive of the radical repentance and trust which he expects of his Body. If we probe beneath the surface of this book, we find several significant convictions with regard to the way in which Jesus Christ will consummate his victory over his enemies. Charges against John should be held in abeyance until these key convictions are weighed.

In the first place, the power that will conquer is the power revealed and released through the humiliation and exaltation of Jesus. From first to last the dominion and majesty belong to him. What is often said of earthly power does not apply to him or to his Body, namely, that power corrupts and absolute power corrupts absolutely. What must be said of him and his Body is this: Love redeems and absolute love redeems absolutely.

In the second place, the method by which heavenly love overcomes earthly power in the future, final events of history is the very method by which the old age has been already terminated by the new. Heavenly love was subjected to earthly powers in order to subject those powers. Through humbling himself absolutely, Jesus was granted the power to draw all men to himself, freeing them from the tyrannies of the rulers of darkness. To the prophet on Patmos came the vision of how the faithful servants and churches were carrying forth this design of being at once subjected and exalted. His visions of violence are subordinated (though not, perhaps, wholly) to the realization that all vengeance belongs to the Lord, that the ravaging lion is none other than the Lamb, and that the King can conquer the kings only by using weapons of gentleness which they do not keep in their armory. It is by the "blood of the Lamb and by the word of their testimony" that the brethren conquer their accuser (Rev. 12:11).

In the third place, in anticipating the future in the light of the cross, the prophet knew well the bitterness with which the world counterattacks the offensive of divine love. He therefore underscores the continuing accumulative animosity of Satan to the Body of Christ. He assumes that the devil will use the same weapons against the Church that he has used against its Head. All kinds of external buffetings and internal doubtings will continue to afflict the soldiers of the Kingdom. But in all this warfare it is the deceiver of the world, and not his human dupes, who constitutes the enemy.

In the fourth place, the prophet has already experienced the fruits of the old age, and it is not surprising that he pictures the final judgment in terms of the self-defeating character of the enemy's work. Bloodshed, famine, defeat in wars, epidemics, the frustration of earthly ambitions — all these will mark the judgment of Christ *which the age draws upon itself*. They are the fruits of the old age, not of the new. Men reap despair as the fruit of their own sin, because that is the seed which they planted. In the end, they will see that it is a merciful God who punishes their deeds with death. Only through such a manifestation of the travail of all creation will the moment come when every tongue confesses the sovereignty of Christ.

This final victory is not yet. Christ's mission is still proceeding. But only as the Church realizes that this final victory is "at hand" will it face the future as Jesus faced it and find in that future the redemption of the world. Such, at least, is the testimony of Christ to and through his servants. The coming Day is so close to the morning star, and the consummation of this Day is so integrally related to the joy already poured into the hearts of faithful servants, that any cautious or fearful weighing of intervening time spans can mark the ruin of the disciple or of the Church.

The true Church is content with the image of this future salvation given in the Lamb that was slain. When he has fulfilled his mission of reconciling the world to God, he will turn his Kingdom over to God. When the individual runner has completed his race and won the crown, he will cast that crown before God, content to glorify him and to enjoy him forever. When the Church has fulfilled its task, it too will cease to exist as a separate entity and will sing its glorias to Him who has conquered. In the Holy City there will be no temple; the only temple will be "the Lord God the Almighty and the Lamb" (Rev. 21:22). When all things are summed up in one fellowship, when all antagonists have been united in one new man, then God will be all in all.

CHAPTER

10

THE TESTING OF FAITH

A BIT of retrospect may be in order before entering upon a new section of this study, even at the risk of excessive repetition. Life in salvation, according to early Christians, is a pilgrimage along the road of faith. The journey begins when a man is baptized into Christ's death and is raised to life in the new Day (Chapters 4-6). It ends when his obedience is made perfect and he apprehends that for which he has been apprehended (Chapters 7-9). Along the road his mind and heart are placed under the tutelage of this memory and hope. Whether he considers the past or the future, he finds there a Lord who directs attention to the immediate duties. His task is to become what he already is: a son called to become a son. He becomes a son through the progressive deepening of humility and the extension of love and the integration of will.

This means on the one hand a process of greater and greater chastisement. "If you are left without discipline, in which all have participated, then you are illegitimate children and not sons" (Heb. 12:8). The pilgrim knows, on the other hand, that this chastisement is for his good and that God will not try him beyond endurance (I Cor. 10:13). Each disciple must admit that in his struggle against sin he has not yet resisted to the point of shedding blood (Heb. 12:4; Rev. 3:19). His life story, therefore, becomes a sequence of temptations, each successive trial a God-given examination in the curriculum of sonship. Behind each test of his faith the son can therefore discern the Father's hand, rejoicing in sufferings (Rom. 5:3-5) and content with hunger or plenty (Phil. 4:12). All situations, however formidable, thus receive a common denominator; they are intended as means for refining the gold of faith (I Peter 1:6).

This outlook explains much of the distinctive emphasis to be noted in the New Testament, an emphasis reflected in the number of teachings dealing with temptations. On the one hand the necessity for temptations is frequently recognized. Those on whom " the end of the ages has come " are subjected to the keenest struggles and should never be surprised when these struggles take the ominous shape of an ordeal by fire (ch. 4:12). On the other hand, each new outburst of the refiner's fire should be met with the greatest soberness and the clearest judgment, because it may prove to be the occasion of stumbling. It is a beginning of the final judgment upon the household of God (v. 17) and conceals within itself both the prowling of the devil and the hand of God (ch. 5:6–8). Always under stress, the disciple has available adequate weapons for resisting his adversary, but always these weapons of meekness and trust are made to seem impotent by the subtle suggestion of the tempter.

Wherever the perspective of the New Testament becomes obscured, there also is its teaching concerning temptation distorted. So foreign is the perspective that it has become very difficult for modern men to appreciate the pattern of attitudes applied to temptation. Many things that people assume to be true temptations are not so considered by the Scripture, and many things that are viewed most soberly in the Scripture are now viewed casually. We identify the tests of faith too readily by applying our own current standards of what is decent and fair, of what threatens the virtue of the individual or group, without considering the structure of relationships created and sustained by the gospel. For many people the very word " temptation " has become either obsolete or objectionable or trivial. There has been in recent times little effort to recover what we might call the anatomy of temptation.[21]

In outlining this anatomy it is well to begin with the conception of faith as that reliance of the believer and the Church upon Christ which makes Christ the actual Head of the Body. Every potential choice is recognizable as temptation when it threatens the sovereignty of this Head, and every temptation rightly met becomes the means of knitting the Body together and of being strengthened by it. But the Head, who presumably rules the Body, is invisible, inasmuch as Christ is no longer visibly present. The disciple must love him " without having seen him " (ch. 1:8, 9). The relationship to him is as strong or as weak as this love. Because the object of love is invisible, the point of attack is upon the apparently tenuous character of this bond. Because the word of this invisible master is heard through three primary means of communication, those lines must be broken or otherwise made useless.

Christ is not now seen, but he is remembered. He is heard through the memory, through the tradition by which the congregation becomes contemporaneous with the ministry of Jesus. If this memory then can be obliterated, if men can be induced to forget, or induced to remember other things more sharply, the communication becomes distorted. To despair of the reality of the death-resurrection event or to deny one's baptism or to forget it in absorption with other concerns — these are signs that the tempter has achieved his major objectives.

Christ is not now seen, but he is at work at the present moment. One area where his work may be recognized is in the common life of the Church. Fellowship with other disciples is intended as an open line of communication with their mutual Lord. Here are means of grace where the Holy Spirit continues its work of linking each act of penitence, mercy, and joy to the power of the living Christ. The entrance of temptation can therefore be detected in the impoverishment and perversion of family ties. Satan is constantly at work to make the relationship of the brother to the family one of earthly idolatry rather than heavenly glory.

Christ is not now seen, but his return is anticipated. Hope is a necessary bond of dependence and of communication with him. Christ dwells in the heart through hope. This hope makes its demands and issues its warnings. To be successful, therefore, temptation must sterilize this hope, or substitute other hopes in its place, or otherwise trap men into various forms of despair, whether conscious or unconscious. But at bottom all such forms of despair are a denial of the control over the future wielded by Jesus as the Omega. Beginning with this diagnosis of the tests confronting the pilgrim at each step of his journey, we will turn to the analysis of various forms assumed by these three temptations according to the New Testament.

A. A Defective Memory

Lot's wife provides an epitome of the disruption of the bonds of faith's memory expressed in the desire to return to the old age. Finding the new life too arduous, the exile seeks repatriation in his former country, preferring friendship with the world to faithfulness to God (James 4:1–4). Sometimes this takes place through immorality and bold carousing together, "looking after themselves" (Jude 12). Passions are allowed to take control. Desires for economic security deflect the mind, inducing men to accept again the worries as well as the illusions of mammon (Mark 4:19; James 4:13 f.).

The institutions of society exert their lures, enticing the runners to revert to " the futile ways inherited from your fathers " (I Peter 1:18 f.). Christians of Jewish extraction are pulled back into a reliance on the works of the law (Gal. 3:1–5), or on the efficacy of the sacrificial cultus. Those of pagan extraction relapse into a new subservience to their hallowed religious customs — festivals, diets, the worship of angels, self-abasement, and severity to the body. All these observances appear to be desirable, but they easily force the free man into an arbitrary schedule of piety (Col. 2:8–23).

Other disciples are more vulnerable to the perversion of freedom into license. Grateful for the Spirit's destruction of the law, they use this freedom for unrestrained self-expression, priding themselves upon this proof that they are strong in faith. But to use the Spirit to satisfy unconverted desires is a devious way of returning to ancient bondage. The " desires of the body " constitute the motivational structure of the world, whether the individual be a conservative or a Bohemian. To use the new freedom as a surrogate for self-centered defense of one's own rights destroys that freedom. Through these temptations the disciple must learn that he is no longer his own master. He belongs to Christ, and only in recognizing this does his body become truly his own. He must learn the subtle ways in which true freedom is related to all the lesser freedoms, how the law of Christ can be obeyed in observing the lesser laws. He is called into freedom from all the laws of the old age, but he is called to become a son and not an anarchist. He must learn how all the laws are summed up in the one law of love, and he can learn this only through continued examinations in the school of life.

An even more deceptive return to the old nature starts whenever Christ's follower takes pride in his new status. Each work of faith may be made the occasion for temptation. " Lord, Lord, did we not prophesy in your name, and cast out demons in your name, and do many mighty works? " (Matt. 7:22). A man may boast, either to himself or to others, of his almsgiving, his speaking with tongues, his knowledge of the mysteries. He may even glory in the fact that he has given his body to be burned. But such boasting cancels love, without which none of these works count for anything (I Cor. 13:1-3). By claiming to have faith without faith's penitence, he condemns his own faith as moribund (James 2:14-26). Conceited faith is the mark of supreme faithlessness, for it is more deeply enslaved to the law of superiority by which Satan dictates his will.

All forms of the desire to retreat to the old age indicate a divided mind (James 1:5-8; 3:11-18; 4:4-10). A single mind can be restored only by the act of dying, each situation affording a new occasion for self-denial. The form of the denial is determined by the particular lure that Satan is using. To share in the death of Jesus does not mean to seek the gallows or the stake; rather, the type of temptation may demand that the disciple die to fleshly passions (Gal., ch. 6), to the law (ch. 2:19 f.), to the elemental spirits (Col. 2:20 f.), or to his own superior orthodoxy or piety. In any case, each particular lure opens the way to victory on a new front. The way to a single mind, to an integrated heart, remains ever the same: " Humble yourselves before the Lord " (James 4:10). In the very vortex of struggle, joy springs from the assurance that " the testing of your faith produces steadfastness " (ch. 1:2 f.).

The runner encounters another type of hurdle in the deceptive feeling of helplessness before the austere demands of his Captain. This despair may be compounded of several ingredients: a keen sense of the perfection required of a son; an acute awareness of the powers of resistance in the hostile world; a recollection of a long succession of personal failures: " I am too weak, too cowardly to run so rigorous a race."

A faith rightly controlled by the memory of Jesus, however, can probe to the roots of this despair. To be sure, a companion of Jesus is expected to imitate his blameless holiness. But Jesus' example proves that his Way, though extremely narrow, offers a possible option for each current decision. What is impossible for men becomes possible for God — and for his sons, who through faith seek to make their adoption sure. When a command appears least possible for the disciple, then it becomes most imperative (cf. pp. 63 f., 109 f.). The disciple, however, is not expected to meet all future contingencies at once; he must not daydream about future dilemmas; he is responsible only for today's action. This action may be much simpler than he supposes: to give a cup of water in Christ's name; to bind up a victim's wounds; or to plod patiently through trivial duties (Luke 17:7–10; 10:29–37). He who scans the horizon for some heroic gesture may discover that his assignment is nothing more than to wait or to watch. In this strange race, ability to stand may be the most effective way of running. Neither Paul nor Jesus tried to hasten the day of martyrdom, goading their enemies into violence in order to pride themselves on their courage. The perfection of love demands first of all a going lower down, a humbling of self in self-forgetfulness, not the self-directed effort to climb to the top by heroic daring or ascetic practice. The " nobodies " in a community are more responsive to such demands than the " somebodies," for the latter always want to do the dramatic, the significant thing. Meekness is undramatic. If one refuses to repent, to forgive, to forget self, this can hardly be excused on the ground of weakness, especially since it is God who performs such work in the truly humbled soul. To remove oneself from the range of obligation because of the rigorous perfectionism of the ideal is nothing but a hidden despair of God's wisdom and power, a self-deception that capitalizes on self-concern. The disciple can learn through such temptations the subtle line of distinction between genuine humility and its false substitutes.

" But the world is too hostile for me to endure its sarcasm and hatred." So runs another plea of faked weakness. Jesus, of course, did not minimize the hazards of discipleship, but made the consequences plain to all (Matt. 10:17–27). He knew that ridicule and resentment would cause many to fall away, yet he knew the blessedness of those who accept this form of discipline. He called men to learn from him how to find courage for the hour of trial, though he was suspicious of any sign of a martyr complex. He taught men to prepare their hearts beforehand so that they would be ready for a sudden baptism with fire, but this teaching took the form of cautioning them not to worry in advance as to what they would do when that fire was kindled. The Holy Spirit will be an adequate counselor for future contingencies, providing that one learns from it how to meet the present tensions. The real crisis of faith usually precedes the external calamity which everyone labels a crisis. It is through learning patience in today's struggle that fears of future disasters are allayed (Rom. 5:1–3). The disciple's faithfulness is not measured by his ability to forecast future acts of cowardice, but by his conquest of today's anxieties.

" But I am too weak even to overcome today's hurdle." To this complaint, faith finds various answers. It listens to the testimony of its heroes: "Who is weak, and I am not weak?" " "My power is made perfect in weakness." Weakness is an opportunity, for only in true weakness can God's strength be seen for what it is; on the other hand, to use weakness as an excuse is an inverted form of pride. One is really complaining because he is not stronger, pitying himself and wishing that he were someone else. He resents the fact that the Creator made him so obscure and insignificant. His very complaint is a bid for recognition, both from God and from men. This is the inferiority complex which society instills, rather than the penitence of Jesus. Successful encounters with false inferiorities is the avenue for learning to distinguish between the false and true weakness.

" But I am afraid." Again the temptation masks an opportunity, offering the possibility of a new discovery by Christ's apprentice. Jesus does not deceive men into thinking that absolute fearlessness can be learned in one easy lesson. He proceeded by subordinating a lesser fear to a greater. Man must choose, not between hysteria and fearlessness, but *whom* he will fear: either him who can destroy the body or him who can destroy both body and soul in hell (Luke 12:4, 5). If one is more afraid of the first, this is not truly fear; it is slavery to a lie. The disciple who confesses that he is a coward convicts himself of fraud. He is more afraid of the father of lies than of the God of truth because, in spite of his profession, he actually gives the former the status of God. But if he comes to himself and learns that his fancied cowardice was nothing but self-deception, if he learns properly to fear Him who alone has power over history, the struggle with himself will have added to his knowledge of God and to his own freedom from fear of death. If he fails so to learn the lessons of discipline, he becomes an example, not of fear but of faithlessness, because he has repudiated the Fatherhood of God. He refuses to abide by the dictum of his Master: " It is enough for the disciple to be like his teacher " (Matt. 10:25; cf. Luke 6:40 f.).

All temptations thus derive their power from a will that is not yet integrated, and provide an opportunity for such integration. They stem from a partial allegiance to Christ, and point to the way by which that allegiance may become total. They disclose an area of life not yet oriented around the axis of personal relationship to Christ, where Christ has not yet been accorded full control over mind and heart.

Especially is this true if one's retrospect betrays him into denying or forgetting that " Jesus Christ has come *in the flesh.*" Such a denial undercuts the significance of historical conditions as the scene of redemption. It repudiates the movement of salvation as a movement downward into the lowest level of human experience. Only by holding fast to the fact that Jesus was tempted in all points as we are can we find purpose and meaning in our temptations. To deny his full participation in our life and death is to deny his victory over the world at the points where the world maintains its power over us. And to deny this is to deny the possibility of our victory over the same antagonists. Those who thus break the bond of mutuality between the human Jesus and themselves are left with only a vague heavenly hope that deprives today's earthly existence of its only genuine significance. They will succumb to the lures of asceticism, trying to escape the conditions of fleshly existence by arduous self-generated and self-seeking exertions. Or they will succumb to the lures of license, of a self-willed repudiation of worldly restraints because the soul is already assured of its salvation irrespective of the deeds of the body. In either case they actually worship the lords of the old age, unaware that Jesus has defeated them on their own ground. This is true even if they imagine that they can now ignore these lords, forgetting the fact that only by subjection to them did Jesus manifest the faith that overcame them.

Whether the offense takes the form of self-despair or self-trust, despair of the world or trust in the world, the disciple may be kept from stumbling by memory of Jesus' victory. The disciple remains in the world as Jesus was in the world, using that context for doing the works of love (I John 4:17). Temptation enables the believer to recognize the presence of sin in the conditions of his own existence, to recognize the ubiquity and pervasiveness of death; yet at the same time it may remind him of how Jesus won his victory *in, through,* and *over* sin, how he defeated death through dying. This redemptive retrospect is surrendered whenever he despairs of himself or of the world, because such despair implicitly denies either the full humanity of Jesus or the full power of the resurrection. At its roots such despair is a despair of the forgiveness of sins; it blasphemes the Holy Spirit by denying his effective presence in one area of God's creation, for it yields that area to the final sovereignty of evil.

B. A Defective Fellowship

Still another occasion for the refining of faith is the temptation to misjudge the present activity of Christ in the Church. A disciple despairs of the Church ostensibly because he fails to find there the authority of its Head. He may consider himself superior to his brothers, his distress over their imperfections masking a complacency over his own goodness. Judging them to be tares, he tries to pull them up before the harvest. Nor is it difficult to find reasons for weeding the wheat field, because the tares are so numerous. One can locate within the Church all the sins of the world: ambition and apathy, greed and hate, caste prejudice and adultery — yes, the whole repertoire of the devil's lusts. Applying his best scale of Christian virtues, the disciple asks: " Is this really a communion of saints? Can Christ actually be found here? Can he overcome such treachery? If this visible fellowship is the mark of his victory, how partial and uncertain is that victory! "

In the New Testament this form of despair came to the surface in the posing of two questions. The questions seem to be innocent enough, but at times they hide a real bewilderment concerning the relationship between Christ and his Church. And this bewilderment is the occasion by which individuals lose their power of hearing God speak through his chosen people. The two questions are these: How many men will be saved? How shall we deal with the tares in the wheat field?

Both these queries were presented to Jesus. When he was asked the first, he did not reply directly by giving a quantitative figure or an objective prediction; he responded with the stringent injunction: " Strive to enter by the narrow door." Either extreme of quantitative estimate, whether it envisage the salvation of all men or of only a few, may betray a false relationship of disciple to lord.

If the disciple is too easily assured of the salvation of all men, he may be deluding himself by the conviction that he, with all other men, can rely upon the long-suffering God. Thus he may be " improving " upon the lesson of the cross by underestimating the world's resistance to God or by lessening the rigors of judgment. He may be impugning God's right to judgment or complaining against the justice meted out by the

Messiah. If so, the questioner in thus posing his question has adopted a position outside of faith; his salvation then requires the repetition of Jesus' command in all its stringency: " Strive to enter." It is the business of the Church to proclaim this command to itself.

On the other hand, he may in the fancied defense of orthodoxy deny that God's love is creation-wide. This denial may spring from the desire to limit the range of divine grace to his own narrow specifications. Seldom does such a person exclude himself from the elect: seldom is he free from a perverse joy in the divine exclusion of his enemies. Subtly he turns the miracle of God's personal providence into the arbitrary working of an impersonal fate. Lack of repentance and lack of love thereby alienate the disciple from the Messiah who suffered, and continues to suffer, for the sins of the whole world. If such a disciple is to be saved, the apostle must again show him that in holding such self-centered attitudes he stands at the outer entrance to the needle's eye, where he must surrender his pride in being among the chosen. The Church must again confront itself and its members with the word of the cross, in both its exclusiveness and its inclusiveness. Again the elect must experience the awesome selectivity of God's justice and the unlimited range of God's love. This way is indeed so narrow that few find it, but it is also the way by which, in God's mercy, all creation will be redeemed. For example, the apostle Paul, caught in the torment of his love for the Messiah and his love for recalcitrant Israel, saw the truth that God prunes dead branches from his olive tree, grafts new branches in their place, and yet retains power to cut out the new branches and revive the dead ones (Rom., chs. 9 to 11). Only the love that bears all things, including the sins of the world, can hope all things, including the redemption of the world.

What, then, is to be done with the tares? In the first place, hope for their salvation is required in the light of Christ's forgiveness of the greatest sinners and his power to create fellowship among the most hostile groups. Only perfect love has the right to final judgment. Therefore, the Church finds its solidarity in the need for forgiveness, not in the achievement of a stated level of righteousness. It is by the sacrament of humility that its members preserve their communion with God and with one another. Any judgment of the tares that proceeds from self-righteousness simply conceals the sin of the judges, and is an invitation for them to examine their own hearts.

In the second place, however, the Church cannot encourage its members to view with casual indifference the presence of treachery. There *are* tares; there *are* false teachers and prophets; there *are* those who by their apathy crucify Christ anew. Brothers should never forget that the Messiah begins his judgment in the Church (Heb. 10:26–30). Some followers will have their names erased from the book of life; some congregations will have their lampstand removed from its place in heaven (Rev. 2:5; 3:5). Just as the individual finds the battle front between the two ages located within the divided loyalties of his own heart, so also the Church finds the crucial struggle being waged within the context of its corporate life. It must say to itself: "We are not the fire, but we live where it burns." Its own baptism by fire is the sign of a true Church.

In the third place, the disciple must examine his motives in judging the Church. If he assumes complete identity between its membership and the Holy City, he may jeopardize his faith at vital points. Such an assumption may be due to complacency, pride, a false claim to immunity, or a desire to sin "that grace may abound." He may forget that the Kingdom comes near to the Church only in a repeated dying to the world and for the world. The fellowship of believers is a sign of the Kingdom's power, but woe to the man who interprets that sign with another mind than the mind of Christ.

If, on the other hand, he sees too sharp a chasm between the Church and the Kingdom, this may but reveal the sin in his own eyes. False teachers, in their self-confidence, often divide the Church according to their ideas of "the righteous remnant." They are inclined to require the realization of perfection as a ticket into the Kingdom and thereby cancel the gospel as the good news of God's grace to sinners. They find it difficult to imitate Jesus' confidence in his disciples, when during the Passion he appointed them to a place in his Kingdom — these men who fled in fear when he was arrested.

The apostles were keenly aware of both the spiritual glory and the imperfections within the communion of saints, but they did not try to arrange disciples along a staircase of attainment, nor did they try to fix the boundary between those who were inside and those who were outside the Kingdom. The Kingdom comes near by precipitating conflict, by creating awareness of sin, and by providing resources for victory in the midst of struggle. Only on the battle line does the Christian fellowship encounter and participate in the powers and gifts of the Messiah. Only when the Messiah returns will the final relationship between Kingdom and Church be made known.

Until he returns, to be sure, the Church must defend itself against wolves in sheep's clothing, but in this defense it must rely upon the guidance of the Spirit as that Spirit speaks through the word of the Messiah, his apostles and prophets, and the corporate judgment of his community. Where the spirits of various prophets contradict one another, the spirits must all be tested by love, and this very test of love makes it quite impossible to arrive at any final classification of Christians into those inside or outside the range of God's grace.

C. A DEFECTIVE HOPE

The denial of Christ's humanity and of his present power over the Church is closely related to despair over his coming again. Broken faith means a broken hope, a defective trust in God's future promise. In the early stages of the Christian race, the typical fault is to believe that the date of Christ's return is too close or, in fact, that he has already come. Fruits of this outlook are idleness and breathless watching for the day and the hour, impatience with present sufferings, frantic desires to escape the disciplining process, an excited by-passing of the ordinary duties of the world. At a later stage the opposite fault emerges. " My master is delayed." " Where is the promise of his coming? For ever since the fathers fell asleep, all things have continued as they were from the beginning of creation " (II Peter 3:4). If the pilgrim stumbles over this obstacle, he ceases his forward movement, goes to sleep, loses himself in preoccupations, or succumbs to the muted bitterness of blind resignation. He could run a hundred-yard dash but not a marathon.

The Lord's disciplining of sons requires both waiting and hurrying, both patience and alertness. The would-be son discovers that either a passive, inert waiting or an impatient expectancy is easy, but that a combination of alertness and patience is most difficult. The young in faith can be eager, but they must learn patience. The old can be resigned to the slow march of days, but they must learn expectancy. Expectancy without the endurance of faith is juvenility. Patience without the alertness of faith is senility. Without faith, patience and eagerness are incompatible worldly virtues based on a human sense of time. With faith, the two virtues are transfigured, for a time-enclosed world has been replaced by a God-enclosed time. In this new time, waiting may be expressed by sober activity, judiciously planned and executed (Matt. 24:43-47); running may be expressed by quiet confidence in a prisoner's cell (Phil. 3:12 f.). Each disciple must learn by experience which of these duties is his at the moment. How he learns to distinguish his particular assignment as given by the returning Master may be indicated by the answers to two questions.

The first question is this: How soon will the Messiah return? What are the motives that lie behind this question? In the New Testament it usually arises from disciples who are engaged in the struggles incident upon faith, and it represents the temptation to make their immediate vocation easier than the Master's. The answer of the Master will accordingly depend upon the character of the immediate temptation, for the Master is primarily concerned with the state of the disciple-Master axis. Unless this is kept in mind, the answers found in the New Testament will seem to be flat contradictions. On the one hand, Christ's return is announced as happening " much sooner than you think "; on the other hand, men are warned that he will come " not so soon as you think." [22] Both answers may be true when the truth is measured by the actual relation of a particular disciple to his Lord and by the shape of the current temptation.

Some disciples, for example, are inclined toward laziness. Because they believe that the Lord tarries, they neglect their lamps and beat their servants. Called to be watchmen of the day, they sleep soundly and comfortably. To them in the middle of the night the alarm is sounded: " The Lord comes." And waking, they discover that their treasures have already been taken by the thief (Matt. 24:48 to 25:13; Luke 12:35-40).

Other disciples, believing that the Day of Christ is almost upon them, are so excited by the prospect that they become irresponsible and shiftless, relying upon the Church for support. They unsettle the brothers with their hysteria and gossip. Breathlessly they hail every untoward event as a direful portent of the end, and flock after every strange teacher as a potential Messiah. The true apostle corrects this perversion of faith with the declaration, " The end is not yet " (Matt. 24:3-28).

Still others are distressed by a seemingly endless sequence of hardships. Their eagerness to know the end is a mark of impatience. With enthusiasm they had entered the road of the Messiah, but, unlike him, they are unwilling to endure all things in joy and to place complete trust in God. To them the word of the Messiah must be proclaimed: "By your endurance you will gain your lives" (Luke 21:10-19).

When such temptations strike, they induce disciples to assume or to crave more definite knowledge concerning the end than has been granted to them. Such knowledge would give them more time to sleep or would increase their hysteria or would buttress a poorly supported faith. To grant this knowledge would contradict God's intention, for it would relieve them of sharing to the full in the suffering of the Messiah. The apostle views the very appearance of the question as a token of wavering faith. When faith is at its full strength, the disciple endures every trial in joy. The prevailing mood in the New Testament is voiced in the hallelujahs and not in the petulant "How soon?" The true disciple is content not to know the day and the hour, for he is busy plowing toward the furrow's end, empowered by the energies that the Messiah instills. Only when, in the Master's judgment, this work is done will its fruits be garnered into the everlasting granary.

The second question in which temptation easily finds expression is this: "How are the dead raised? With what kind of body do they come?" [23] Whether or not the disciple who raised this question was ill-advised, the question itself was inevitable. Ultimately it is only by raising the question that the congregation of believers learns to distinguish between an unsure and a sure hope. Improvement of communication with a Lord who is expected to return involves questions concerning the character of the coming transformation. New Testament answers to this query again appear to be contradictory, even when allowance is made for the fluidity of metaphorical images. It has become the fashion to explain these contradictions as due to the diverse cultural legacies of the various authors. Much may be said for this explanation, since any writer expresses himself most naturally in the idiom of his native tongue. Christians of Jewish heritage are naturally inclined to stress a physical resurrection (The Revelation of John); those with Hellenistic thought-forms naturally stress more ethereal concepts of immortality (the Fourth Gospel); Paul, as heir of two cultures, tried to combine the two mutually incompatible doctrines. In Paul's case the result has been called an unstable equilibrium, an imperfect fusion, or a perfect paradox. This interpretation of the development of Christian thought has a certain plausibility, but it fails to penetrate to the real character and logic of the apostolic witness.

The decisive determinants of their attitudes toward the resurrection body are to be found, not primarily in inherited concepts, but in the revelatory event around which all their thinking and acting was oriented. The data on which these attitudes depend are the same data that shaped their other attitudes. Sufficient evidence for the *fact* of resurrection is provided by the exaltation of the Messiah, as certified to them by his continuing activities in their midst (I Cor. 15:12-19). The clues to the *form* of the resurrection are given by their relationship to this Messiah as a "life-giving spirit," "the first fruits of those who have fallen asleep" (vs. 20-28). Knowledge of the life that belongs to those who "bear the name of Christ" is communicated to the disciple who is "in peril every hour," who knows what it means to "die every day" (v. 30). Denial of the resurrection is appropriate only from those who refuse to share this "dying life," where the Christian finds his key to "knowledge of God" (vs. 32-34).

In this context, the customary Jewish doctrines of a revivified body prove to be patently inadequate to do justice to the disciple's present dependence on a living Lord. In neither Revelation nor the writings of John or Paul does faith require objective proofs of a reanimated body. Faith is the response to present, powerful activities of a glorified and heavenly Lord, who sits among the seven candlesticks, who is the vine, who reveals things that "no eye has seen." A doctrine of physical re-animation would not in itself be able to convey the reality of the mysterious otherness of this heavenly King. Nor was it adapted to describe the mystery of the believer's inner transformation, his own participation now in the life that has no end (Heb. 12:18-24; 13:8, 20, 21). To insist upon the prior necessity of a reanimated body, according to doctrines that later became formalized, would violate their experience of the "first death" as marking the point of decisive transition: Such insistence would not help to explain the work that the Messiah has already accomplished among them. Their victory over the "first death" is the basis of confidence that what lies ahead in the "second death" is merely a sleep, a moment of departure to be with Christ, a time for putting on a new body of glory. To require prior proofs that the same body will be reanimated would be, in effect, a denial of the life that is "now hid with Christ." Likewise it would be a denial of the transfiguration of all creation which has been accomplished in the cross.

On the other hand, the disciples found that prevalent pagan conceptions of spiritual immortality were also inadequate to the truth which they had learned from Christ. To be sure, such doctrines on the surface seemed congenial to the realization that " flesh and blood cannot inherit the kingdom of God," that " this perishable nature must put on the imperishable." But on deeper levels, the insufficiency of these doctrines becomes clear. To be content with them would imply, for the Christian, that the Messiah had not actually died and that his exaltation was no new miracle of grace. It would imply that the body is not the Lord's, that it lies beyond the reach of God's redemption. It would imply that the earth in its fullness is not the Lord's. It would imply that victory has not actually been won over Satan, this world, and that last enemy, death. It would mean that the Christian's victory does not take place in the arena of concrete historical reality, that it does not redeem the stuff of which earthly existence is made. If this were true, then the question of how he lives in the flesh becomes a matter of indifference. If this were true, then the disciple is not now participating in the process by which all things are being subjected to a single Master. This would deny both the power and the love of the Messiah. To be true to their faith in him, Christians must insist both that death has spread through all creation and that new life is now delivering all creation from its bondage. In the context of genuine faith, the thirteenth chapter of First Corinthians is as much a description of the character of " future life " as the fifteenth chapter, and neither chapter is complete apart from the other (cf. II Cor., chs. 3 to 5; Eph., 2; 3).

Knowledge of the Messiah based on his knowledge of them, and love of the Messiah based on his love for them — these are the grounds for the disciples' trust in God's Tomorrow. The truth of the end of history derives from the truth that has already been made available in Christ. The first followers knew that they did not know many things about the coming Kingdom of God, or about the future course of earthly events. But what they knew about the Kingdom of Christ freed them from slavery to false hopes, from the deceptive lures of an elusive Paradise. Faith posed many problems, but it also furnished the way by which those problems might be solved through living according to God's purposes. The New Testament as a whole is a witness to this power to transform every test of faith into an opportunity for the refining of gold. Those who faced each successive temptation by reliance on the truth of the gospel experienced the Lord's faithfulness in keeping his pledge: " Fear not, little flock, for it is your Father's good pleasure to give you the kingdom " (Luke 12:32). To them this proved supremely good news, for the gift included unending peace, joy, love, and life, but this " proof " was accessible only to those who learned to participate more faithfully in the mission of bringing all creatures under the single rule of God.

11

THE GIFT OF FREEDOM

IT IS a distinguishing mark of the New Testament that in it all the manifold associations of man are conceived in fully personal terms. Even the relation to such mammoth social entities as empire and industry are reduced to the dimensions of the immediate responsibility of person to person. This trait of early Christian thought stems from the realization that every man is one for whom Christ died. It stems as well from the fact that every earthly relationship conceals an ultimate opportunity wherein to distinguish the competing voices of invisible rulers. To hear one voice and to obey it is to stumble; to hear the voice of the Messiah and to obey it is to march forward toward reunion with him. In the choice of whom to obey the pilgrim comes to know most fully his own selfhood in all its weakness and strength. When his will is most fully subject to faith's memory and hope, then too does he become most fully alive to other men as persons. Through remembering Jesus' temptations he has the clue to victory in his own. Through imitating Jesus' faith he learns how to accept the Father's chastisement of his sons. Over and over again, when he is baffled by the riddles of life and unsure of his direction, he hears the risen Lord say, " I am the way."

One expression of this intensely personal relationship to Jesus is the axiom that recurs frequently in the First Epistle of John: " As he is so are we." This is virtually equivalent to the definition of life in the Gospel: to abide in him. To believe in Jesus is to abide in him, to do his works, to live as he lived. To this life there are many facets, at a few of which we should look. All, however, accent the conviction: The Way of Christ is the path to perfect freedom.

A. Sonship

"As he is so are we in this world" (I John 4:17). The station in which Jesus was called is the station in which we are called — the world. We cannot expect a different environment from that accorded him. This drives out fear and gives confidence for the Day of Judgment, because we face no conditions more difficult than his. Subjected to all the conditions that apparently frustrate God's will, he found in perfect love the victory over the world. This love transformed those conditions from formidable obstacles to redemptive opportunities. By abiding in God, Jesus transposed the worst conceivable situation into the greatest conceivable glory, the fulfillment at once of the Father's will and his own vocation. To abide in him while *in* the world is the path to his crown.

This means that the disciple must not "love the world or the things in the world." He hates what the world covets, fending off the desires that the world seeks to instill in men: "the lust of the flesh and the lust of the eyes and the pride of life" (ch. 2:16). A world oriented around such motives is destined to emptiness, because these motives exclude the single-minded love of God. Because the logic of this love is so different from worldly calculations, "the world does not know us" as "it did not know him" (ch. 3:1). It was the fate of the Saviour of the world that when he was in the world "the world knew him not; he came to his own home, and his own people received him not" (John 1:10, 11). It is the disciple's fate to be rejected by the same world, for this world has not changed its lusts or its lies since the coming of the Lord.

This very alienation, however, is evidence that what is true in him is also true in you: "The darkness is passing away and the true light is already shining" (I John 2:8). The darkness represents the hatred of brothers, which is the ultimate hallmark of the world's blindness. The light represents the love of brothers, in which there is no cause for stumbling. As Jesus hated the world by his love of the brothers, so too the disciple hates the world by his love of men in the world. And this hate-love indicates that he has stepped from night into day. By his deeds in the world he gives witness to the fact that he is now living in the dawn of the new time.

Henceforth the requirement laid on the disciple is to "walk in the light, as he is in the light." This light, shining *in* the world, produces penitence for sin, cleansing from sin, and fellowship with one another (ch. 1:6–10). It is by confession of sin that the disciple walks according to the Master's word and is purged by that word (John 15:1–5). To keep his word is "to walk in the same way in which he walked" (I John 2:6) and to love as he loved. The rigor of this love is not forgotten. "By this we know love, that he laid down his life for us; and we ought to lay down our lives for the brethren" (ch. 3:16). It is only through such love that "we know that we have passed out of death into life" (v. 14). Only through such love can we be righteous "as he is righteous," enabled thus to "overcome the evil one" (ch. 2:14). To hate men rather than to love them is to be overcome by the evil one and to remain "in death."

This personal dependence of the servant on his lord in the age now present establishes the rocklike confidence in the coming fulfillment.

> "Beloved, we are God's children now; it does not yet appear what we shall be, but we know that when he appears we shall be like him, for we shall see him as he is. And every one who thus hopes in him purifies himself as he is pure" (ch. 3:2, 3).

Thus the brother begins to experience the point-for-point correspondence between his will and Christ's will, his death and Christ's death, his glory and Christ's glory. This is what it means to be God's son. The test of sonship is not simply the deeds that are done, though they are of course significant; the test is the personal relationship to the Father to which those deeds testify.

Relation to Christ becomes the determining factor in the day-to-day pilgrimage. This relation is multiple and mysterious, best indicated in grammar, perhaps, by prepositions and participles. At least that is the way by which Paul was accustomed to describe the link between Christ and his servants. In the Epistle to the Ephesians, for example, these prepositional phrases give to his letter a steady rhythm: before him, under him, from him, of him, through him, and in him. It is the prepositions that underscore the intimate relationships, but it is the participles that convey the wealth of what God does through those relationships: Blessing, choosing, destining, bestowing, lavishing, uniting, forgiving, promising, enlightening, accomplishing, working, subjecting, filling. All sentences of this passage focus upon the direction of God's purposes for men and of how these purposes are realized in and through Christ.

> "He destined us in love to be his sons through Jesus Christ" (Eph. 1:5). "He chose us in him . . . that we should be holy and blameless before him" (v. 4). "We . . . have been destined . . . to live for the praise of his glory" (v. 12). "For by grace you have been saved through faith; and this is not your own doing, it is the gift of God — not because of works, lest any man should boast. For we are his workmanship, created in Christ Jesus for good works, which God prepared beforehand, that we should walk in them" (ch. 2:8–10).

The frequent recurrence of these statements throughout the New Testament indicates their centrality in God's design for history. God is engaged in creating sons through Jesus Christ. He does this in and through love; this love can be known, yet it surpasses knowledge; to receive it fully is to be filled with God's fullness. Sonship, however, includes the quest for holiness so that man's life is directed toward the increase of glory. Surrender to love is nothing less than sharing the fullness of God's glory. To live thus produces good works, yet these good works are so designed as to prevent any man from boasting, for the man who does them is himself a work of God and the deeds are themselves prepared beforehand by God.

In these verses the purposes of God may be summarized in two objectives for the disciple: perfect holiness is the positive expression; the confession of sin is the negative expression. The negative is essential to the positive, because only a perfect penitence can assure the fulfillment of perfect holiness as God's work rather than man's. Progress toward total humility is progress toward total love. Thus is the final integration of life accomplished.

At the source of this paradox of holy penitence and penitent holiness lies the teaching of Jesus. It was he who first realized that the gate to the Kingdom opens only to the meek, that the final gift of the Kingdom is granted only to those who ask in surprise, "When did we see thee hungry and feed thee?" To him the measure of perfect charity is for the right hand to be ignorant of what the left hand is giving. Such a high calling is obviously difficult to realize. One can readily imagine a second episode in the story of the Pharisee and the tax collector, a sequel in which the roles are reversed: the tax collector revels in the peace of God which blessed his prayer in the Temple, and the Pharisee, finding that his pious exercise had been utterly devoid of God's forgiveness, repents of the self-deception. Yes, the sequel could tell a story the reverse of the first and yet illustrate the same message. Similarly the minds of the two sons in the parable of the forgiving father might again have changed, the morning after. Thus can repentance be transformed into sin the moment one becomes conscious of it as a merit. Subtract from it the continuing judgment of God and it becomes impenitence and impertinence.

Even so, the cross persists in turning this new pride back again to humility, so long as one subjects himself to its light. It continues to display a power and a wisdom contrary to all human expectations, revealing each new sin with sharper penetration. God persists in choosing "what is low and despised in the world, even things that are not, to bring to nothing things that are, so that no human being might boast in the presence of God" (I Cor. 1:26–31). Since the Master remains as the "wisdom," the "righteousness," and the "consecration" of the disciple, the only boasting permitted by God is a boasting in the Lord. The author of The First Epistle of John states the same truth in a different form: "If we say that we have no sin, we deceive ourselves, and the truth is not in us. . . . We make him a liar, and his word is not in us" (I John 1:6–10). It is the confession of sin that opens the door to sonship. Also in the same book we find the other pole of the paradox: "No one who abides in him sins" (ch. 3:6). The door which confession of sin opens is able to exclude sin, simply because the door is a forgiveness of sin and not its extenuation. It opens the way to God's righteousness, but forever excludes self-righteousness, either on the part of the sinner who glories in his sins or on the part of the sinner who glories in his holiness. And for this reason this is the only door to perfect freedom. (The Christian remembers, of course, that this door is a person, a Person on a cross.)

B. FORGIVENESS

One reason why God permits sin to reign, as we have seen, is that man might learn what sonship means, and learn as well the scope of the Father's mercy. Educated by temptation, the son discovers ever new dimensions in the operation of God's judgment and forgiveness. He learns that judgment falls on all men, and that this is the basis of hope for all men (Rom. 11:11 f.). God has entrusted the work of judging all men to his Son, so that men may grasp both the rigor and graciousness of his purpose. The Son's standard of justice is quite the opposite of the standards of worldly wisdom, thus condemning those standards and freeing men from them.

The objective of Jesus, however, is to bring men to judge themselves, thus assuring them their freedom. In placing himself under God's judgment, man participates willingly in the final judgment. He passes from death to life and the future has no more terrors for him, so long as he continues under this judgment. But if he refuses to bend the knee to the humble Messiah, he will ultimately come to realize how that refusal has pyramided his guilt; for him God's judgment, ratified at last by self-judgment, will be inexorable torment.

God's aim to place every creature under self-judgment is therefore an eternal purpose which is hidden or revealed according to man's response to his Word. His Word is perennially close, as near as man's opinion of himself. However difficult it may be for a man to humble himself wholly, it is always just as possible as his awareness of the demand. Here is a standard of holiness that does not require climbing up an endless ladder of moral or religious attainment, but simply invites one to descend; one is always able to step down to a lower level, because his pride is *his* pride. What makes it seem difficult is one's involvements in social intercourse where prestige depends upon the maintenance of superiority. That is why resistance to God's purpose is so deeply imbedded in corporate as well as personal attitudes.

This cluster of convictions concerning judgment is well presented in the Fourth Gospel, whose author was greatly concerned that men should understand Christ's work as the Judge who does not judge except through bringing men to the point of self-judgment. For brevity's sake we have brought together the important teachings:

"The Father judges no one, but has given all judgment to the Son" (John 5:22). "God sent the Son into the world, not to condemn the world, but that the world might be saved through him. He who believes in him is not condemned; he who does not believe is condemned already" (ch. 3:17, 18).

"For judgment I came into this world, that those who do not see may see, and that those who see may become blind" (ch. 9:39). "He who hears my word and believes him who sent me, has eternal life; he does not come into judgment, but has passed from death to life" (ch. 5:24). "He who rejects me and does not receive my sayings has a judge; the word that I have spoken will be his judge on the last day" (ch. 12:48). "I judge no one. Yet even if I do judge, my judgment is true" (ch. 8:15, 16).

"Now is the judgment of this world, now shall the ruler of this world be cast out" (ch. 12:31). "This is the judgment, that the light has come into the world, and men loved darkness rather than light, because their deeds were evil" (ch. 3:19). "They replied, ... 'No prophet is to rise from Galilee. ... Can anything good come out of Nazareth? ... He has a demon, ... he is mad. ... He ... called God his Father, making himself equal with God. ... This man is not from God, for he does not keep the sabbath. ... We have a law, and by that law he ought to die. ... If we let him go on thus, ... the Romans will come and destroy both our holy place and our nation. ... It is expedient ... that one man should die for the people, and not that the whole nation should perish. ... Away with him, ... crucify him!'" (chs. 7:52; 1:46; 10:20; 5:18; 9:16; 19:7; 11:48, 50; 19:15).

"I can do nothing on my own authority; as I hear, I judge; and my judgment is just, because I seek not my own will but the will of him who sent me" (ch. 5:30). "As the Father has life in himself, so he has granted the Son also to have life in himself, and has given him authority to execute judgment" (vs. 26, 27). "How can you believe, who receive glory from one another and do not seek the glory that comes from the only God?" (v. 44). "He who speaks on his own authority seeks his own glory" (ch. 7:18). "[You] loved the praise of men more than the praise of God" (ch. 12:43). "You judge according to the flesh" (ch. 8:15). "Do not judge by appearances, but judge with right judgment" (ch. 7:24). "If you were blind, you would have no guilt; but now that you say, 'We see,' your guilt remains" (ch. 9:41).

Through the mission of Christ, God placed the whole world under judgment in order that no man may boast, for to bow the knee to Christ is to follow the humblest man in history. The cross is the event that epitomizes the character and process of judgment; the disciple's rebirth is the event when a man, confessing his blindness, accepts that judgment upon himself; the receiving of full adoption as a son is the end of the process by which a man's penitence is being realized. The return of Christ is the end of the judgment of all creation, including those men and institutions and rulers who now resist his work. The Fourth Gospel pays little attention to the forms of this future return, partly because it concentrates on the immediate response of those who have already heard the Word ("these are written that you may believe"), partly because it sees this present judgment being extended throughout the world by the work of the Counselor, but chiefly perhaps because it knows that the final judgment will do no more than demonstrate the fact that the ruler of this age has already been judged.

> "When he [the Holy Spirit] comes, he will convince the world of sin and of righteousness and of judgment: of sin, because they do not believe in me; of righteousness, because I go to the Father, and you will see me no more; of judgment, because the *ruler of this world is judged*" (ch. 16:8-11).

One function of the Holy Spirit is to lead the disciple from one level of penitence to a deeper level. As one learns from the story of Peter, the first desire " to flee from the wrath to come " does not bring a full understanding of how subtly one's desires are woven from the stuff of the dying age. Peter trusted too fully in the prestige of Israel, until the Spirit broke down this trust (Acts, ch. 10). He was bound more tightly then he knew to the prejudices engraved on his mind by the law. Each successive act of penitence was more than a momentary regret for a recurring misdeed. It was a discovery of an unsuspected depth of rebellion against God. It was a discovery of a wider sense of responsibility and of the stubborn hold exerted by the law, the Temple, and the race, as those institutions had been perverted by sin. It was a revelation at once of greater slavery, greater obligation, and greater freedom. To abide in Jesus' word leads to a progressive intensification of the sense of responsibility for social sin and of slavery to social judgments. The disciple learns that he is still deceived by the fog of illusions which self-judgments and social judgments create. Yet he is responsible for his blindness, and he is free to be healed if he will confess his blindness. He who learns to be a son through God's disciplining comes to know how infinitely complex is his involvement in the world's sin, how intimately responsible he is for that sin, and how utterly dependent he is on God's forgiveness if those chains are to be broken. "To me, though I am the very least of all the saints, this grace was given " (Eph. 3:8). But the recognition that he is lowest of all qualifies the saint to be a steward of the mystery, a witness to the unsearchable riches. Integral repentance before the judgment of God leads to integral forgiveness by God; and such forgiveness is the key to perfect freedom. God does not delight either in the punishment of the sinner or in placing him under perpetual scrutiny. He takes the initiative in offering to forgive sins in order to emancipate man. Similarly, it was Jesus' mission to "proclaim release to the captives " (Luke 4:18). Consequently it was the mission of the apostle to invite men to receive this gift in gratitude. And the apostle who was most effective in this work was the Pharisee who had once been most tightly yoked to captivity (Gal. 5:1).

C. Freedom

Freedom from what? Freedom from sinful bondage to the law, to the prejudices of the race, to the processes by which social institutions foist their mind upon the members. The disciple who returns to the pattern of social judgments that rule his religious community enters again into a yoke of slavery. By the desire for social approval and for public recognition of his goodness, he cuts himself off from Christ and no longer lives by the truth (vs. 1–12).

Progress in repentance is thus progress in freedom, a true fulfillment of God's purpose. This is the point of the promise of Jesus: " You will know the truth, and the truth will make you free " (John 8:32). Few of the promises of the gospel are more frequently misused than this one. This is due, in part at least, to the fact that readers ignore two elements in the context. In the first place, they overlook the *if*, the condition on which the promise is based. Two forms of this condition are stated. " If you *continue in my word*, . . . you will know the truth." Or alternately, " If *the Son makes you free*, you will be free indeed " (v. 36). The context makes crystal clear the fact that the listeners did not fulfill this condition. Their will was so estranged from God that they could not bear to hear the word, much less to continue in it (vs. 43–47). So long as they sought to kill him, the Son could not make them free. In other words, the door to freedom is just as narrow as the door to true faith, because it is the same door, " and those who find it are few."

In the second place, by lifting this promise out of its context, readers give to the words " truth " and " free " a meaning very different from that of the gospel. What is the truth that makes men free? First of all, it is the truth about Jesus, or it is Jesus who as the Truth frees men. It is the truth that comes from God through Jesus. To know him, to abide in his word, to be his disciples, to obey him — all this is included in knowing the truth. And how does this truth free them? By revealing to them their present bondage to sin. As long as they are unaware of this bondage they cannot be freed from it. When they reply, " We . . . have never been in bondage to anyone " (v. 33), they close the door to the truth and bar the way to their own emancipation. Reliance on Abraham as their father proves that they are not Abraham's children, but rather sons of the devil, who is " a liar and the father of lies " (vs. 39–44). Such parentage can be changed only by a new penitence, new desires, and a new will. Only the true Son of God can make them sons who will continue in the Father's house forever.

The Son who thus frees his disciples also promises that they will do " greater works." They are qualified by repentance for doing these works. But this very repentance means that their works are actually the *works of Christ* (John 14:14), just as Christ's works are the *works of God* (v. 10). Thus the disciple in his activity of penitence participates in the global purpose of the Father. Penitence is an act of power, for only penitence can cast off the chains of the world's power. Perfect obedience to Christ is the road to perfect freedom. More than this, it is the sign of Christ's redemption of the world. For this freedom has one sovereign purpose — to emancipate the world from " many ' gods ' and many ' lords.' "

He who receives forgiveness must therefore spend his efforts in making the same opportunity accessible to others. Reconciled to God, he becomes a messenger of reconciliation. In and through his own gentle meekness he is given power to bring hope to the despairing, recovery of sight to the blind, release to captives. As heir of the promise, his inheritance can be received only by being shared. This mission means living as a sojourner in a foreign land, like Moses and Abraham. It means self-denial and surrender, like that of Jeremiah and Jesus. It means that the word that rebukes the world's rebellion will bring ostracism and persecution to those who carry it. Despised and rejected of men, Christ's slave fulfills his mission, and experiences in his suffering the blessedness and joy that God has promised. His blessedness is a mark of his freedom. His joy comes from the confidence that " in the Lord your labor is not in vain " (I Cor. 15:58).

The fruitfulness of the labor does not, however, stop with the release of other men from the tyrannies of the old age. It stops only with the reconciliation of God's ultimate enemies — the principalities and powers. This cosmic goal of the ministry of reconciliation is the subject of the following chapter.

12

THE MINISTRY OF RECONCILIATION

THE documents of the New Testament were written by men who had been freed by Christ from bondage and written to others who shared in that gift. The prevailing mood is therefore one of gratitude, wonder, and buoyancy. Worship was to them a true celebration, and their writings were permeated by irrepressible rejoicing. It was a sober rejoicing, of course, because it was pervaded by a sense of infinite indebtedness and was directed toward the meeting of daily trials. Since surrender to Christ was the entrance to freedom, the buoyancy of release was channeled into the tasks of the Church. One of these tasks was to announce the opportunity of freedom to men who were still in bondage. But underneath this task lay a more far-reaching one — that of serving as Christ's agents in bringing into subjection the principalities which keep men in bondage. Christ had descended in order to take captivity captive (Eph. 4:8). His Body is therefore commissioned to make the wisdom of God known to the rulers in heavenly places (ch. 3:10). In discussing the victory of Christ (Chapters 5, 6) we have seen that it is the usual thing for New Testament writers to distinguish between human rulers and the invisible powers lying back of those human agents. We have seen how victory over human adversaries was made possible only by victory in the heavenly places. We now need to trace the thoughts of the New Testament with regard to the twofold ministry of reconciliation — the freeing of slaves and the bringing of their former "rulers" under the power of love. Obviously this double work of reconciliation is carried on by the same agents, working through the same means, so that any division of the task applies primarily to the consequences rather than to the methods. We may begin by summarizing what has already been said about the freeing of other men, adopting for the sake of brevity a paraphrase drawn from the confessions of freedmen. Then we will explore the specific ways in which these men were trained for the reconciliation of their former lords. First, then, the composite confession:

A. RECONCILIATION ON TWO LEVELS

" Jesus Christ died for us while we were still sinners, while we were still subjected to the sovereignty of Satan as expressed through the misused institutions of society (Rom. 5:6–21). For this reason we are freed from the fear of anything that Satan may now do to us through those institutions. No longer can any earthly power, any form of social organization, any historical catastrophe, separate us from God's love or God's power (ch. 8). No set of environmental conditions can avail, apart from our consent, to deprive us of the life in Christ. By freeing us from fears, Christ frees us from the illusions through which the demonic forces in a particular civilization claim for themselves a specious ultimacy.

" By forgetting and betraying Christ we can, of course, forfeit this freedom, placing ourselves once again under other masters. We may make of our freedom an opportunity for the flesh to reassert its power, for pride to exalt itself, for righteousness to become self-righteousness, for ourselves to deny the freedom of others (Gal. 4:5). Such temptations may be detected, however, when we recall the way in which Jesus became free, the way in which he freed us, and the purpose of our freedom (Matt. 4:1–11; Heb. 2:14, 15; I John 2:14). His freedom is a freedom to love God and neighbor, to witness to the powerful presence of God's Kingdom, to invite other slaves to accept his yoke, and to challenge the hold exerted over men by Satan. We are freed to become Christ's servants in the battle he continues to wage against principalities and powers.

" The scene of the battle is ' the state wherein we were called.' Satan knows that where full obedience is given to God, he loses his control, so he employs every trick to prevent such obedience. He takes advantage of every trace of self-concern and social attachment. He appeals to the judgments of the world, trying to instill fear of social ostracism, economic insecurity, persecution from religious or political officers, the power that social agencies hold over our earthly fame and fate. He creates dissension among us by encouraging teachers to rely upon alien ideologies or by encouraging brothers with various cultural backgrounds to insist upon the necessity of their own ecclesiastical or social customs. He wants to draw us back again within the world's field of influence, making us its friends, subservient to its desires, fearful of its power, and deceived by its wisdom.

"Yet our captain is engaged in the struggle with us and through us. He supplies a full set of armor and power adequate to our needs. Guided by his Spirit, we are constrained by his commands: to repent, to forgive our enemies, to love all men, to seek first his Kingdom, to wait with alert patience, to deny ourselves, to pray without ceasing, to be joyful and thankful in every situation, to yield our hearts in perfect trust and hope — in short, to carry his cross. These are his commands. More than this, they are his beatitudes, because they yield the first fruits of eternal life (Matt., chs. 5 to 7; Rom. 12:1-18; Gal. 5:22 to 6:5; I Peter 3:8 to 4:11).

"Like our lord whom we serve, we are sent into the old age to bear witness to its redemption. Called out by him as citizens of his new city, he sends us back into our former countries as pilgrims and sojourners. Having freed us from the prince of darkness, he commissions us to wrestle with that prince until his power is spent. Our connections with the old age are not terminated but transfigured, for each of them becomes an arena where we share the agonies of an old era and thus the power of the new. The joy that fills our hearts during this struggle is itself a signal to Satan that his territory is being reclaimed by its rightful ruler."

The question must now be raised: *How* does this work of Christ's slaves actually serve to emancipate *the very rulers* by which they had earlier been enslaved? How does God bring the dominions of darkness under subjection to Christ, so that God may fill all creation with his fullness? Before dealing with this matter, there is need for reviewing what was said earlier about the social structure through which Satan maintains his authority, remembering above all the two levels on which such authority operates: (1) the relation of one man to another, of the superior and the inferior; (2) the relation of both men to the invisible seat of authority that sets their respective tasks and rewards their performance.

Reducing this pattern of forces to its simplest equation, i.e., to a single set of relationships, we may visualize two men, X and Y. According to the existing organization of a particular segment of society, X is superior to Y, a superior status defined by greater authority, independence, privilege, prestige, and power. Both X and Y have a common responsibility under a common law, but their responsibility, like their rights, is defined in accordance with their differing status. In certain areas it is the duty and right of X to command Y, and Y to obey X. In this area, the one obeyed may be termed the human lord, the other the servant. In this situation, two courses are open to each, when only the shape of the external act is considered: X may utilize his right to command, or he may waive that right; Y may fulfill his obligation to obey, or he may refuse to do so. The continuance of the established relationship will depend upon the decision of both. The decision to rule must be accompanied by the decision to obey; a decision by X to abdicate or by Y to rebel disrupts that relationship. Either abdication or rebellion threatens to some degree the order under which both live. Freedom, in this case, requires successful abdication or rebellion, initiated by either party; but either freedom becomes an evil from the standpoint of the order as a whole. To be sure, any stable organization of human behavior must provide a limited flexibility in these relationships. It permits a certain amount of rebellion and abdication, and men will judge the system by the degree of " freedom " that is officially encouraged. Where X and Y are alike content with this degree, they will not chafe against the differences in status. But in the best of systems there will be frustrations, and these frustrations will stimulate an awareness of bondage and a desire for greater liberties than are allowed. The goal of freedom will be determined mainly by the area where the order of authority is felt to be an order of unjustified tyranny. Here the one who desires greater freedom locates the wall that must be broken down.

In this situation, however, the possibilities of action exceed the original *four,* because the dreams and motives of both X and Y must be considered. X may rule or abdicate, but he will do either from diametrically opposed motives: from self-regarding efforts to improve his status, or from self-forgetting efforts to serve Y better. Likewise Y may accept or reject the commands of X, either through self-regarding fears and ambitions, or through self-forgetting love for X. It is in this area of motive that the New Testament locates the primary issues, for it is in this area that the relationship of X and Y becomes fully personal, and this is the sphere where either God or Satan will claim the victories. The power quotient of Satan is the human desire (whether of X or of Y) to climb higher, to become superior, to claim for oneself a greater freedom than others, to fulfill one's ambition to become wiser or wealthier or more prominent — in short, to become more of a lord. The power quotient of Jesus is the eagerness to take a lower seat, to become a servant, to become least and last of all, to become as a little child. When either X or Y acts according to the former principle, he acts as a suppliant of Satan, though of course that fact is hidden from him, for " he is blind." When either acts according to the latter principle, he is a son of God, though he does not stop to think of himself as such. Freedom in this case may not mean any external change in status, but it will mean freedom from Satan and from the world which he rules. In this case the first wall to crumble is not the external distinctions between lord and servant, but the inner distinctions, the engrained hostilities. And with the crumbling of this rampart a second wall crumbles, the wall that protects Satan's whole realm. For the principle on which the wall between X and Y is built is a principle that underlies all human institutions as such, so far as they have become the occasion of blindness. With the collapse of the walls of this prison, the prisoner is truly freed from all dominion and power, except that of his emancipator.

The existence of this wall thus depends upon the inner choice of the prisoner himself. Most prisoners are not aware of this invisible wall and are consequently blind to their actual slavery; and so long as this blindness continues, the wall remains unbreached. This is the blindness that Christ heals, by first making men aware of it. Similarly, the existence of Satan depends, not upon the structure of external societal authorities, but upon the alignment of men's loyalties. This it is that makes the question of Satan's existence such an ambiguous one. The blind man thinks that the existence of this inner wall, this invisible prison, is an illusion, but by his act of subservience to the principle of superiority he makes that illusion real. The man whose eyes have been healed must wrestle against that principle and its power, but by his act of faith he makes that reality ineffective. For him in this act there is only one Lord, and therefore he is free.

For the same reason, his task is a difficult one, both to describe and to perform. For he is commissioned to proclaim freedom to others who by their deeds establish the reality of that which they think to be unreal (" many ' gods ' and many ' lords ' "). He must convince them that they blind themselves to their real prison by denying that it exists (" We . . . have never been in bondage to anyone "). And at the same time he must heal that blindness so that for them the real prison, the present evil age, no longer exists in power, since they are now free sons of God, living by the powers of the coming age.

The complexities of this procedure may be clarified by examining specific examples of imprisonment and emancipation. We have selected three, to each of which a subsequent section is devoted.

B. Jew and Gentile

Among those who first heard the gospel, the highest walls among human institutions were to be found at the boundary between Israel and the Gentiles. This wall had been erected presumably upon the covenants between God and this peculiar people, set apart as his inheritance. The shape of the wall was provided by the Torah, circumcision, and the Temple, institutions divinely ordered, which had become disordered by being made the basis of invidious distinctions. Through centuries of tragedy, the conflicts between Jew and Gentile had served to make permanent this division in the collective unconsciousness of mankind. Jews and Gentiles alike were born and reared in a climate that engraved this barrier on the heart, feelings, and thought of each individual. Their prejudices were prefabricated in this climate, so that few were the activities in which this barrier was not felt as an inescapable reality. Neither those who accepted these restrictions nor those who rejected them, neither those conscious of them nor those unconscious of them, were wholly free from the social effects of this particular history. Jews might glory in their prerogatives or they might resent them, but they could not destroy the invisible line that separated the religiously superior from the religiously inferior. They were made conscious of the wall by all their personal, professional, business, and political contacts.

Now the followers of Jesus stoutly affirmed that the law is good. God had called Israel as a servant, to share in the fulfillment of his purpose for all history. He had intended the institutions of Israel as instruments of his will. He had spoken through the prophets, had guided the fathers, had revealed his deeds to Moses, had called the people out of Egypt, had blessed them with innumerable gifts, had yearned over them with an inexhaustible love.

Yet, in spite of his continuing mercies, the law had become the instrument of evil, because of the way in which men had used it. Intended to carry out the saving purposes of God, it had come to be the tool by which Satan's futile purposes were being served. At present "the god of this world" was using the law and the covenants to deflect men's allegiance from God, without their being conscious of this trick. In fact, the more ardently they thought they were serving God, the more fully they served his adversary. Wherever Israel served Satan through the Torah, it had become Israel-according-to-the-flesh. Only when Satan was divested of his hidden authority could Israel-according-to-the-Spirit be reconstituted.

The marks of Satan's sovereignty may be described in various ways. A law which God had created in his freedom had been exalted above God, thus limiting his freedom. A covenant which had been meant to be a door leading men to God had become a barrier excluding them from God's presence. Meant to keep men humble, the law had become the basis of pride. Meant as a gift to show their dependence on God's grace, it had been used to establish priorities of merit. Called out of nothing to be a light to the Gentiles, this people had allowed its claims of racial superiority and exclusiveness to shut out the Gentiles. Called to be holy, this nation had so hedged about its holiness with ceremonial safeguards as to confuse holiness with external purification. The house intended for all nations had become the symbol of national isolation. The demand of God for other-regarding love had been twisted into deceptive rationalizations of self-regarding love. A people sustained by the promise of a Messiah had so perverted that promise by self-centered worldly conceptions of power and glory that they had been unable to recognize the true Messiah in the form of a servant.

Jesus came as an Israelite, loyal to the law. He had been true to Israel's original mission. He had interpreted the covenants according to God's initial intention, as a means to humble love rather than to proud self-assertiveness. He had repudiated Satan's deceptive claims, which took the form of defensive appeals to the Scriptures. He had broken through the circles of exclusiveness which sanctified themselves by implicit assumptions of superior righteousness. He had obeyed the law, subject to it as a divinely created instrument, but this obedience had never been an expression of ambition, the desire to be known as a righteous man and not as a sinner.

But his own people had killed him, thinking that they were serving God and protecting the Torah. As Christians later came to see it, the watchword of the scribes was, "We have a law, and by that law he ought to die." When he affirmed that his understanding of God's will in the law was true, they classified him among the worst of sinners, those who tried to destroy the law. Yet he knew that this rejection was a sign, not of their perversity as individuals, but of their blinded loyalty to Satan. He was carrying on God's battle against this blindness, which made them serve powers of evil without knowing what they were about, and not against them as persons. Satan had successfully trapped them into subservience to sin by appealing to their fears of sin.

A vivid testimony to this situation is given by the apostle Paul.[24] Blameless according to the standards of the law, Paul had persecuted the followers of Christ. To him, circumcision, racial purity, legal zealousness had seemed a "gain," inestimable in worth. But when his "reason for confidence in the flesh" was destroyed, when he had learned to "count everything as loss," when he had learned from Christ that true circumcision consists in humble love rather than in superior righteousness (Phil. 3:1–11), he learned that the law, which was good, had been used to make him a "wretched man," so that when he had thought he was doing good, he had actually been fighting against God.

When the implications of this struck home, he realized that Christ had permanently demolished those walls so that they could never again be used to separate inferior from superior. Israel-according-to-the-Spirit could use the law to indicate men's oneness in sin and their duty to love all others without fear of compromising their own purity. Humble love for all is in fact the only true holiness; therefore in the new Israel "there cannot be Greek and Jew, circumcised and uncircumcised, barbarian, Scythian, slave, free man, . . . male and female; for you are all one in Christ Jesus" (Col. 3:11; Gal. 3:28). Christ thus eliminates distinctions that rest on the basis of sex, race, nation, economic status, and religious background. He also deprives any generation of the right to consider itself superior to other generations, for his Kingdom embraces men of faith from all generations (Luke 13:28–30; Heb., ch. 11;

Rom. 3:21–31). In a kingdom so constructed that no man shall boast it is impossible for men to use any human institutions as the basis of superiority. (When the congregation does so, it excludes itself from Christ's domain.) Satan is thus robbed of his control over those institutions. In Christ, God has created "one new man in place of the two, so making peace" (Eph. 2:15), because no two institutions, when deprived of the pride of superiority and subjected to the law of love, can remain hostile to each other or alienated from God. And since Jesus Christ has demonstrated his power to reconcile the two *most stubbornly hostile* segments of humanity, he represents God's design "to unite all things in him, things in heaven and things on earth" (ch. 1:10).

Now there are many people, Jews and non-Jews alike, who protest against the extremity of the apostle's condemnation of Israel. At first sight there are good grounds for their protest. In plain justice one cannot include all Jews under the same condemnation. There were in their number humble servants of God who gave their lives in obedience to the law, without thought of fear or favor, in service of their fellow men. Moreover, the level of life in Israel was actually in many ways higher than the level among the Gentiles. To treat them so harshly is but evidence of the erection of a new wall which makes the Gentile now superior to the Jew, a new prison for self-righteous Christians. If the issue is stated merely in terms of the reconciliation of Jew and Gentile, to damn the Jews in such rigorous terms would forever prevent such reconciliation. When the objective is merely to free an individual Jew and an individual Gentile from their mutual animosities by attacking their mutual prides, it will not be attained by such a denial of the human achievements of either. The apostle, a Jew himself, would be the last to fan the fires of anti-Semitism, either in his own day or in ours.

But this is not the issue. God's design is to level an invisible wall, the basis for all walls among men. His objective is not only to emancipate both Jew and Gentile from the hostility of their particular relationships but also to free them permanently from all bondage to idols. This is why the apostle never tires of reiterating that all are included under the same condemnation and that all are included in the same promise. This is why, when either Jew or Greek is reconciled to God, there can be for them no longer any boasting, any self-regarding distinctions. Their relationship has been redeemed at its heart and not merely on its surface. The principle on which their captivity is based has been taken captive. They are free, indeed, not because they cease or continue to be Jew or Gentile, but because they cease to measure superiority before God by any such criterion.

In most, if not in all, cases, the free man chooses to continue his work in the state wherein he was called. He cannot carry freedom to others by becoming stateless and lawless. If he is called while a Jew, he does not cease to be a Jew, but he is no longer held to the law by the desire for superiority. He no longer accords to the law in itself the power to save or to condemn, to bring him to God or to separate him from God. To a Jew he becomes as a Jew in order to make clear God's true purpose in Jewish institutions. To the Gentile he becomes as a Gentile in order to make clear God's intention in Gentile institutions. In both cases he tries to emancipate other Jews and Greeks and to reconcile them to each other. His sole fear is that by observing rules and regulations he may be drawn again into a false reliance on " the flesh " and may become again a person " better than thou." By the libertarians he is charged with prudish inhibitions; by the legalists he is charged with libertarian selfishness; but he recognizes that the accusations from both sides are motivated by pride and defensiveness, whereas his only standard is the freedom-in-subjection of Christ's concern for others (I Cor., ch. 9).

C. Household Relationships

The same principles of reconciliation are applied to all social institutions within which men's existence is ordered. The disciple remains in the state wherein he was called, this subjection becoming the instrument by which he loves God and his neighbor. The subjection is not merely a bit of practical advice, but a divine mandate; more than a mandate, it is the means by which God seeks to redeem the superior-inferior relationship from self-regarding infection in either party. It is an incident in the battle by which Christ subdues whatever ruler " in heavenly places " has been using that relationship to create friction among men.

The common conscience of the apostolic community is this: We must obey our earthly masters, whether it be in the relationship of child to parent, wife to husband, slave to owner, commoner to king, Jew to the law, or Gentile to his laws (I Peter 2:13 to 3:7; Eph. 5:21 to 6:9; Rom., ch. 13; Mark 12:13–17; I Cor. 7:17–24).

This command of obedience is not hedged about by pragmatic conditions and exceptions. [25] Obligations to an earthly master are not made contingent upon whether he is a Christian or a non-Christian, a patron or a persecutor, a friend or an enemy. Nor does it depend upon whether the master's policies appear to his slave as just or unjust, advantageous or dangerous. Rather, the transformation takes place in the invisible lord that is served through this visible hierarchy of status. Both the one who commands and the one who obeys must *serve* the Lord and him alone. The eye must be single, everything being done through love. In no case can the free man seek first of all to please men, obeying them through fear of them. The free man does not concede his loyalty because of anxiety for his own future or to win the peace that the world can give and take away.

If the inferior rebels for the sake of enhancing his own status, if he chooses to cast off his yoke by violence, he is refusing to follow the example of Him who for our sakes took upon himself the body of our humiliation, subjecting himself in humble love to the law, to the body of flesh, to sin and to death (II Cor. 5:21; Heb. 2:14–18). On the other hand, when Satan uses that earthly power to command an allegiance that belongs to God alone, the inferior cannot comply and at the same time be a servant of Him who accepted the cross and despised the shame. The reconciling ministry of Jesus included simultaneously obedience to earthly authorities and refusal to serve the heavenly principality whose power operated through the systems of authority prevalent in his day.

How, then, can a man know which lord he is serving? One slave may obey his earthly master through fear of death; another may obey him through love of Christ. How can the truth be known? The servant of Christ accords to his Master alone the power and wisdom to determine the faithfulness of his servants. The free man cannot rely on earthly authorities to judge what constitutes true obedience. In crucifying Jesus, the authorities judged his obedience to be disobedience. Nor can he rely upon his own criteria to determine when a fellow disciple is obedient and which master he is serving. He does not trust even his own judgment of his own freedom, for his service of the Lord may be lip service only. Only one is the judge, and he knows the recesses of the heart that are closed even to oneself. It is he who calls us in each successive situation to humble ourselves, to subject ourselves, to accept the burden of the world's suffering.

This is clearly the pattern of thought underlying the New Testament injunctions concerning the wife's duties to her husband. For that very reason these injunctions have caused difficulties wherever society has adopted other criteria of status and responsibility. In a culture where feminine duties are defined in different ways, Paul's counsel is naturally resented by many of both sexes. That counsel is now taken to be an element of disorder rather than of order, because it runs counter to conventions and laws. If the apostle meant to chain women's status to that of a perpetual menial, then freedom requires the repudiation of his commands, or so it seems to many of us. Here again, however, we must distinguish the two types of prison, and remember that the gospel is directed against that prison which is hidden in all systems of domestic economy. Accepting the actual system of his day, Paul's attention was directed not alone at the relative status of a single man and wife, let us say of Aquila and Priscilla; he was dealing with the attitudes of both toward that principle of self-advancement which is the source of slavery in any society. He was enjoining the wife to obey her husband *in the Lord,* with the accent falling on that last qualification. To seek to become superior to her husband, or to become less submerged by insisting on her rights, is not true obedience *in* the Lord or *to* the Lord. Her status in society does not determine her freedom; only the Lord does that in accordance with the faithfulness of her motives.

We seldom protest against the rigorous demands that Paul directs at the superior in this relationship, that is, the husband, yet they were every whit as important to the husband's true freedom as the demands made of the wife; and the obedience of the husband *in the Lord* is just as difficult as that of his wife. In fact, it often appears more difficult for the superior, in the midst of his onerous responsibilities, to win true freedom. Authority is not an easy thing to wield *in the Lord,* whether it be the authority of the father, the husband, or the master (Eph. 5:25; 6:4, 9). These superiors are counseled not to abdicate their position, as if they could thereby ease their burdens and secure greater liberty of action. No, they are urged to use these positions as means of redeeming a relationship that is otherwise corrupted by self-directed power. They must, in subjection to Christ, treat their inferiors with love, treating them as if they were dealing with the Lord, overcoming every temptation to pride and self-aggrandizement by remembering

Christ's descent. They must avoid using their authority in such a way as to place a stumbling block in the path of their dependents. Fathers must not, by unjust actions, provoke their children to angry resentment. Masters must not threaten their servants, causing them to stumble through sinful fear and " eyeservice." No less than his servant should his master expect his reward from the other, but only from Christ. No less than his servant the master must follow the example of Jesus, using every situation as an opportunity to love those dependent upon him, and thus overcoming every thought of using his position as a base from which to claim special privilege (chs. 5:21 to 6:9). For master as for servant this course of conduct requires God's armor for success. The ultimate enemy of each is neither the other man nor the existence of differing social status, nor the particular distribution of power in the community as a whole, but the invisible power that has estranged men from one another and from God by its appeal to pride and resentment, to selfishness and fear.

We may glimpse an example of this ministry of reconciliation in the dramatic story of the slave Onesimus — a story, however, that must be reconstructed by reading between the lines of Paul's letter to Philemon. We may assume that Onesimus had been a slave all his life. We can only conjecture what the conditions of his servitude had been, but one thing is sure, namely, that he had come to desire liberty so intensely that he was willing to risk death by planning and executing an escape. One hardly risks death in such a situation unless a long period of frustration and resentment has built up an explosive readiness to try anything. Either he considered death as preferable to a continuance of his bondage or he dreamed of the benefits of freedom as worth the chance of death. In any case, Onesimus took the risk, and, furthermore, he succeeded. He fled to a large city (perhaps Rome) and evaded detection in that polyglot metropolis. Freed at last from his galling inferiority, he was his own master. His dreams had come true, and all through his own adroitness and courage.

But something happened — we do not know what it was — and he found himself in prison. The charges were probably not serious, because he was soon released to go his own way again. The freedom that he had temporarily lost was regained. But while he was in prison something else happened. He met the apostle Paul, " a prisoner for Christ Jesus." From Paul he heard the story of Jesus as a gospel that had taken captivity captive. He was persuaded to become obedient to the humble Nazarene, born again through the "fatherhood" of Paul (Philemon 10). We cannot trace in detail how this conversion took place, nor his thoughts during the process. But the basic facts seem to be clear, whatever vocabulary or metaphors one may use. As a slave he had gained his liberty from Philemon. In his freedom he had discovered a more deeply engrained slavery — to self and to the basic principle of self-concern by which the world defends itself. From this slavery to one invisible master, of whose existence he had once been unaware, he was freed by another master, Jesus, of whose presence he had also been unaware.

This new master, in freeing him, made him rethink his earlier attitudes toward social status and toward men, and in particular toward one man whom he had defrauded. What now is his duty to Philemon in the light of his duty to Jesus? In this dilemma he no doubt counseled with Paul, but without question Paul left him free to make his own decision. And that he did. He would return to Philemon, ask his forgiveness, and accept again the yoke of human servitude, not in order to please men, but out of loyalty to his new Lord. He had overcome his fear of Philemon or of what Philemon might do to him. In returning he would again risk his life, for the former master was legally entitled to kill a runaway slave. Yet the compulsion of an invisible lord was stronger than the fear of the visible one. His act of returning was his witness to *all three lords* concerning his new freedom, and an act as well that was aimed not at justifying the institution of slavery but at reconciling this area of human relationships to the humble love of God.

When Onesimus returned, he took with him a note from Paul to the Christian master. And in his letter Paul reminds Philemon of his obligation to Christ. He must answer to Christ for his treatment of the returning fugitive. His punishment, if it be such, must be done before God; it must be done through Christian motives. What now was Philemon's response? We do not know. But we know what Paul considered essential in his decision. His action toward Onesimus must be taken on his own initiative (v. 14). He should look for the deeper significance in Onesimus' treachery, some purpose that God had in mind for both master and slave (v. 15). In his heart he should receive Onesimus back, not primarily as a slave but as a " beloved brother." He should receive him in the same way that he would receive Paul (v. 17). And he should look upon this new circumstance as an unexpected opportunity to serve the Lord (v. 20). Only the dramatist can portray the decision of Philemon and the new relationships that pertained between him and his " chattel." If reconciliation resulted, it would be nothing less than a work of Christ, realized through the obedience of Onesimus, Paul, and Philemon, a triumph testifying to a common freedom which all had received from the Lord.

D. Ruler and Citizen

God's design for creating peace also operated within the realm of political organization. For a typical statement of the New Testament outlook, attention comes sooner or later to the most controversial passage of all, Rom. 13:1–7. Considering the tortuous history of the efforts to understand this passage, no expositor can afford to be too certain of his conclusions, whatever they may be. Yet no expositor can evade dealing with the subject. The more difficult segments of Scripture may be the more rewarding, if they are used as clues to a solution not yet rightly assessed rather than as proofs of a predetermined position.

We may begin by granting the authenticity of this passage as representing Paul's attitudes, and by assuming that these attitudes are in the main supported by the New Testament as a whole.[26] It is not difficult to read what action Paul commanded: " Let every person be subject to the governing authorities." But it is very difficult to reconstruct the motives and logic that lie back of that command. This difficulty lies in part in the interpreter's haste to draw a direct line from this point on the periphery of Paul's thought to a point on the periphery of our own action. We should first reconstruct the line that runs from the center of Paul's faith to this point on the circumference of it, and only then ask how that same line may be drawn in our situation. The subsequent exposition will seek to take the first of these necessary steps. *Why* did Paul arrive at this conclusion concerning subjection to governing authorities? And *how* did he relate this conclusion to the process by which God reconciles the world to himself?

Let us begin by reviewing Paul's previous experience with " governing authorities." As a Jew, Paul had been taught due respect for political rulers on the basis of the axiom that " there is no authority except from God, and those that exist have been instituted by God " (Rom.

13:1). This axiom, of course, has a double function. It enjoins upon the governed a respect for their superiors and upon the governors their obligation to God. In this case Paul was in a position to speak *only* to the governed, but in counseling obedience by the governed Paul does not consider governors to be self-created absolutes. As a Jew, Paul knew that absolute power and authority belong to God alone. God can both establish rulers on the throne and dethrone them. He can use evil rulers as well as good to fulfill his purposes.

As a follower of Jesus, Paul knew at first hand the story of conflict that had greeted the gospel. The Messiah had been killed at the order of the procurator, Pontius Pilate. Pilate and his successors had imprisoned and executed other apostles of Jesus. When Paul visited Corinth, he met Priscilla and Aquila, who had been expelled from Rome, perhaps because of their allegiance to Christ. Or, to come closer home, Paul himself had received many unjust scourgings from Roman soldiers. Before writing the Epistle to the Romans he had endured many beatings and imprisonments, living in constant "danger from Gentiles" (II Cor. 6:5; 11:23–26). And in this epistle he addresses, among others, at least two who had served a jail sentence with him (Rom. 16:7) and others who had "risked their necks" for him (v. 3).

Nor should we forget, as Paul would not forget, the precarious status of the people in Rome to whom he was writing. They did not constitute a state Church. They were not legally recognized, although they generally shared at first — we do not know for how long — in the recognition accorded to Israel, and the inbred hostility of Gentiles as well. Moreover, many Jewish leaders were eager to disown any responsibility for this new sect. Early records are very inadequate, but they seem to show that the followers of Jesus in Paul's day were either ignored or frowned upon by the Roman officials. In the earliest references by secular writers they were commonly called vermin and filth; they worshiped a criminal, they were led by ex-convicts. If they had not yet been generally condemned by legal action, they were subject to the whims of lesser magistrates, in some cases cruel, in others lenient. At best their position was not a secure one, and their history offered little hope for an improvement.[27]

Nor should we overlook the initial occasion for Paul's command that every disciple should subject himself to the governing authorities. Such counsel is called for only because those to whom he wrote were inclined to resist tnese authorities. They were not eager to appease the existing order, but rather they were looking for a justification of rebellion. And what justification was nearest at hand? The reasons are implicit in Paul's cautious remarks. They were advising resistance " for the sake of conscience " (ch. 13:5): " We have no ruler but God. In obedience to him, we must repudiate our earthly rulers. We have no king but Jesus. Loyalty to him cancels our obligation to other kings " (vs. 1, 2). " God's Kingdom has come, freeing us from all other kingdoms and all other laws, even from the necessity of paying taxes and of showing respect to our superiors " (vs. 6, 7). " The authority of these fraudulent kings cannot be from God because they are a terror to good conduct. They are enemies of Christ and of God. They use their power to destroy us. They prevent us from carrying out our mission. With them in authority our cause is hopeless. We must either resist them or surrender our faith in God's kingdom " (vs. 3, 4). Such seems to have been the reasoning of Christians in Rome to whom Paul is addressing his appeal.

Having noted the predicament of Roman Christians, we should notice too the literary context of Paul's command. In the first eleven chapters of his letter, Paul has delineated the essence of the gospel, its power for salvation, its revelation of the wrath and mercy of God. These chapters as a whole constitute the premise to which the *therefore* of ch. 12:1 is the conclusion: " I appeal to you *therefore*, brethren, by the mercies of God, to present your bodies as a living sacrifice." The central thrust of this *therefore* is to create a mind so transformed that the whole existence of each brother represents his body as " a living sacrifice." The subjection to governing authorities, on the part of a person who would otherwise resist them, is one of the acts of a renewed mind, a fruit of the total revolution that has taken place. The attitude toward pagan superiors is fully in line with the genuine, humble love in which men outdo one another in showing honor (ch. 12:10), in line with the mandate to " bless those who persecute you " and to " repay no one evil for evil " (ch. 12:14, 17). The prohibition of resistance to rulers is directly implied by the more general prohibitions: " Never be conceited " and, " Never avenge yourselves." More significantly it is an imitation of the divine method of overcoming evil with good (ch. 12:16–21). As Paul wrote the letter, there is no break in logic between chs. 12 and 13 (although there may be a change in literary forms). Nor is there a break between the political duties in ch. 13:1–7 and the law of love, so explicitly made supreme in the following verses: "He who loves his neighbor has fulfilled the law." One should observe, too, the vivid contrast between night and day (ch. 13:11-14), in which violent resistance is associated with covetousness, quarreling, and jealousy, as works of darkness.

In this context it should be clear that the apostle is not intending to provide a formal religious justification for the policies of pagan rulers. He is not propounding a philosophy of political justice. He is not evaluating the good or evil character of a particular regime, nor counseling Christians with an eye to practical expediency. He is trying to expunge from the hearts of potential rebels the sins of jealousy, conceit, hatred, fear, anxiety, and contentiousness. He attacks these sins because they seem to be justified by the plight of the Christian community. But he knows how Satan uses such a predicament to draw the minds of brothers back into conformity to the ways of the world. The way of self-seeking rebellion is not God's way of humble reconciliation.

The rulers are not, as persons, approved; nor are their brutal policies sanctioned. If one must classify them, they belong among the enemies who are to be loved, the persecutors who are to be blessed by their victims, and the guilty who fall under God's wrath (chs. 12:19; 1:18-32). They endanger the disciples, not by abusing their authority (although they may of course so abuse it), but by tempting the brothers to adopt in rebellion the goals and means by which they lord it over men (Mark 10:35-45). The judgment that the disciples must fear is not the penalty inflicted by these rulers, but the judgment of God upon their own love. God will condemn all those who in pride think that they know better than God what circumstances are good or bad, what forces will defeat or advance his purposes.

At several points, however, the wording of Paul's command seems to run counter to this exposition. In Rom. 13:3 there is the bald statement that "rulers are not a terror to good conduct, but to bad." This may be construed to mean that in Paul's opinion all governors may be trusted to discern the difference between good and evil, and may be expected to administer an even-handed justice. How can this have been the intent of a writer who remembers Jesus' execution? How can one say this who has himself suffered imprisonments and floggings because of his allegiance to Christ? Paul may have meant to say this, but if he did it is most curious if not most contradictory. He might be expected to be more consistent than that.

There are two terms in this statement that call for closer scrutiny: *terror* and *good conduct*. We must construe these words, not by reference to another's vocabulary, but by reference to Paul's. What does he usually mean by terror? [28] It is fear on the part of an inferior in his reaction to a more powerful superior. And how does faith view such fear? Neither Jesus, nor Stephen, nor Peter, nor Paul was subject to terror because his superiors imprisoned and executed him. Their love had cast out such fear. Their love had replaced such fear of what men might do by fear of God, the God of love. This love is known by its fruit: the good work, which has here been translated "good conduct." To the Christian, the only work that is genuinely good is the act of humble love that frees the lover from fearing any enemy. Good conduct is such conduct as Jesus' forgiveness of his persecutors. The one who accomplishes this good work is frightened by nothing. But the one who accomplishes an evil work, i.e., any loveless and impenitent act, is shackled by fear, whether he supports or resists a political regime. "Would you have no fear . . . ? Then do what is good."

The rest of this sentence, however, poses an even more difficult problem of translation and interpretation, for Paul has written: "Do what is good, and you will receive his approval, for he is God's servant for your good." As commonly understood, the words "his approval" refer to the praise given by the governor to the governed for his act of obedience, while the words "your good" refer to the compensation given the law-abiding citizen in the form of external security, peace, and prosperity. But again we must consult the attitudes prevailing through the New Testament as a whole. If we do this, we will observe that this usual interpretation runs counter to less ambiguous evidence. Consider first the teaching of Jesus: "Woe to you, when all men speak well of you" (Luke 6:26). Consider, too, the example and experience of Jesus. He neither coveted the good opinion of the rulers nor received their praise. Or observe the accents of Paul when he warned the brothers not to be "men-pleasers," not to seek the peace and the pleasure that superiors can give. The practice and experience of the apostle was wholly in line with Jesus' injunctions. The only approval that he sought, through the welter of human conflicts into which he was plunged, was the "Well done" of Christ and of God. How, then, may these words be so construed as to fit historical fact and these other testimonies?

Let us deal first with the words " his approval." Let us remember that this word " approval " is usually reserved in the New Testament for God. All praise belongs to him and all genuine approval comes from him. In Christ he gives his full blessing only to the act of genuine self-forgetting love. The commoner's acceptance of the king's authority provides the opportunity for the commoner to serve the Lord and receive his blessing. But what, you say, shall we do with the pronoun " his "? In the passage we have cited, this seems to refer directly to the ruler; at least the rules of grammar point toward that conclusion. However, even should the pronoun " his " be applied to the earthly governor, one should observe that the time when he will bestow his praise on the subject remains undefined. We should recall that Paul is here dealing with the dynamics rather than with the date of reconciliation. He is confident that good *will* overcome evil, that in the end those who love their enemies *will* behold those enemies bend the knee to the power of Christ. But he was too experienced in suffering to suppose that persecutors are immediately converted by their victim's forgiveness. To be sure, in his own case his praise of Stephen had followed soon after he had joined in stoning that disciple. Perhaps, also, he had watched the miraculous transformation of a jailer or two (Acts, ch. 16). Well he knew that the power of meekness could humble its enemies, but he did not set time limits within which this humbling process must bear fruit. In our passage he may have been expressing the assurance that in the coming manifestation of Christ all persecutors would join in praising the good conduct of those whom they had persecuted. (Compare this passage with I Peter 1:6, 7; ch. 2:12; Matt. 5:11–16). In the end kings would bring their glory into the Holy City (Rev. 21:24).

There remains one further phrase that causes confusion. Paul speaks of the governor as " God's servant for your good." But what is this " good " that will accrue to the obedient? The answer may be found by a careful perusal of the eighth chapter of this same letter. Here Paul speaks as a personal participant in " the sufferings of this present time." We are weak. We groan in agony. We wait in patience for the hope of glory that is yet to be revealed. Like Christ who suffered the loss of all things, we " are being killed all the day long." By adversities we are tempted to fear death, angels, principalities and powers, which seek to 'cheat us out of our inheritance. But none of these powers, whether earthly or heavenly, can separate us from God's love, for we know "that in everything God works *for good* with those who love him." It is this same *good* that results from subjecting ourselves to those in positions of authority. Our rulers are servants of God, because whatever they do to us God will bring good out of that " evil." If we love as Christ loved us, though the governor kill us, he becomes an instrument of God, unwittingly contributing to praise, honor, and glory at the revelation of Christ. If self-concern leads us to resist the magistrate, then whether we escape the sword or not, we have made ourselves slaves to that fear which is itself a sign of God's wrath on us. In either case, the sword-bearer, wholly apart from his intentions in the matter, is a servant of God for our good. But this true good is realized only when we participate with God in his work of reconciling enemies by re-enacting Christ's loving humiliation.

Again we note how important is the distinction between earthly authorities and the invisible authorities in heavenly places, between the two levels on which reconciliation proceeds. The existence of a hierarchy of earthly rulers is not in itself evil. It becomes the occasion for sin when men, either as conservatives or rebels, express their enslavement to heavenly rulers through self-centered action. It becomes the occasion of emancipation when those same men obey their earthly rulers "in the Lord," i.e., in fearless love. God thus transforms the superior-inferior relationship from within, purifying the blood stream of social life. He dispossesses Satan from his control over man's heart, and thus demonstrates the ultimate nonexistence of the invisible rulers. He uses the free heart to show earthly authorities the only door to their own freedom, the use of their station to serve the Lord in humble love. Thus is the king reconciled to the commoner, and both find a union in one Body, a Body that is surrendered to the service of its true Head. When the governors praise their meek victims, then will Satan's power be at an end.

Until that unity and peace are wholly consummated, the disciple retains his particular assignment. Plodding toward the goal, he is not to be surprised when he is overtaken by the fiery trial that befell his Lord. He carries his cross daily, however the Zealots or the nationalists treat him. Their hostility is a step that prepares them for an unexpected disclosure of God's mysterious purposes for both the cross bearer and the cross giver. It would seem that the cross bearer has by far the heavier load, but it is not so, if we are to believe the New Testament confessions. The disciples do not so much chafe at the tragic weight of the cross as they sing for joy at its amazing lightness. Christ's yoke is easy because he himself carries it. It is light because it is itself the channel of redemptive power. The moment of suffering is the moment of joy, because the love that occasions the suffering is the only power that can restore the heart to its freedom and health, the only power that can defrock the rulers of darkness. Only a power " made perfect in weakness " can exorcise the power of Satan. Only the wisdom of God can renew men's minds and melt the frozen patterns of the world's thought. Only a righteousness made perfect in humble love can deliver man from the curse of personal and institutional self-righteousness.

This is the power and the wisdom that animate the Body of Christ, enabling it to grow by fulfilling its earthly vocation. This is the mystery that the Body of Christ declares to the hierarchy of spiritual authorities that sinful men propitiate (Eph. 3:10; I Peter 1:12; chs. 3:17 to 4:6). But the only form that such a manifesto can take is the continuation of his meekness and love, his obedience unto death in order to redeem those who are under sentence to death (Matt. 5:11-16; I Peter 4:12-19; Heb. 9:15-28; II Cor. 4:7-12). It is thus that Christ continues to level the walls of alienation among human groups, whether political, economic, cultural, or religious. It is thus that he is creating peace among things in heaven as well as on earth, restoring all creation to its intended unity and fullness under God. Apart from each successive manifestation of his glory, we are blinded again by the darkness of the old age. The activities of organized society provide promises and obligations through which the Prince of this world conforms our minds and wills to the law of sin and death. When Christ's glory is manifested to us afresh in a contemporary situation, these same activities are seen to be the necessary medium through which the Lord of the new age transforms our minds and wills, and through us our social relationships, into conformity to the eternal purpose of God. Now each work of love is an event of redemption, a first fruit of the eternal Kingdom, a reaping of the seed that God has sown.

PART
III

"THINE IS THE KINGDOM AND THE POWER"

13

THE MYSTERY OF THE KINGDOM

O UR study began with the vision of the scroll, tightly bound by seven seals, expressive of the way in which the mind is baffled by the riddles of historical destiny. In sharp contrast to that bewilderment, we set forth the audacious manifesto of the apostles. Two prisoners, John and Paul, had told all who would listen how God had disclosed the secrets of the ages through the wisdom and the work of a crucified Galilean; how he was proceeding upon his work of redeeming the world from death to life. These stentorian announcements, seen against the background of their authors' predicaments, posed the problem that we have explored through the subsequent chapters. We have sought to restate in their own terms, so far as possible, what they understood the eternal purpose of God to be; to grasp the inclusive scope of what they called " good news," and how they had come to accept this news as the only gospel by which men may be saved. We have seen how they related God's design to the varying dilemmas and situations encountered in daily experience as they tried to follow step by step the path of the Messiah. Now that we have finished the exploration of the major implications to them of the good news, there is need for a backward glance, first at the riddles of history with which any news must deal if it is to be considered truly good and genuinely new, then at the ways in which God's activity in Christ enabled men to come to terms with those riddles.

Whatever may be our estimate of the validity of their faith, we should at the very least admit this much: It represents a view of the meaning of history that is strikingly different from all others. Perhaps, too, even the non-Christian may concede that the apostolic attitudes toward history, however complicated or baffling, seem to be remarkably integrated and coherent. Once the basic axioms are accepted, once the event of Jesus' death and resurrection is actually taken as the central clue, there comes into operation a logic that links every detail to this core of meaning. The thinking stems from a common mind, not from an anarchy of voices. Perhaps the non-Christian may venture even farther, going so far as to grant that this mind, whatever the truth of its answers, was not unaware of the intricate problems that concern every interpreter of history. Let us look again at these problems, merely to note that none of them is wholly neglected in the New Testament perspective (cf. Chapter 1).

The first is the problem of beginning and end, of unity and direction in history. Obviously, the gospel contains a specific answer to such questions, though it may revise the form in which the questions are put. There is a beginning and an end, both comprehended within God's activity. He is Creator and Redeemer; he has revealed in Jesus Christ the character of his creative and redemptive acts. There is unity and direction in history, both stemming from the sovereignty of one eternal purpose. However difficult it may be to trace the working of that purpose, however anarchic the course of historical events may seem, the life story of every creature remains subject to God's dominion.

This question involves the second: whether any uniformities may be observed in the welter of change, any recurrent pattern in the flux of happenstance. Here too the gospel presents a positive answer. In all the affairs of men the apostles could see the rhythm of rebellion-and-return, which was counterbalanced by the rhythm of divine judgment-and-forgiveness. They could trace, in the old age, a dynamic movement forward from its beginning in Adam to its end in the cross. And as heirs of the new age they knew themselves to be participating in a process wherein the pattern of the Messiah's Way was being repeated in the experience of disciple and Church. To be sure, they do not locate these rhythms in the areas where men ordinarily look for them, i.e., in the evolution of biological species, in the rise and decay of nations, or in the changes in modes of economic organization. Primarily, they are the basic patterns in the relationship of men, individually and corporately, to God. Yet these patterns pervade every sort of social affiliation and confer upon those affiliations a significance which they would not otherwise possess.

What is the power that propels men and events, the momentum that produces historical change? To this question the New Testament gives clear-cut answers. In the central event of history, the hearts and wills of the actors are decisive: e.g., Jesus, Peter, the priests, Pilate. In every event in history, the genuine source of movement is personal rather than mechanical, intentional rather than adventitious. The false gods may lure men into worshiping fate or chance, into fearing the massed might of impersonal institutions, into calculating the prospects of the future by reference to quantitative estimates of power. But that which is truly new and free emerges only where the will of God acts and the wills of men respond. Only the perfect integration of these wills can produce unity in the self, fellowship with other selves, and the perfect communion of the Holy City. The only true changes in human fortunes, whether for better or worse, stem from the devices and desires of men's hearts, and the invisible lords who command these hearts will determine whether the movement be toward life or death.

How may men measure progress toward one end or the other? By what milestones may true distance be computed? The gospel has an answer. On the one hand, it maintains that before faith comes, all measurements are faulty, all milestones misleading, because neither the true end nor the means of progress toward that end are rightly known. On the other hand, after faith comes, the disciple may recognize in all the hidden works of God the maturation of the divine purpose. God's deeds mark the true milestones, and the faithful can discern those deeds by viewing them in the light of the greatest deed of all, the cross. Correspondingly, the disciple can assess in the successive decisions of men their progress or regress; their responses indicate their position on the Way. In the sequences of ordinary daily experience may be noted genuine advances toward the goal of perfect penitence, self-denial, truth, freedom, joy, and love.

The disciple receives help too in dealing with the problem of the relative importance of the various environments of life. He knows which environments are more transient and which the more enduring, on which man is dependent and of which he is independent. He has placed his faith in the Kingdom of God as the environment that continues throughout all the changes in history. It is the true context within which are to be placed all the events and scenes of life. He recognizes, too, that life in this Kingdom can be mediated to him in every local scene. It has the power to transfigure all the chains of cause-effect relationships. Its laws include all the lesser laws. He does not enter the Kingdom by fleeing from the transient, by escaping his earthly environment, by defying the lesser laws; rather, the eternal comes to him now in the midst of the transient.

The New Testament also gives succinct though controversial answers to the perennial problem concerning which men and movements are the chief bearers of meaning in the process called history. The divine purpose, of course, permeates the existence of every creature, the least sparrow being of importance to God. But God has chosen a people for a special role. To them he reveals the eternal purpose; to them he gives the mandate to proclaim this purpose to men and to their invisible lords. Ultimately all men are to be drawn within the community where God dwells. The first-born of this humanity is a man called Jesus of Nazareth. Those who are reborn according to his image become members of his Body. Each of his members becomes a bearer of historical destiny, whether he be an apostle, prophet, teacher, or obscure and anonymous believer. His Church also becomes a corporate bearer of historical destiny, with a mission for the whole world. In a still deeper sense, Jesus Christ is the sole bearer of destiny, for through him alone does God fill all things with his fullness.

Perhaps we need not review the other riddles that confront the interpreter of history. What has been said is enough to support the thesis mentioned above, namely, that the gospel does present some sort of answer to those riddles. It discovers the answers through using its distinctive key: the work of Jesus Christ in reconciling the world to God. To disciples, the story of Christ unveils the mysterious and majestic way in which God moves to establish his Kingdom over all. He has given the Kingdom to " the Son of his love " (A.S.V.). The whole of human life before faith comes is a preparation and a promise of this event. After faith comes, the whole of history is viewed as a movement from the sowing to the reaping of this seed. The humiliation and glorification of the Son (Jesus and his Body) mark the boundary between the night and the Day. To those who walk by his light, the Day has dawned, and all history becomes the stage where this transfiguration is being effected. From the beginning of history to its end, the design is furnished by God's Kingdom. In all its intricate affiliations, this reality is the ground for faith's confidence in the significance of everything that happens.

The term "Kingdom of God," however, strikes most moderns as too mysterious to be helpful. For some, it is more entangled with riddles than the more obvious historical processes it purports to illumine. The reign of God is a far more elusive reality than the kingdoms of earth. And the design of this Kingdom, as disclosed in Jesus, runs counter to the conceptions of the plot that most actors in the drama hold. To introduce God into the story as an aid to deciphering its meaning is for many interpreters of history either an evasion or a vain detour. Even those who affirm allegiance to God's Kingdom may not discover therein a sharp tool for the explication of contemporary predicaments. Its reality fades into fuzziness as compared with the harsh actualities of an age of atoms and airplanes. Men know what kingdoms are, but what and where is God's Kingdom? No subject of Biblical research has provoked more varying definitions than the meaning of this special Kingdom.[29]

We shall summarize the preceding discussion and at the same time attack this prevalent confusion by indicating seven necessary conditions for understanding what the New Testament means by the Kingdom of God.

In the first place, this reality is the Kingdom *of God*. It is the king who defines the kingdom. To be sure, the term "kingdom" represents an analogy between visible and invisible realities. Like human empires, God's Kingdom is a sphere for the operation of power, authority, and glory, a sphere where citizens obey and adore and fear their sovereign. Yet God's Kingdom is "other" than human empires. It cannot like them be touched or shaken or destroyed (Heb. 12:18–24). It cannot be located or dated by an external boundary: "Lo, here it is!" It respects none of the lines of time or space that men draw on their maps. It is the city of the invisible God, a city that can never grow old or corrupt. No census may be taken of its population, nor may its citizenry be purged by antisedition legislation. Knowledge of its walls and doors, its streets and its buildings, may be gained only by knowing the purpose and character of its ruler. And this knowledge only the king can convey. Men who seek to enter may enter by the door which this king has opened, a door through visible historical experiences into the realm beyond the yeil. Men are bound to misunderstand this reality so long as they construct diagrams of God's Kingdom by projecting into infinity the arc of earthly measurements.

In the second place, the Kingdom of God is to be apprehended through its continuing warfare with an enemy kingdom; both these realms are invisible, yet both now exert authority over men. Through his messenger God declares war on his enemy and establishes a beachhead in hostile territory. Every act of the Kingdom is in this sense an act of war. But who is this enemy? We must know the answer if we are not to misjudge the line of battle, as well as its odds. But can the frontier be located with accuracy since it shifts so frequently? Certainly it is hazardous to trust any hasty or fixed definition of the boundaries. The New Testament is not content with any single formula, and it is doubtful if any of the current modern formulas is wholly faithful to the apostolic mind. We are accustomed to formulas, for example, that locate the final struggle along the line between spirit and flesh, eternity and time, heaven and earth, God's empire and Caesar's, the supernatural and the natural, the realm beyond history and the realm within history. All these formulas do violence to the New Testament witness; all utilize too readily the philosophical antinomies between one factor that is known and one that is unknown. The New Testament seems much more content with the distinction between two ages, and between the two rulers of those ages, both of which are " unknown " and invisible. God has engaged in a struggle, not with flesh and blood, but with heavenly principalities, with the rulers of this darkness (Eph. 6:11 f.). The crucial frontier penetrates the heart of each man, the inner character of each empirical association, the spirit of every social activity, the Zeitgeist of every culture. God and Satan are battling for the souls of men, and the place of battle is creation-wide and history-long. Human resistance stems, not from flesh and blood as such, but from those blind men who think that they can see because they have succumbed to the enticements of Satan. God seeks to win the souls of these men so that as soldiers of the cross they may be liberated from the kingdom of evil and join in the fight against its prince. Is all this mystifying? Not to the early Christians, because Jesus had dispelled the fogs with the sharp light of actuality. By word and deed he had demonstrated that the power quotient of Satan lies in the practice of self-seeking pride and superiority, and that the power quotient of God lies in the practice of self-giving love and voluntary humiliation. To live in the flesh does not constitute rebellion, because life in the flesh may also be a life in love and a life in the Spirit. What constitutes rebellion is to live according to the flesh, to guide one's own destiny in supposed freedom according to one's desires and fears, power and wisdom. Yes, these appear to be one's own, but they actually indicate subservience to the father of lies, who makes evil appear to be good, and good to be evil. The mind of Satan has become the mind of the world, and this mind blinds men to the presence of God's Kingdom, so that they cannot comprehend its superlative goodness and power. When men get an accurate glimpse of the mysteries of God's purpose because God has touched their eyes, they are enabled to participate in " death of death, and hell's destruction." In the ensuing discipline of trials they discover the interplay between knowledge of God's Kingdom and knowledge of its true antithesis. They discover too why the design of God *is* a mystery and why it must *remain* such until everything secret is disclosed at the final manifestation of Christ.

In the third place, the Kingdom of God is recognized as a new age, a time of fulfillment that terminates the former age and imparts to its heirs a new sense of duration. The temporal sequences of life take on a new meaning when they are seen as the way through which God creates and redeems his creatures. To every creature he assigns a period of flourishing, during which the God-implanted seed grows toward a fruitful harvest. In revealing the nature of his purpose and the character of the harvest, he imparts to each disciple a sense of the importance of each moment in the maturation of his vocation. Apart from faith, man's sense of time proves to be the source of self-deception. He interprets the significance of his days by reference to self-centered memories and hopes, by reference to the ambitions that the world has engrained in his heart. He measures change by what happens to him, yet is aware that all his fortunes are subject to the ticking of the clock and the ceaseless marching of the months. His existence and its significance are checked by the calendar, past and future finding their tiny inch on the long time line of the historian. He subordinates the meaning of his life span to the life span of other creatures: an institution, a nation, a civilization. Or he supposes himself to be bound to the recurrence of fate's wheel, or tries to take frantic advantage of whatever accidental opportunities may be offered by Dame Chance. Or in bland indifference to the glacial movement of centuries he exalts his ephemeral footprints over the marks left by other less prominent individuals. Many are the devices by which Satan tempts a person to enthrone an impersonal "time" as an elemental power that chains the free movement of both God and men. When these devices are successful, Satan prevents men from realizing either their own freedom or God's true sovereignty over all the times. He prevents men from entering a Kingdom that marks the completion of the age of promise and the beginning of the age of redemption. But when, by faith in Jesus as Messiah, men join the exodus from the realm of darkness, they participate in a revolution that alters their evaluation of both time and space.[30] No longer do they view the work of Christ merely as proceeding within the horizons permitted by previous conceptions of time (although that is quite possible); now they view all the ages within the horizons of the work that Christ is carrying to completion. To understand this Messiah and his Kingdom, therefore, it is not enough for the historian to place the Kingdom and its events within the context of his own time line; he must place himself and his time line (including his own desires for professional competence and accuracy as well) within the context of God's all-inclusive design.

This suggests a fourth point, which is this: The Kingdom of God is a realm into which man enters by a new birth, by a reconstitution of his selfhood as a son of God. "Unless one is born of water and the Spirit, he cannot enter the kingdom of God" (John 3:5). The truths of the Kingdom are accessible only when Christ dwells in the heart through faith. It is of the very essence of the Kingdom that one cannot be told in advance exactly what it contains. Even the greatest apostle was given only a partial knowledge, and this fragmentary knowledge contradicted his previous expectations. The pattern of rebirth does not follow a course that can be explained in advance, a fact that nettled Nicodemus (ch. 3). Indeed, the disciple must leave behind him even the image of conversion, the understanding of what conversion entails, which he has absorbed from his previous life in the old age. He cannot know in advance precisely what sacrifices will be required and how those sacrifices will become the ingredients of good cheer and zestful mirth. He may feel that he already knows what it means to love, to suffer, to repent, to rejoice, but he learns that in Christ these experiences have a new dimension. "Blessed are the meek," but only the meek learn of what that blessedness consists. This is one reason why the image of death is inseparable from that of conversion, because none of us knows until he dies what death is and what lies within and beyond it. One's knowledge of dying and rising is itself transfigured by each event of dying daily. Knowledge of the Kingdom cannot therefore be handed like a parcel from one person to the next; it can only be transferred by the Spirit that is at work in both hearts.[31]

The Spirit alone brings the joy, peace, and righteousness that sustain the common life in the Body of Christ. Its presence, guiding the prayers and acts of the saints, relates each historical situation backward to the beginning of the new age and forward to its consummation. All the fruits of life in Christ are gifts of the Spirit. The Spirit too has its antagonists, but these antagonists are not the "natural limitations" of birth and death, space and time, man's existence in the body and in history. The Spirit has demonstrated its power to operate *in, with,* and *under* such factors.[32] The Spirit transforms these factors from limitations to opportunities. It is the mind of the old age that blames men's bleak fate upon such factors. To speak of the human situation as a limitation reveals the influence of spiritual powers in heavenly places that are the real opponents of the Holy Spirit. The Holy Spirit is the source of genuine prophecy; its enemy speaks through the voice of false prophets. Only a genuine faith, itself the work of God's Spirit, is enabled to detect the word that is truly from God. Any interpretation of the Kingdom that is not itself, in part at least, a work of this Spirit is a source of misunderstanding; and the more impressive the interpretation, the more dangerous may be the deception.

In the fifth place, God's Kingdom is inseparable from his glory and his power. Where one is, there are the others also. This is why God's adversary seeks to implant in human hearts a false image of glory and a false conception of power. In so far as human institutions contribute to these illusions they become ramparts of the kingdom of blindness. In so far as earthly authorities witness to the true glory and power, they become the signposts of God's Kingdom. This is precisely what they do for the followers of Jesus. The power of their leader is not simply an extension to infinite proportions of the power that enslaves and corrupts. His power has wholly different dimensions, since it is made perfect in weakness; it is the power of the meek to inherit the earth. Because God's glory is manifested in the person of Jesus, that glory is not a grandiose display of earthly grandeur, a fusion of all the stupendous colors of the honorific spectrum by which men adulate their superiors. God does not bask in pomp and ceremony, but quietly proceeds to fill all creation with his invisible glory. His is a glory that requires sharing; the more it is shared with the Church and men, the more it abounds. It has already been shared with the Son in his perfect obedience and humble love, and through him with the congregation of his brothers in accordance with their faith-full penitence. Men who weigh power and glory on the scales of their own ambitions will substitute their utopias for God's Kingdom, but they will be repeatedly frustrated and ultimately disgraced by those vain dreams. Those, on the other hand, who see that God's glory is actually manifested at its brightest in the face of the gentle Jesus will be grateful for the hope of the same glory that abides in their hearts. It was at the cross that God glorified Jesus, and it is at the same cross that he glorifies other sons, sharing with them freely the inexhaustible riches of his majesty and grace. In his effort to describe the Kingdom of God, the expositor will fail if he neglects to make the cross the key to the manifest power, wisdom, and glory of God. He will also fail if he classifies the hope for the Kingdom among the long succession of wistful dreams of a harassed humanity, a dream to be measured by the same criteria that secular historians apply to other dreams.

In the sixth place, the New Testament insists that God's Kingdom will be realized and known only through the fellowship of the kindred minds who inherit it, only through the communion of saints. One source of confusion in the attempt to define this realm lies in the difficulty of drawing the boundaries of this community. There can be no king without subjects, no kingdom without a group of citizens. The king is known by his will to govern, the subject by his will to be governed. So much is clear. Moreover, these subjects are men and women; consequently the saved community cannot be set over against all human associations as such. The organization of people into familial, economic, and political groupings cannot in itself be considered evil. Yet, on the other hand, the communion of saints is not to be charted on the maps which society provides. It is a new order that makes its way *in*, *with*, and *under* all the organized forms of society. It spans all generations, climates, and races. It does not depend upon the principles of exclusion or inclusion that prevail in the world. It does not define friends or enemies by the same tests of agreement or disagreement. It does not choose its leaders and apportion praise and blame according to the same scales of historical greatness or influence. Its sanctity and superiority are not defended by the same weapons. Its future is not assured by the same techniques. Only those who have become citizens in this commonwealth can understand its "constitution," and even their knowledge is imperfect because their citizenship is yet to be perfected. They are unable, therefore, to draw a sharp line between those who serve Christ and those who serve his adversary. Small wonder that those whose perspectives on community have been molded by the competing, demonic pretensions of historical institutions should misinterpret the character of the communion of saints. Since God's Kingdom constitutes the only true community, it is therefore unique, and only those who share its peculiar memories and hopes can understand the mysteries of this eternal fellowship.

Finally, God's new order has been disclosed as "the kingdom of the Son of his *love*" (A.S.V.). The various requirements for apprehending the nature of this order may be compressed into one simple word, "love." God is love, and all his far-flung creative and redemptive activity is comprehended within a single work of love. God loves each creature with his whole being; the total story of that creature is thus a single work of love. God loves the world so much that he gave his only Son, to sum up the story of mankind in this deed of love. His purpose is one, his work is one, his power is one, his victory is one. Thus the epitome of the story of all creation and of every creature is found in the work of love to which the apostles witnessed; "in this was the love of God made manifest." It is in Christ that every creature and all creation are redeemed by the exhaustlessly expended love of God.

The "person of Christ" is the true synonym of the word "love." What is the antonym? Not *human* love, because Jesus Christ is human. Nor is human *hate* a satisfactory antonym, for even Jesus speaks of hating one's father and mother. No, the ultimate antonym is the power principle by which Satan extends his kingdom, using laudable lesser loves to serve higher selfishness. Satan appeals to man's power to love and directs it to false objects or false ways of loving. And he confuses man's ideas of love by making true love appear hateful and true hate appear lovable. The kingdom of Satan is permeated with human loves, at least with what men call love. It takes a concrete revelation from God to make clear what love actually is, and what love of God and love of neighbor actually demand. It takes a life subjected to that demand to yield sure knowledge of the Kingdom.

God's love is characterized by the marks that Jesus taught and enacted (cf. pp. 56–59). It is embodied in repentance, in total renunciation, in a humbling that is complete. Love that is unrepentant is demonic. True love is embodied in expectancy, an eagerness to love God now as a preparation for God's Kingdom. A man's ultimate hopes are expressed by whom and what and how he now loves. "Love . . . believes all things." Love that does not rely on and anticipate a blessed future is demonic. True love is embodied in the act of giving and forgiving, without stint or stipulations, without anxiety or compulsion. The forgiven is not made dependent upon the giver, but upon a free uncoerced love. Love that does not channel perfect forgiveness is demonic. True love is embodied in integral obedience to one Lord. It springs from the response of gratitude for his love. It seeks no exemption from God's command and discovers that what God wills can be done. Love that is not thankful obedience to God is demonic. True love is embodied in utter confidence in the power of God. It endures all things and hopes all things. It never doubts God's desire to give good gifts to them that ask him. Love that is anxious and fretful, that insists upon a certain reward in advance, is demonic. True love is embodied in the constant recognition of the goodness of God which makes the lover entirely unconscious of his own merit in loving. He loves the neighbor, not himself through his neighbor. He even forgets that he is a lover so intent is he upon the needs of the beloved. He is so conscious of the source of love and the end of love that he confesses, "I can do nothing on my own authority." Love that is self-conscious, calculated, measured, made the occasion for public or private commendation, is demonic. True love is embodied in the repeated dying to the self, a death so genuine that the lover forgets the problem of his own destiny in his concern for others. It does not require a guaranteed reward, but finds ample reward in the love itself, a joy that marks the final emancipation from the bondage of an introverted existence. True love is the love of the martyr who discovers life in what other men fear as death. Love that denies the self only to a certain point, love that protects the innermost kernel of selfhood from ultimate surrender, love that covets the immortality of the self as a necessary prize, is demonic, for in seeking to save that inmost citadel of selfhood one forfeits the hope of the resurrection.

Such is the character of God's love shed abroad in men's hearts through his Son. His Kingdom is the realm over which this love exerts its sovereignty. The experience of his loving-kindness throws a needed light upon the six clues that have just been outlined as requisites for understanding the Kingdom of God. This is the first: the Kingdom *of God* is the Kingdom of the Son *of his love*. This Kingdom is therefore unlike all other kingdoms to the degree that this love is unlike all other loves. And this unlikeness is not to be minimized when one considers the cross as the measure both of his love and the world's unbelief in it. Yet this love, in its sovereign majesty and its all-encompassing humility, invades every other kingdom with its patient power to elicit love from the beloved. It motivates all God's acts, is communicated through all his gifts, guides the entire process of chastening, and insures the final triumph of his will. His love alone enables men " to comprehend with all the saints what is the breadth and length and height and depth."

In the second place, love indicates the contrast between God's Kingdom and the realm that futilely resists that Kingdom. The two ages produced two minds that are most clearly distinct at this frontier. The mind of Jesus was permeated and controlled by his love; the loves of the world are permeated and controlled by the mind of the world. He who shares the mind of Christ will share the conflict that his love precipitates, the subtle antagonisms and tensions that arise when true love clashes with its demonic substitutes, the suffering that is the cost of loving the world as Jesus loved it. A conflict not precipitated by this love cannot be a final conflict, but wherever there is a true work of love, there will meet both final struggle and final victory. It is while he is engaged in this struggle that the lover discovers the character of Satan's kingdom and knows by contrast the brightness of the new Day.

In this struggle, too, the lover is caught up into a new relationship to the sequence of days — past, present, and future. A new momentum is given to his deeds, which in turn imparts a new understanding of the significance of temporal duration. God's love enters the heart only through today's response; this response is contemporaneous only when it exerts a judgment upon the old self and a constraint on the new. When this happens, it affects the lover's memories and expectations, thus transforming his past and his future. The acceptance of a new constraint becomes a new yesterday; the pressure of the constraint creates a new tomorrow. Now, in looking back, he recalls what he has been doing with his "time" and is humbled; he recalls what God has been doing in spite of resistance, and is overjoyed. The grace of effective penitence, forgiveness, and gratitude frees him from the guilt of the past, for that guilt had been compounded of self-regarding memory and hope. Yet, in reflecting upon the past, love never despairs because of the length of time that has elapsed or because of previous failures to love. "Love . . . endures all things." In its estimate of today's possibilities, love creates its own interim, in which each moment has an urgent significance. It interprets each day as an opportunity for the refining of gold. It communicates its own patience to enable the lover to endure the continuing march of moments, by teaching him why the Kingdom is so near and why it still tarries. It is as near as the present task, and as distant as the perfect fulfillment of that task. Like its Kingdom, love does not wait for a perfect environment that will make its task easier, but accepts the present environment as the only point where the potential may become actual, and may thus create a new environment. Love hopes all things, refusing to depend upon the visibility or the nearness of the beloved, and by its hope creates a new situation.[33]

Love becomes the clue for understanding how the Holy Spirit gives a new birth to the sons of God, for love has power to beget love, to create the good that it seeks in the beloved. The experience of genuine love discloses the actual texture of personal relatedness, showing that life flows, not from the separate deeds of independent atoms, but from the attraction of spirit to spirit. Love makes it clear that the Kingdom is not an external something, independent of men, but a purposed unity of wills — God's will done on earth through the ligaments of love that knit together the body of the one new man. The power of the Holy Spirit to create such a fellowship is demonstrated by genuine love. The Spirit is able to re-enact the work of Christ in the life of the disciple, to weave together the gossamer threads of vital concern that establish the unity of the present with the past and future, and the unity of one man with all men.

Does anyone wish to understand the unique power that God wields over his Kingdom? Let him discern in Christ the power of love. Let him experience the ways in which this power can win its victories over every earthly and heavenly power. It can humble the wisest and proudest; it can supplant the strongest fears by the most buoyant freedom; it can create peace in the midst of war and joy in the midst of suffering; it can reconcile the most stubborn antagonists and redeem the most evil days. Does anyone wish to glimpse the highest form of glory? Let him glance at the majesty of God's love. The love that humbles a man is the love that exalts him. He who abides in Christ's meekness is blessed, for he abides as well in a celestial mansion where the whole panoply of divine splendor is shared with him.

This was the love that was the final truth of life to that captive of Christ who, caught up by the Spirit, saw "a Lamb standing, as though it had been slain" (Rev. 5:6), a Lamb to whom all power had been given over the destinies of men. In his confinement on Patmos, John was subjected to all the temptations that had beset the Lamb, to doubts concerning the reality of a new City, to despair concerning its power, to a loveless fear and resentment against his earthly adversaries. But in the midst of his personal Gethsemane he received his own assurance that into such a place and at such a time God comes down to make his dwelling place with men, to share with them his ineffable glory. In his vision he saw "a new heaven and a new earth," "the holy city . . . coming down out of heaven from God." He heard again the promise of the Messiah to give to every faithful witness the power to reign with him forever and to have a part in the healing of the nations. In this City the chief rule is this: "The last will be first." Here there can be no salvation for the individual apart from the salvation of all men, because each person is qualified as a citizen by his love for all. Here there can be no pride in superiority, because love makes the lover conscious of his own unworthiness. Here is a land where everyone in honor prefers another to himself, where everyone considers himself the least because an inexhaustible gift has been received by men who know they are quite unworthy of it. Love here creates an enduring community that is different from all other communities, yet this love wins its victories within the earthly associations of the lovers and the beloved. It crosses every temporal boundary and pierces every iron curtain: the borders between nation and nation, between slavery and freedom, between eternity and time, between heaven and earth, between life and death. By crossing these borders and making the two one, love batters down every compartment of terrestrial life so that the Kingdom may come. The act of perfect love is the perfect fulfillment of all history, uniting in final glory the work of the individual disciple, the work of the Church, the work of Jesus of Nazareth, and the work of God.

14

THE RELEVANCE OF THE MYSTERY

THE preceding chapters have been directed mainly to the task of historical exposition, although we have observed the demand made by this particular history upon the expositor, that is, that he must share the history in order rightly to interpret it. We have sought to sketch the scope of the gospel as its first heralds proclaimed it and as its first servants obeyed it. This gospel has called for a double focus: the concentration of interest on those events that disclose the structure and meaning of all events, and on those persons to whom was given the wisdom for grasping the eternal purpose embodied in those events. The key event is to be found, according to the gospel, in the victory of the Lamb that was slain; the key person is he to whom God gave all wisdom and glory, dominion and power. To those who share in the suffering and the triumph of the Lamb, he communicates his wisdom and glory. They give their witness to his power to transform their whole existence: their hearts and minds, their relationship to God and the devil, and all their associations with men. So far as possible we have sought to preserve the idiom and vocabulary and perspectives of these first witnesses.

A. The Question of Relevance

The reader who has been patient enough to read thus far may well have gained several impressions of our historical exposition. The first of these may be the feeling that the author has indulged in a professional parade of platitudes, relying upon ecclesiastical eulogies and romantic rhetoric. The phrases of the New Testament have become so mouth-worn that they sound both innocuous and insipid in many ears. When we reconstruct the historical circumstances of the first disciples, however, these anemic words are seen to be courageous thrusts at very real foes. When we live with them through scourgings and temptations, through ridicule and lonely imprisonments, their fearless shouts of emancipation lose their drabness and antiquarian mustiness. When we consider the whole range of problems with which their interpretation of history came to grips, their hymns of joy sound not so much like ecstatic gibberish as like coolheaded testimonies to the actual experience of having passed from death to life. On the lips of later preachers and teachers, these same testimonies may, in fact, easily become platitudinous rhetoric, but for that act of plagiarism the original martyrs were not responsible.

A second reaction, equally natural, may be the sense of bewilderment and bafflement in trying to comprehend the whole structure of early Christian thought. It is so alien to the contemporary mind, its pattern of accents is so different, its logic is so tightly woven by a strange loom of events, that one does not know where to begin in the effort to assimilate it. One can admit that the perspective is remarkably integrated, and that for the first disciples it served to orient them to the whole gamut of human experience. One can recognize that to do justice to this perspective one must accept or reject it as a whole. Yet a person cannot assimilate a totally strange perspective all at once. Would it not be better to discuss the meaning of ancient ideas one at a time, translating each category one at a time into modern speech? Then, having built up a dictionary of equivalent terms, we would be better prepared for dealing with the structure as a whole.

This, undoubtedly, is the way in which our minds work in their usual effort to assimilate alien ideas. In this case, however, something more radical is necessary. Here one must understand the interacting wholeness of the perspective before attempting the needed work of translation. In this case, one can hardly translate the text of the gospel merely with the help of a dictionary, finding equivalents for the separate words one at a time. For the gospel is not the sum of so many verses; it is a single message that one must first understand in its integral simplicity before proceeding to the work of comparing the vocabulary of its first witnesses with our own. Moreover, the gospel demands that the mind of its auditors be changed radically, that the presuppositions and criteria of that mind be transformed, that its present desires and scales of value be "put to death," before the new mind can exert its mysterious constraints. And a mind is not really transformed when it absorbs ideas one at a time into its previous structure. The gospel is tantalizing because it is so different, but unless it were so different, it would not be a gospel.

One popular way of dealing with the foreignness of the gospel is to attribute its strangeness to a faraway place and a long-ago time. It utilizes thought patterns from first century Palestine that have long been outmoded. Had we lived then, we could have grasped the meaning with ease, but today's world has rendered that message archaic. He who would recommend for twentieth century Occidentals the viewpoint of ancient Orientals is an archaist, a term that no one covets. There is enough truth in this reaction to make it both attractive and deceptive. When we begin to search for them, we can locate archaists on every hand, most of them unidentified. Some of them are found within the Christian community, trying to bind modern thought and experience into an idolatrous strait jacket of conformity to some earlier fashion, whether of the first century, of the sixteenth, or of the nineteenth. But is the believer's "imitation" of New Testament faith inevitably archaist? Several considerations should be weighed before a final judgment is rendered.

First of all, the charge of archaism is usually appended to a particular position because one does not for *other* reasons approve it. Seldom does one actually say "No" merely because of its archaism, for if he, a living person, accepts a given position, it is to him and to that extent not ancient but contemporary. One may note that even in the New Testament period men could explain their rejection of the Christian proclamation on the grounds of its archaism.

Secondly, we should recall that this gospel seemed as strange to many men of the first century as it does to us. But what made it most foreign was not the unfamiliar verbal clothing, but its radical challenge. The simple confession, "Jesus is Lord," is made up of words each of which is readily intelligible in any century. The phrase may easily be translated into any language, but what is difficult is to translate the *hearer* from one slavery to another. The apostles knew the difficulties of communicating their message to those who used an entirely different vocabulary and did what they could to bridge the chasm (as their successors must do in any generation), but the question at bottom was the allegiance to lords rather than to languages.[34]

A third consideration, and the decisive one, is this: From the perspective of Christian faith, the important distinction is not the conscious, arbitrary choice of which century to live in, the first or the twentieth. The important distinction is one that runs through all history: the contrast between the old age and the new. To the extent that the New Testament understanding of the world is true, to that extent men of the twentieth century have the same options as men of the first. They cannot, without some fantastic hocus-pocus, become men of the first century, as those men cannot be expected to become theologians according to twentieth century patterns. But, apart from faith, men today belong to the same age as did the unbelievers then; conversely, in faith men from all centuries may find an inheritance in the same new age, even though they use various equivalents for the word " age." The gospel is neither archaist (calling for a leap backward into the first century), nor futurist (calling for a leap forward into the twenty-fifth century), nor modern (trying at every moment to fit the specifications of what men assume is up-to-date). The gospel is a message of redemption, a proclamation of an age that draws near to every generation that hears the Word. It points to an ever-new work of God, which unbelievers will always think of as remote from their situation, because the distance is measured, not in calendar years, but in rebirth and its travail-filled joy. Because it is God's ever-renewed deed, the love of Christ is as near to us as it was to Peter and Paul. It remains, now as then, God's advancing of his future into our present, not the forceful projection of Paul's theology from a past grave into modern minds. In short, God's Kingdom transcends the times by being the one new Day.

A third reaction of many readers justifies more extended treatment. They may be willing to grant the intrinsic grandeur of the Christian epic, but they fail to see how it can be applied today. They can admit its power for men of a remote place and time, they can recognize that many fruitful influences have stemmed from it, they can join in praising the heroic stature of its earliest ambassadors, but how is it relevant to our own historical predicament? What light does it throw upon the urgent tasks of healing the schisms between races and classes, of fending off the demise of our society, of creating one world of peace and brotherhood? What we need is more direct and more compelling information concerning God's design for our ultramodern world. In a word, the cry is for relevance. What is irrelevant is by that token unimportant.

B. The Definition of Relevance

What, then, is relevance? According to one dictionary, it is " the quality of being pertinent to the case in hand." In evaluating the relevance of anything, we must first define what is *the case in hand*. Here it is well to distinguish four different spheres in which the *case* may be located.

First of all, one may focus attention on the area of man's heart, his deepest self, the source of his hopes and fears, a realm lying so deep that even his conscious thoughts may be unable to plumb its caverns. How healthy, how well integrated is this subconscious selfhood? Is he free from inner rigidities and submerged nausea? Is the bloodstream of his life infected? Does he defiantly repudiate this inner core of consciousness, or does he try to ignore its existence? Is man confident of inward peace and joy, sustained by the spontaneous uprush of integrity and health? If the central problem is located here, that which is most pertinent will be that which heals and cleanses this inner relationship of the self to itself, and this relationship will be purged only when it is rightly oriented to its ultimate context.

From this inmost self we may distinguish a second sphere, that of man's mind. By conscious thought, man distinguishes truth from falsehood, right from wrong. By conscious thought he accepts certain values and ends of action, and then weighs, records, and censors what happens by reference to these values and ends. Here he judges the men whom he meets, approving or disapproving them in terms of his prior scales of judgment. His mind becomes an arena where different systems of values and ends collide with one another. Here the tensions of human relationships are felt and refracted, being either intensified or resolved. In this area he must force the world of manifold impressions into some kind of conformity to the pattern of ideas and wishes, or he must allow this pattern to be constantly reshaped by the ceaseless impact of changing events. What, then, is the state of this mind? Is it unified and healthy, at peace with its self and its world? Can its stock of wants and emotions, its bent and its grain, be trusted? Does it achieve and maintain equilibrium through all the noise and turmoil of the city's streets? How well established are the supports on which it relies? Does a man locate in this area the problems that constitute for him the "case in hand," which in turn will affect his conception of what is relevant?

The third sphere where we may locate the crucial problems may be called that of the world, although obviously the problems of mental health are closely enmeshed in the problems of world health. It is the world that lends to man its vocabulary, its stock of values, its routines of custom and law, its sense of rightness and truth. The world organizes man's activities, regularizes his relationships, categorizes his significance in its pigeonholes of status and achievement. It lays down for him the paths of behavior, like the streets of a great city with busy traffic circles and shifting traffic lights. It is in the world that his personal wants and social needs are cultivated, and either denied or fulfilled. He is dependent upon the world and its health for that modicum of familial, economic, and political security which accrues to him. He is presented by the world with that particular hierarchy of communal authorities to which he should be subservient, and with such liberties as society deems appropriate to his rights. What is the state of this world? Is it at peace with itself? Are its institutions neatly co-ordinated to provide justice with security, freedom with order, opportunity with responsibility? Are the processes of social living sufficiently integrated to produce the accomplishments and emoluments that men desire and deserve? Does the mind of this society accurately mediate to its members a common mind that is not too greatly divorced from the truth about life?

Heart, mind, and world are all parts of a more inclusive area, that all-inclusive context whose horizons exceed the powers of imagination to draw. In its heredity, heart, mind, and world are each related to the hidden origins of life; the problems in each area are in part the fruits of this long parentage. The environment of each area reaches out far beyond the range of the largest telescope, far beyond a future that can be charted, and this widest environment has its bearing upon the narrowest datum of experience. Whether we call this largest frame of meaning "nature" or "history," it transcends the life span and valuational structure of any societal entity. What is the state of things in this large context? Is perhaps the denial of peace to man due to a history that is perverted from its beginnings? Are the dilemmas with which he struggles traceable to the invisible wheels of a diabolical machine, or the uncontrolled winds of a cosmic tempest?

When the " case in point " may be chosen from so wide a range, it is not surprising that one man should differ from another in his definition of relevance, nor that one man should change his mind in estimating the pertinence of a single idea or event. Actually, our estimates of relevance do change, and they change continually and sometimes radically. They are altered whenever there is any alteration in our conception of what the case in hand is. They are altered whenever there is any real change in us: our purposes and ends, our hopes and our values, our minds and our hearts. It is what we want that conditions our awareness of the obstacles in our path. And something will be relevant if it offers us help in removing this particular obstacle to this particular goal.

The character and the shape of both wants and obstacles will depend upon how we conceive of our particular role in history. For example, we may think of ourselves primarily as spectators watching the ceaseless caravan of pilgrims along the highway. If this is our role, that will be relevant which gives us a clearer view of the caravan, a higher tree up which to climb perhaps, or an improved lens for our camera which will combine both a sharp focus and a long range. In this situation it is the action of our curiosity that determines the degree of relevance.

On the other hand, we may visualize ourselves simply as marchers in the caravan itself. We have no desire to photograph it; in fact, we are hardly conscious that we are on a pilgrimage of any sort. Long-term goals are not in themselves of keen concern. We don't know where we are going, but we are on the way, our minds and hearts quite hypnotized by the ceaseless changes in the roadside and by the fluctuations in weather from day to day. In this case, we resemble blindfolded donkeys on the treadmill. The only things that have a mild significance will be the actual length of the day, the tolerability of the weather, and the alternation between the pleasure in a bag of oats and the pain in the crack of a whip.

Few of the readers of this book, however, are content to think of themselves in either of these two roles: as marchers in the caravan or merely as onlookers. They will be more likely to visualize themselves as guides to the other pilgrims, chosen according to their station or ability. They will be trying, for the sake of the marchers, to find a better route, or a more promising goal, or a more feasible method of transportation. The section of the journey that lies ahead is uncharted. In it lie many hazards to be avoided and short cuts to be chosen. The guides must have superior vision, knowledge, and ability to lead the way for a contingent, at least, of the vast company.

To qualify as guides, however, they must share the conditions of the journey with their fellows. With the others they must know the meaning of fatigue, frustration, despair. And the pains and pleasures of the journey, for them, are factors that affect their own spirits. Being responsible for leadership, they are aware of their own ignorance. Understanding the heartaches of the others, they are conscious of their own responsibility. They know what it is to mislead their followers because they themselves have been misled. And this knowledge is assimilated inwardly, becoming an added cause for apprehension. In short, men may view their roles in history as either that of *sufferers* or that of *leaders,* and if either of these functions is understood in its ultimate spiritual terms, then the two functions are fused together: The leader is specially qualified to suffer, and the sufferer is qualified to lead.

Let us assume, then, that the person who raises this question concerning the relevance of the gospel does so because he takes seriously his function of bearing his own burdens and at the same time bearing the burdens of others, by providing the light and power that will enable them to bear those burdens. Now let us recall the four spheres in which problems appear that will determine the relevance of the New Testament message: (1) the heart; (2) the mind; (3) the world; (4) existence as a whole. And let us concentrate upon problems that appear in the two intermediate areas, asking whether the apostolic proclamation is pertinent to their solution.

C. PEACE OF MIND

Our society currently places a high premium upon the attainment of peace of mind, an indirect confession that such peace has been lost and is difficult, under current conditions, to regain. Men are quite ready to itemize at length the excessive strains in modern living that produce abnormality. Our asylums are full of the mentally sick, and most of those who need a refuge have not yet found it. The world that induces chaotic neuroses in its members summons its specialists to minister to its casualties. It calls impatiently for physicians who can devise a defensive armament adequate to offset those weapons that have been turned against that most sensitive organ: man's mind.

These surgeons of the mind, themselves both sufferers and leaders, now face a case in hand, and ask whether the gospel of the Kingdom of God is pertinent to their task. The answer will depend largely upon how they analyze that task. They may analyze it in the terms of the perspectives of that society which in the first instance has destroyed peace of mind; or they may analyze it in terms of the new realm opened to the sick and demon-possessed by Jesus.

If they choose the former, both the diagnosis and the prescription will proceed along carefully, though subtly, controlled avenues. Society assumes the possibility of mental sanity on its own terms, although it never speaks with one voice concerning what those terms are. This very Babel with which it defines the integrated personality is one of the basic reasons why such integrity is impossible. For example, it encourages each individual to cultivate peace of mind *for his own sake,* so that the imbalance of others will not disturb his own balance, and so that he may view his own hardly won equilibrium with complacency and pride. At the same time, however, it insists that stability of mind shall contribute to the betterment of the existing structure of social relationships. The sane mind must not show its disdain for society by adopting a monastic seclusion; it must not exhibit its independence by vigorous action to change the present balance of economic or political power; it must continue to take a " loyalty oath " to the reputable institutions; it must avoid any behavior that would mark it as snobbish or eccentric. The person who thus achieves peace of mind by mastering the more obvious fears endemic in a society thus salves the society's conscience for feeding those fears. Such a person will draw praise for his success in dealing with problems in this intermediate area of concern; but he will need to avoid the problems in the ultimate areas (1 and 4), because in those areas questions are raised of existing institutions that make them unsure of their own ultimate validity. By preaching the desirability of inner equilibrium with reference to the intermediate areas, the world opens the door to the achievement of a modicum of mental security and health, provided only that the cured person maintains a delicate balance between common sense and unusual wisdom, between conventional virtues and heroic greatness. Should the cured person become too concerned about the situation in the ultimate areas (1 and 4), he may well be called a fanatic by his fellows, for he makes them subconsciously aware of the problems they wish to forget for the sake of their own peace of mind. For society, like the individual, wants to ignore its own mortality, its own slavery to narrow perspectives, its own divided allegiances, its own elevation of relatives to the rank of absolutes, its own segregation of problems into categories where its professionals feel competent to deal with them.

Where, then, lies the relevance of the Christian message to the contemporary quest for mental sanity? Certainly the Christian does not wish to deny or evade the existence of an illness that is taking epidemic proportions. The Christian as such is moved by compassion to share the suffering of his fellows and to mediate the healing grace of Christ. But he will recognize that the primary threat to health is man's allegiance to false gods (areas 1 and 4). And he will recognize how the existing world and its mind furthers the spread of the disease. He knows that the only true peace is that which comes from God, and that the world can neither give nor take away this peace. The advent of such peace does, in many cases, alleviate the difficulties encountered in the intermediate areas (2 and 3), but victory must be won over the fatal schism in the human heart and the fatal schism in all creation, before true reconciliation will alleviate the tensions of distraught minds. And this victory has been won in Christ. The announcement of the acceptable year of the Lord is authenticated by the healing of the blind and the casting out of demons. The gospel is relevant to every case of mental sickness, but this pertinence may not be rightly evaluated by doctors or patients who measure effects by the world's assessment of causes.

In some cases, they will observe that many sick minds achieve relative health quite apart from any conscious relation to the saving power of God, and that the word of the gospel does not suffice to bring healing to other distraught minds. Even where the resources of the gospel seem to effect a cure, other explanations may be found to explain this effect. Even though the work of Christ should be credited with the cure, that work may still be basically misunderstood. It may be used as a tool for realizing purposes not intrinsic to itself, for overcoming obstacles that it does not consider to be the ultimate cause of illness. For instance, the healer may appeal to Jesus as an example of one who maintained personal serenity under adverse circumstances, but the reasons for his serenity may be quite ignored. His words may suffice as soothing ointment, but his power to subdue hearts and demons to the purpose of God (areas 1 and 4) may remain quite untapped. Men may thus judge the gospel to be relevant to a limited range of problems, and thereby empty it of its true scope and power. They may reduce it to a substitute for sedatives or for a " shock treatment " and be quite unaware of the victory that has been won over all the powers of " the enemy."

D. Peace of Nations

A second goal which men seek today with great earnestness is the better ordering of political organizations as the basis for the recovery of other harmonies. The lure of this new order is described in glowing terms: brotherhood and justice, equality of opportunity, the guarantee of cardinal freedoms, the actualization of human rights, the termination of war, the eradication of disease, the extension of universal education, an abundant life of prosperity, security, and happiness. These at least are some of the dreams that have proliferated under the stimulus of modern inventions, modern means of transportation, modern mastery of physical power, modern doctrines of evolution, and the cultural climate of the day.

There is much that is laudable in such goals, much that strikes a spark in man's imagination. The minds of most of us are permeated by such dreams. Nor should we repudiate them out of hand, even if we could. The Christian, even more than his fellows, should sense the tragic " groaning " of creation and share the longings for international accord. Yet the loftier the aspiration, the more grim the obstacles: a famine-ridden world, nations peopled by exiles, an economy based on and producing scarcity, the holocaust of racial antagonisms, the rapid mechanization of personal relationships, the secularization of culture, the atomic bomb and germicidal warfare.

What now will be considered relevant to such a scene? And who shall be the judge of its pertinence? Society will insist that any message, if its relevance is to be granted, must affirm these dreams and attack these obstacles. Its message and strategy must be of some weight in shifting the existing balance of power among competing nations, classes, races. It must be capable of being rushed immediately into the arena of international diplomacy, into the center of a race riot, into the legislative halls or scientific laboratories, wherever and whenever the world shouts, "Crisis." The world thinks it knows what it wants, and what is standing in its way. It needs a tool for circumventing the obstacles and for carrying it toward the goal. Can the Christian message justify itself in this predicament?

Before answering, one should consider the process by which human utopias are manufactured. The architects of utopias are confident that they themselves are radical rebels against the *status quo*. Yet their dreams in a subtle way often prove the opposite — prove, in fact, that they are slaves of the world against which they are at odds. Their heavens are constructed out of forlorn desires, desires that the world has created and then frustrated. Crusaders for world order increase the disorder by trying to force their dreams upon their fellows. Their loyalty to their cause aggravates their enmity toward crusaders following antithetical paths. Only by abolishing all but one panacea can the effectiveness of that panacea be proved — something that never happens in human affairs. Since this is true, no prescription for the world's malady can ever be completely validated or invalidated. All utopias remain mirages, which retain their power because one of them might conceivably turn into an oasis. But the purer the utopia, the more distant it actually is, and the less probability there is that the world will ever arrive there. Thus the utopian remains vulnerable, in an acute form, to the inner despairs that characterize that world whose sickness spawned his dream.

Any plan for attaining world order is shaped by a segment of the world in such a fashion that the accomplishment of the goal would enhance and solidify the interests of this segment. The Zealots of Jesus' day, assuming the prior importance of solving the political problem, dreamed of a day when the most righteous nation would be free and supreme. They had scant patience with the legalists, who assumed the prior importance of solving the religious problem and who dreamed of the day when community life would be wholly organized around the regulations of the Torah and when the most faithful servants of the Torah would be supreme. The apocalyptists, or some of them at least, were aware of the impracticability of nationalism and legalism alike as solutions of the problem. Since all nations are evil, they are all disqualified from participating in the Kingdom of God. Only God can abrogate national sovereignty and establish the rule of his elect, a community in which the apocalyptist himself will be given a long-denied honor. In all utopias, the dreamer assumes that he will have a prominent place therein, and that he is able to define what things must be changed in the organization of society before the dream will take effect. His hope is always subject to the despair of repeated postponements. Thus the world creates hopelessness that is greatest in the hearts of those who hope for the utopias that the world, by its negative logic, encourages.

Obviously the gospel of Jesus is not a ready-made answer to the problem of world order such as the world seeks. Jesus did not die simply in order to be a tool by which the world can save itself. Christianity does not announce itself as a vehicle for saving a particular civilization from collapse. It begins by proclaiming a fiery judgment to which all men and nations are subject. The good news of the cross announces its revelation of the wrath of God on the body of sin and death. The mind and the institutions of society must justify themselves before the truth of God, and not vice versa. God's strategy does not first require drastic revisions in social organization of power in order to yield the desired security; it first of all creates sons with new hearts (area 1) and casts from heaven the principalities and powers (area 4). It brings the Kingdom of God near to men so that eternal life may be received now, at the very point where world peace seems most distant and where all utopias seem impossible. The peace of God is shed abroad in men's hearts, and from his act of forgiveness the work of reconciliation proceeds to invade all areas of man's existence. It transforms the fruit of man's actions; it transfigures the relation of husband to wife, slave to master, citizen to ruler. It is able to do this because humble love has forced Satan to reckon with a new power which he cannot destroy. The utopian considers such peacemaking to be trivial in comparison with the transformation of battlefields into playgrounds. Yet this trivial "event" is actually the way by which God transforms the whole battlefield of creation into a realm of joy and peace.

Is this message relevant to the peace of nations? The humble assent, though the proud cannot. The pure in heart see God, but those whose allegiance is divided cannot. The meek inherit the earth; the warriors attempt it but fail. The blind see it and are healed, while those who think they can see are blinded. The merciful receive a forgiveness that betokens a new Day, but the unmerciful are excluded. The Kingdom remains a mystery, but it is a saving mystery to those who respond to God's invitation. This invitation makes its recipients share in a new way and to a new degree with the travail of creation, but it also frees their hearts, heals their minds, and orders their world, by overcoming the enemy in heavenly places. As a result, their role in history has become that of ministers of reconciliation and stewards of God's mystery. As stewards they well know what obstacles to peace of mind and to world peace may be found in all areas of human wisdom and social organization, but the weapons for overcoming these obstacles are placed in their hands. If they were wrestling merely against other men and other institutions, an earthly armory might be sufficient, but since their battle is against demonic influences that corrupt their hearts and the world's mind, they are given weapons whose power over both the demons of mental disease and the lord of the demons has been demonstrated. The world sees little efficacy in such weapons, but the world is not fighting the same antagonists or seeking the same peace. When the world locates truly the enemies of its real peace, then it will find use for this archaic armor: " the shield of faith, . . . the sword of the Spirit, which is the word of God " (Eph. 6:16 f.).

NOTES AND INDEXES

NOTES

1. Whether the Epistle to the Ephesians was or was not written by Paul is a question that arouses much disagreement among scholars. This is a question, however, that we cannot discuss here. It is legitimate to use Ephesians for the purposes of this book, because our primary aim is to explore the witness of the New Testament as a whole, and few would dispute the right of this letter to be considered a genuine expression of early Christian faith. Furthermore, it is generally recognized that at most points this letter holds faithfully to the central line of Paul's thought. Where it is important for the argument that my reference to Ephesians should be a reference to Paul, there will usually be found supporting evidence from other letters whose Pauline authorship is practically certain.

2. New Testament scholars should read, if they have not already done so, the essay by Professor DeZwaan of the University of Leyden which appeared in the *Journal of Theological Studies* in 1947 (July–October issue). In this essay he not only summarizes the common witness of New Testament writers along the lines we have followed, but he also indicates the function of technical scholarship within the context provided by God's revelation of the meaning of history.

3. Few writers since the apostolic age have had a more vigorous awareness of the *skandalon* underlying the story of Jesus than Søren Kierkegaard, and few have given so acute an analysis of the different ways in which this offense was felt by the contemporaries of Jesus. The reader who wishes to follow this cluster of problems, as it has emerged into recent theological discussion, may well begin with Kierkegaard, *Training in Christianity,* tr. by Walter Lowrie (Oxford University Press, 1941) and his *Philosophical Fragments,* tr. by David F. Swenson (Princeton University Press, 1936). If the student uses German, he will find a full-length treatment of the history of the Biblical concept in G. Stählin, *Skandalon* (Gütersloh, 1930).

4. In *The Choice* (The Westminster Press, 1948), I have tried to tell the story of a single Christian disciple of the first century, an imaginative ac-

count of how Clement of Rome first heard and responded to the Christian message, was persuaded and drawn within the fellowship, and was taught both in the Church and in his own experiences the meaning of discipleship. In writing the story, however, I was constantly made aware of the impossibility of reconstructing the whole story of any individual, of the infinite variety of ways through which different people in that first generation must have experienced " rebirth," and of the infinite flexibility of diction in which they must have described that experience to themselves and to others. Yet, in spite of such difficulties, every historian of ideas needs to recapture the developing pattern of ideas on the part of a single man if his history is to achieve verisimilitude. And every student needs to keep his study of the past oriented around the life of specific individuals.

5. The unity of the New Testament, as well as the unity of the Church, is ultimately comprised in this confession of Jesus as Lord. A more general summary of the evidence may be found in F. V. Filson, *One Lord, One Faith* (The Westminster Press, 1943) or in A. M. Hunter, *The Message of the New Testament* (The Westminster Press, 1944). A more detailed historical examination of the earliest creeds is now available in English in O. Cullmann, *The Earliest Christian Confessions,* tr. by J. K. S. Reid (Lutterworth Press, London, 1949).

6. Some readers at this point will feel the need for clear-cut definitions that will enable them to know precisely what is meant by " the spiritual powers that rule the world." They will feel that until such a concept can be defined, and the existence of such powers proved, it is confusing to use the concept at all. But, as we shall see, the definition of the concept and the character of the existence of these " spiritual powers " together constitute a major part of the problem, rather than tools for its solution that can be sharpened in advance. We can well utilize such categories, even though their meaning remains hazy, like words whose meaning becomes clearer in the very process of speech as the speakers discover in varying contexts their different affiliations and subtle nuances. There are several ways to define such words: one is the direct method of the dictionary or the philosophical glossary; another is to use the term indirectly in story or discussion. The latter is the way chosen by novelists, dramatists, and the writers of the New Testament. It is the method of describing what a particular " spiritual power " does before appraising the forms in which its existence is to be affirmed or denied. However, the reader of this book who is dissatisfied with our postponement of the question may locate some of the answers by glancing ahead at Chapters 5, 6, 9, and 12. Then, if he is still dissatisfied with the way in which the ambiguities of the existence of Satan are dealt with, he should study Dostoevski's treatment of those ambiguities in his account of Ivan's struggle with the devil (*The Brothers Karamazov*). If he wishes an important current discussion of the actuality of the demonic, and its relevance to the interpretation of history,

he is referred to H. Thielicke, *Fragen des Christentums an die Moderne Welt*, Ch. 4 (Genf, Verlag Oikumene, 1945).

7. Whether or not Phil. 2:6-11 was used as a hymn, its rhythmical, liturgical structure has led many scholars to conclude that Paul is not at this point creating new phrases but is relying upon a common tradition that has become almost a formula because of its long use. Such a conclusion would support our adoption of this passage as an epitome of the common memory of the Church concerning the movement of Jesus' ministry. There are, to be sure, very complex problems involved in any exposition of the section. Not the least among these is the doctrine of pre-existence, which is presupposed, and the problem of defining how Jesus "emptied himself." Preoccupation with these problems has, however, often distracted the attention from the central motif of the section, which is quite clear even at the first reading. This motif is the progressive self-humiliation of God's servant as at once the path to exaltation and the clue to the mind that his followers must emulate. Our purpose in this chapter is simply to accent this motif and to describe some of its more apparent implications.

8. A careful study of these axioms, using the techniques of form criticism, has convinced the author that these proverbial utterances are in the highest degree authentic. Cf. "The Morphology of a Proverb" in *The Anglican Theological Review* (Vol. 21, 1939, pp. 282–292). Few teachings were more widely adapted to multiple situations in the life of the Church, and these situations have left their mark upon the tradition in the Gospels (e.g., the use of the word "cross" in Mark 8:34), but the alterations in the form of the teaching testify to the originality and the vitality of the teaching itself.

9. See note 6. It has been suggested that an understanding of the meaning of the term "Satan" may best be gained by a movement of thought from the story of what Satan does to the question of his existence. Early Christians gained much of their understanding by reflection upon the story of what he had done in encompassing the death of the Messiah. Here his hand most clearly showed itself, both in the minds of those who crucified Jesus and in the minds of those who continued to reject Jesus' message. The chief manifestations of his existence, whatever "level" of reality one may assign to that existence, are to be located in human thoughts and deeds. The references in the New Testament to principalities, powers, dominions, rulers, elements, may best be approached and assessed by keeping central the event of the cross. It is in this event that the basic evidence may be found for measuring Satan's power and weakness, his existence and the termination of that existence. It is hoped that the subsequent chapters may rightly interpret the implications of this evidence.

10. Let no reader suppose that this cry of the Jewish people, "His blood be on us," offers any excuse or extenuation for anti-Semitic feeling. The

Gospels were written, of course, in a period of great hostility between the synagogue and the Church, and not all Christians (then as now) were guiltless of making all Jews per se guilty of the blood of Jesus. Traces of this animosity may be detected in the Gospels, nor should that be surprising. The tenor of the Passion story as a whole, however, is to affirm the guilt of *all* the participants, and not of a selected group of culprits. Moreover, one needs to remember that the same story underscores the Messiah's declaration that none of those who were guilty knew what he was doing. The same story recalls the Messiah's prayer that all be forgiven. The gospel *does* seek to condemn the Jews and all others for their complicity, but the motive of this condemnation is to announce and secure their forgiveness. This is one point where the reference to Satan is significant. None of the participants, Jew or Gentile, is identified with Satan, who is the true adversary of Jesus, yet all of them are revealed to be unwitting servants of Satan. The implication of this is not that the synagogue is the enemy of the Church, but that Satan is the common enemy.

11. The technical historian will observe immediately that in reconstructing this account of the conversion of disciples I have fused together materials from many different strands of tradition and many different writers: the Gospels, I Peter, The Acts, and Paul's letters. One legitimate objective of the historian is to separate these strands and distinguish the attitudes of one writer from another. This is necessary if one wants to recover the developing stages in the history of ideas or institutions. My objective has been quite different, hence a different methodology. I have been trying to assess the significance of an event by pooling the testimonies of many witnesses (in the New Testament use of that word). I am not saying that a particular man whom we know by name went through these successive stages, in precisely this order, and that he described the course of his thought in these particular categories. The evidence does not permit us to attempt this, except perhaps in the case of the apostle Paul. But it does allow us to attempt the other objective: a composite and typical testimony to the major dimensions of the conversion experience, with its contrast between the time before and the time after. In fashioning such a composite description, I am not ignoring, as they could not ignore, the separate histories and vocabularies of the individual converts. Yet those converts, however diverse in background and temperament, were fully convinced of genuine fellowship in a common experience. They were impressed, if not amazed, by the unities that bound them together: one Lord, one faith, one baptism, one hope, one Spirit. Later scholars may conclude that no such unity existed, but that rather it was a pious self-deception. In such an opinion they are contradicted by the opinion of the objects of their historical study — the apostles and their followers — who not only affirmed their mutual oneness of faith in a given generation, but also their oneness with the original disciples and with all the brothers of Christ

in all generations. Once we accept their "opinion," we are bound to adopt a method of historical reconstruction that honors it.

12. In this and subsequent paragraphs, I have incorporated material that appeared in an essay, "The New Testament Witness and Civilization," *Theology Today,* Vol. V, pp. 340 ff. (1948). This material is used by permission of the editor.

13. The significance of Eph. 4:8 has been obscured by the Revised Standard Version, which reads: "When he ascended on high he led a host of captives." This rendering has the virtue of clarity, since both translators and readers can readily grasp the idea of leading a host of captives, but it may be doubted whether this is more accurate than the earlier rendering: "He led captivity captive," which has definite support from the Greek. The real issue in choosing a translation here seems to depend upon each translator's comprehension of the finer nuances of Paul's attitudes toward spiritual captivity (cf. Rom. 7:23; II Cor. 10:5; II Tim. 3:6). When we consider Paul's interest in the invisible sources of man's captivity (e.g., Eph., ch. 6), we are convinced that in ch. 4:8 the focus of attention is upon the captors that must be defeated before the emancipator can give gifts to men. Gerhard Kittel insists that "only the meaning of spirits is possible" (cf. G. Kittel in *Theologisches Wörterbuch zum Neuen Testament,* I, p. 196). This is in line with Chrysostom's identification of the captives with Christ's enemies: Satan, sin, and death (cf. Rom. 7:23; Ignatius, *Ephesians,* 17:1). Of Chrysostom's rendering, T. K. Abbott writes, "In substance this interpretation is no doubt correct, but it is unnecessary to define the enemies; the figure is general, that of a triumphant conqueror leading his conquered enemies in his train" (International Critical Commentary, *Ephesians, ad loc.*).

14. The ambiguities in all the temporal terms in the New Testament constitute one of the major difficulties in exposition. The words "age," "generation," "year," "day," may each be used in the simpler literal sense as an objective reference to chronological duration. But each is also used with a wide range of metaphorical meanings, in which duration can not be measured by reference to the ordinary calendar. For example, "the *day* of the Lord" is virtually equivalent to "the *days* of the Son of man," and this "day" is not a period limited by time because it refers to eternal sovereignty (cf. B. Noack, *Das Gottesreich bei Lukas,* pp. 42 f. Uppsala, 1948). As Paul used this term on occasion (Rom. 13:12 f.), it signified the epoch since the resurrection of Jesus and since the rebirth of the disciple. Those who inherit eternal life, or life in the coming age, are sons of the light and sons of the day. Here, obviously, "day" refers to the whole period of salvation, and is usually indistinguishable from the year of the Lord and from the new age, introduced by him.

Conversely, the word for "night" refers to the age of darkness, the whole period before the fulfillment of God's sovereignty and before the conversion of a man (I Thess. 5:5; Rom. 13:12). Apart from the light, man walks in darkness (John 11:10). To shine as lights in the world means to be blameless "in the midst of a crooked and perverse generation" (Phil. 2:15). The term "generation," when thus qualified by such adjectives as "wicked," "perverse," "adulterous," "rebellious," thus comes to stand for the race as a whole, the people who are bound together by sin, the world that is shrouded in darkness (cf. F. Büchsel in Kittel, *Theologisches Wörterbuch zum Neuen Testament,* I, p. 661). In this sense, the term *aion* approximates the meaning of *kosmos* (Mark 4:19; Matt. 13:22). The wisdom of the world and the wisdom of this age are synonymous (I Cor. 1:20; 2:6; 3:19); "for ages" is equivalent to "before the foundation of the world" (John 17:24; I Cor. 2:7; Eph. 1:4; I Peter 1:20; Heb. 1:2). The evil age is defined not so much by its temporal span as by its rulers (I Cor. 2:6; 4:4). Sometimes the singular *age* appears to be interchangeable with its plural *ages;* elsewhere the plural appears to indicate that the whole course of time may be broken up into smaller units. Viewed from one angle — that of its ruler, its darkness, its sin — the singular is preferable; viewed from another angle — that of God's overarching activity — the plural is commonly used (cf. H. Sasse in Kittel, *op. cit.,* I, 203 f.; also E. Stauffer, *Die Theologie des Neuen Testaments,* pp. 59 f. Geneva, 1945). To be a son of this age is to belong to an evil generation, the direct opposite of being a son of light (Luke 16:8; 20:34). The translators of the R. S. V. reveal the virtual equivalence of "age" and "world" by using *world* to translate *aion* in Luke 16:8 and *age* to translate *aion* in Luke 20:34. The former of these passages may indicate a thin line of distinction between *aion* and *genea;* we may hazard a guess that in their relative symbolisms, *age* focuses attention upon the rulers of the age, of whom the servants are called sons, while *generation* focuses attention upon the processes by which that age begets its children (cf. Col. 1:26, R. S. V., margin). In any case, the above should be sufficient to justify the position that in certain contexts the New Testament writers viewed the "night," the "evil generation," the "world," and the "age" as virtually equivalent categories; and that in such use the quantitative measurement of duration is superseded by qualitative considerations.

15. The treatment of this section is based upon a longer essay which appeared in *Interpretation,* Vol. III, pp. 259-272 (1949). The material is used here by permission of the editor.

16. A qualification should perhaps be made to the assertion that the believer must always react to a threat or a promise as if it were directed to him. Consider, for example, the prediction of the prophet Agabus to Paul as recorded in Acts 21:10 f. Through this prophet the Holy Spirit announced a forthcoming arrest in Jerusalem, an announcement that did not deter Paul

from continuing his journey (cf. Rom. 15:30–32). We note that by the time
The Acts was written, its readers could hardly view this prediction as addressed to themselves; even less can modern readers do so. The same
observation could be made of other predictions in the New Testament that
are similarly outmoded. Their particularity must be fully recognized by
later interpreters. Nevertheless, in recognizing this particularity of historical
utterances and situation, one may distinguish between those messages intended for a single person at a single occasion and those directed at a disciple in such a way that the mission of all disciples is illuminated. The congregation that listens for the Word of God in Scripture may discern even in
the story of Agabus a message relevant to its present situation, wherever, in
terms of its own mission, it contemplates a journey to Jerusalem. It must
of course be alert to the dangers of forcibly wresting from Scripture the
word which it wants, and not the Word through which God's purpose is
manifested.

17. See note 14.

18. There is no space here adequately to support a position that runs counter to much current exposition. There are many who will deny the close
relationships between the coming of the Son of Man to his faithful witnesses
(as pictured in Rev., chs. 2; 3) and the final coming of the Son of Man in
glory (as pictured in Rev., chs. 21; 22). Some of the evidence that supports
my exposition will be given in Chapters 8–10. I do not deny that in New
Testament thought there is frequently drawn a distinction, in temporal
terms, between the end of each disciple's mission and the end of the whole
redemptive process. My point is that the unities to be observed between these
two ends are more important for New Testament writers than the existence
of this temporal distinction, or the chronological measurement of the interim.
There is a unity of judgment: the judgment that now is being manifested,
wherever the two ages meet in the decisions of men, *is* a work of the coming
Son of Man. There is a unity of life: those who lose life for the Messiah's
sake find it, and this finding of life is inseparable from the gift of glory in
the Messiah's Kingdom (Matt. 16:24–28). Those who now see the Kingdom
of God, in and through their own reception of its power, see what all creation will see when the Messiah has been similarly revealed to all creatures.
The new age, which is thus inherited in the act of perfect faith, is at its
center measured by the interdependence between this act and the fulfillment
of God's promise in Christ. Wherever Christ is at work, speaking to men of
judgment and mercy, commanding and inviting them, instilling in their
hearts his own humble obedience, there he is at work *as the coming Son
of Man,* and his work is a sign of that coming. His servants, therefore, from
their point of standing, experience that coming, not as a single instant of time,
determined alike for all men, but as the true fulfillment of their relationship

to the Master. The unity of the "end" stems from the personal will of a single Lord.

19. The significance of this replacement of the natural man's goal of *one* victory by faith's awareness of *two* victories has been discussed by Kierkegaard in various essays. If interested in his analysis of this significance, the reader should consult: *The Works of Love*, tr. by David F. and Lillian M. Swenson (Princeton University Press, 1944); *The Gospel of Suffering*, tr. by David F. and Lillian M. Swenson (Augsburg Press, 1947); *Training in Christianity*, tr. by Walter Lowrie (Oxford University Press, 1941); "Purity of Heart" in *Doors Into Life*, tr. by Douglas V. Steere (Harper & Brothers, 1948).

20. At most points, the view of the nature and unity of the Church that I have tried to express is similar to that presented by Karl Barth in his contribution to Commission I at the Amsterdam Assembly. There he describes the Church "as a congregation, a subject, which is confronted by, and controlled by another primary subject: Jesus Christ as absolute Lord. . . . The Church [as "congregation"] is only a living Church in so far as it is filled with the life of this primary subject, and only if its life is based on this foundation is it a real Church. . . . The congregation exists where, and in so far as, it dares to live by the act of its living Lord" (*Man's Disorder and God's Design*: The Amsterdam Assembly Series, Vol. I, pp. 67 f. Harper & Brothers, 1949). I may add that I read Barth's essay after writing this chapter.

21. A notable exception to this silence, this neglect by historians and theologians of the distinctively Biblical pattern of thought regarding temptation, may be found in an essay by H. Richard Niebuhr on "The Shame and Glory of the Church" (*Man's Disorder and God's Design*: The Amsterdam Assembly Series, Vol. I, pp. 78 f.). Professor Niebuhr chooses as the key to correct appraisals of the shame and glory of the Church the criterion of "repentant faith" and "believing repentance," and rightly distinguishes between false appraisals, which increase the disordering of the Church, from true appraisals, which arise from the ordering process by which Christ continues his work in and through his Body.

22. Rudolph Otto has called attention to the presence in Jesus' teachings of the two apparently contradictory attitudes: the expectation of a speedy end, and the assumption of a continuance of the present earthly circumstances into an indefinite future (*The Kingdom of God and Son of Man*, tr. by F. V. Filson and B. L. Woolf, pp. 59–62, Zondervan Press, 1938). Such a contrast is apparent not only in the Gospels but in almost every book in the New Testament. The existence of this contradiction does not necessarily mean that two authors have been at work or that any author has changed his mind. It is often simply an expression of the faith that the Lord whose

speedy return is anticipated is the same Lord who disciplines his servants in patient endurance. The student who wishes to discover the ways in which this ambivalent emphasis appears may study the following passages, two from each of a number of writings. In each case, the first reference implies a long prospect lying ahead of the disciple, with a consequent need for endurance and perseverance; the second makes explicit the nearness of the Lord's return.

II Thess. 2:1-12	....	I Thess. 5:1-3
Rom. 11:17-27	....	Rom. 13:11-14
Phil., ch. 1	....	Phil. 4:5
Heb. 12:3-12	....	Heb. 10:32-39
James 1:2-4	....	James 5:1-9
I Peter 1:17	....	I Peter 4:7
I John, ch. 1	....	I John 2:18
Rev., chs. 13 to 19	....	Rev. 22:20

Professor E. Rosenstock-Huessy (*The Christian Future,* pp. 71 ff. Charles Scribner's Sons, 1946) has given a provocative discussion of the reasons for this apparently contradictory emphasis upon the nearness and the distance of the Lord's return. He writes: " Theologians have made a great pother about the early expectation and subsequent delay of the Second Coming. The debate is pointless. For one who lives from the end of time, the combined expectation and delay of Christ's return is the contradiction on which the Christian lives . . . a tension which is the paradoxical essence of Christianity." Elsewhere he develops the theme that we have adopted, that is, (1) that God's word is always spoken from the future back into the times (p. 97) and (2) the disciple who lives by that promise will live from the future back into the present.

23. See note 15.

24. A longer analysis of the process by which the apostle arrived at his understanding of the reconciliation of Jew and Gentile is provided by my essay on "Paul the Apostle" in *The Interpreter's Bible,* Vol. I, pp. 200–213 (Abingdon-Cokesbury Press).

25. See note 12.

26. The most important passages in the New Testament that parallel Pauline material are the following: Mark 12:13-17; I Peter 2:13-17; chs. 3:14 to 4:2; 4:12 to 5:11; Heb. 10:32-35. The book of Revelation is usually cited to show that contrary attitudes are supported by the New Testament (cf., e.g., chs. 13;14). Here the Roman authorities are viewed as servants of the beast, who makes war on the saints, who are commanded not to worship the beast. I do not think, however, that any sharp contrast can be fully

demonstrated. On the one hand, Rom., ch. 13, does not give the unqualified blessing of Paul upon the policies of political rulers, which many have uncritically supposed. Paul was quite ready to suffer death rather than worship the "beast," when the rulers asserted absolute power over his allegiance to Christ. On the other hand, the interpretation of Revelation has often failed to distinguish between the authority of the devil, the beast, and specific Roman emperors, and has assumed therefore that John was as outspoken in condemning his captors as Paul in blessing them. Such a contrast is far too strong, as the ensuing interpretation of the two books should make clear. The different situation explains the contrast in accent, perhaps, but too much has been made of this factor. I think it impossible to prove that Paul's attitudes toward Rome changed after he was placed in a Roman prison, or that John's attitudes would have changed after his release.

27. It seems to me that many historians in recent decades have underestimated the extent of friction between Christians of the first generation and the Roman authorities (provincial and local officials in most cases). In part this faulty estimate is due to a dependence upon the book of The Acts, in which one of the motifs admittedly was to diminish the extent of such animosities. In part, the estimate is due to a dependence upon secular historical records. All references to official hostility in the New Testament must be supported by Roman historians. Since these historians mention only a few brief periods of open persecution (under Nero, perhaps Domitian, and Trajan), it follows that apart from these periods the relationship of Christians to the political authorities was quite amicable. Seldom has the argument from silence been put to more extensive use. That argument is weakened when one considers the improbability that all acts of Roman magistrates in the far-flung Empire were recorded, and that all the records have been preserved. It is further weakened when one gives full weight to the Christian records, which not only reflect the atmosphere of hostility but also give firsthand testimony to many specific incidents of conflict with Roman representatives. Paul's oblique references to scourgings and imprisonment should be given greater weight than either the accounts in The Acts or the silence of Roman annalists.

28. The precise connotation of *phobos* in Rom. 13:3 is not accessible from its immediate context, so we are impelled to look at other passages to learn what Paul usually meant by the term. Even in the thirteenth chapter itself, there are two uses of the word which seem to contradict each other. In v. 3, the rulers are not a "terror," i.e., not an object or source of fear for those who do good, but only for evildoers. Yet in v. 7, the brothers are commanded to give "reverence" (*phobos*) to whom reverence is due. To whom, then, should one accord *phobos,* and to whom should one deny *phobos?* When is fear encouraged and when is it forbidden? The other passages, of which there are eleven, provide probable if not certain answers.

In two of these passages, *phobos* is that under which sinners live. On the one hand, they have no fear of God (Rom. 3:18); on the other, their present fear is a mark of sin, a sign of their slavery, their debt to the flesh, their life according to the flesh (Rom. 8:15). In the remaining nine contexts, *phobos* is attributed to the disciples without any suggestion of sin or guilt implicit in it. In fact, this *phobos* is a sign of holiness, a genuine accompaniment of the life according to the Spirit. In no fewer than six of these contexts, the object of fear is specifically mentioned as God or Christ (I Cor. 2:3; II Cor. 5:11; 7:1; Eph. 5:21; 6:5; Phil. 2:12). The other three permit the thought of *phobos* as a godly fear (II Cor. 7:5, 11, 15), but do not permit the idea that disciples should fear their earthly superiors because of what those authorities might do to them. In short, then, to Paul sinners have no fear of God but live in slavish fear of men; those who have been freed from the latter live in fear of God. These latter, in remembering the work of Christ crucified and the power of God, stand in fear and weakness and trembling (I Cor. 2:3). This *phobos* gives them boldness and fearlessness in their encounter with human adversaries (II Cor. 5:11). It is an accompaniment of perfect holiness (ch. 7:1), as they work out their own salvation in the knowledge that God is at work in them (Phil. 2:12). Of all the passages, the two in Ephesians provide the closest parallels to the situation and teaching of Rom. 13:3. In both, the injunctions deal directly with behavior toward authorities. Ephesians 5:21 gives the general rule which covers many different relationships: "Be subject to one another in fear of Christ." In the first example, one notes the parallelism between the wife's attitudes toward her husband (vs. 22–33) and the attitudes of Roman Christians toward their rulers (Rom. 13:1–7). In the second example, however, we find a succinct definition of what the *phobos* of Christ means, and how this rules out the *phobos* of master by the slave. "Fear and trembling" is here identified with singleness of heart, with doing the will of God, "with a good will as to the Lord," with knowing that the only good that one receives for doing good will come from the Lord. This godly service of the earthly master "as to Christ" rules out "eyeservice, as men-pleasers," rules out the rendering of obedience "to men," and by implication rules out the expectation of receiving from men the reward for doing good (Eph. 6:5–8). What is said here is virtually a paraphrase of what is said in Rom. 13:1–7; and what is said in Romans could be said of the slave's duty to his master. In both cases, the man who does good, i.e., whose act is done in the Lord, or out of fear of the Lord, will "have no fear of him who is in authority."

29. Advanced students of the New Testament are already conversant with recent developments and controversies in the interpretation of the Kingdom of God. Those who wish to review this material will find convenient and accurate summaries in the revised edition of Amos N. Wilder, *Eschatology and Ethics in the Teaching of Jesus*, Harper & Brothers, 1950, and in W. G. Kümmel, *Verheissung und Erfüllung*, Heinrich Major, Basel, 1945.

30. I hope that, in the treatment of time in these chapters, some of the misunderstandings occasioned by former writings may be removed. One of these misunderstandings is well stated in Professor Daniel D. Williams' book, *God's Grace and Man's Hope* (Harper & Brothers, 1949, pp. 126, 127). Believing that I have read the Bible too much through the eyes of Kierkegaard, this scholar contends that I have made too sharp the distinction between *chronos* and *kairos*. The result has been that "the day-by-day time [*chronos*] which is the form of our human existence is either treated as irrelevant to the issues of man's salvation, or else it is regarded as the sphere of death and frustration from which we must be saved." If either of these two alternatives is actually the result of my argument, then Professor Williams' protest is justified. He rightly raises the question: "Why must *chronos* be negated? Is it wholly evil in God's sight or man's experience that there should be times and seasons?" We would agree that the answer is "No." Where, then, lies the misunderstanding? Perhaps we may locate it in the excerpt that is made the basis for the protest. It reads as follows:

"The tyranny of *chronos* has been broken once and for all. It stands under the all-encompassing negation of God's judgment. Its boundary has been set by the manifestation of a 'wholly other order of reality.'"

Professor Williams has, I think, overlooked the word "tyranny." It is the tyranny that has been broken, that stands under the negation of God's judgment, and whose boundaries have been set by the manifestation of a freedom that is "wholly other." And what turns *chronos* into a tyrant? The sin and blindness of men, and the ruler of the age. God's saving act in Christ reveals both how widespread and how deep-seated is this tyranny; but reveals too how the evil time may be redeemed. Under bondage to sin, men have made *chronos* the sphere of death and frustration, but forgiven of that sin, men find that God is using *chronos* as the sphere of life and joy.

This rejoinder, however, does not remove all the points of disagreement. It seems to me, for example, that the New Testament's emphasis concerning how thoroughly sin has perverted man's ability to understand what time *is* and what it *means* does not receive adequate recognition by Dr. Williams. Neither does the Biblical witness concerning the radical change that the new life in Christ makes in a man's time consciousness. Dr. Williams seems to assume that a satisfactory definition of *chronos* can be arrived at apart from faith. It is "the form of our human existence." But there lies the real issue: What is "the form of our human existence"? Does the gift of new life in Christ change the form, and change the conceptions we have of that form? If so, then only "the saved man" in faith can rightly appraise what *chronos* means as "the form of our human existence." But we must halt here. The function of these notes does not permit a fuller discussion.

31. These requirements for apprehending the meaning of God's design for our lives serve to underscore the limitations and dangers of all profes-

sional efforts to construct a Biblical theology within which the organized concept of the Kingdom will have its fixed and carefully defined place. The danger lies in the supposition that, when we have satisfied ourselves that these ideas, which have been absorbed as neat paragraphs into our system, are Biblical ideas, we then know what thinking Biblically really means. As J. C. Hoekendijk has pointed out (*The Student World*, 164, pp. 142 f., 1949), we are safeguarded from our systems of Biblical ideas only when we stand " in fear and trembling " before God's act in Christ, remembering his benefits and seeking his promise, only when our reading of the Bible draws our words and concepts within the activity of God; only when we " share with prophets and apostles in their encounter with the Lord of Scripture." Our carefully devised reconstructions of Biblical theology may well hide a new bibliolatry, a new " paper pope," which inhibits alert listening for a new message from God and faithful response to it.

32. The rich meaning of this formula for elucidating the activity of the Spirit and for grasping the mystery of the Kingdom has been explored by W. Stählin, *The Mystery of God,* tr. by R. B. Hoyle (S. C. M. Press, London, 1937).

33. I have seen no recent treatment of the relationship between agape and the unique time consciousness that it produces. This is an area that, so far as I know, has been left quite unexplored by psychologists, theologians, and historians. The last great explorer was Kierkegaard, who developed in his edifying discourses some of the clues that I have merely mentioned. The reader is referred especially to his *Edifying Discourses,* Volume I (Augsburg Press, 1943), and his *Works of Love* (Princeton University Press, 1946), both translated by David F. and Lillian M. Swenson.

34. The relevance of an ancient message may be distinguished (though not wholly separated) from the relevance of an ancient terminology. Many readers will agree with me that the central message of the New Testament is truly free from the charge of archaism, but will insist that the vocabulary and thought-forms of the Scripture are not free from the irrelevance of antique fashions. These readers may well feel that in holding so closely to the first century categories of thought I have unduly bound the gospel to its obsolete clothing. For the proclamation of that gospel to modern men, modern categories should be employed. To be sure, the Biblical theologian must be alive to the truths embodied in this demand for contemporary forms of communication. To maintain the special sanctity of the Biblical language is a subtle form of idolatry which the Bible itself does not support. In this book I have relied (perhaps excessively for many readers' tastes) upon the major idioms of the New Testament writings, using them more frequently than they are used in the original writings simply because, whereas the original writers could take those idioms for granted, modern readers must make a

260 THE KINGDOM AND THE POWER

greater effort to enter into the same thought-world. This reliance upon an ancient imagery spells archaism for many moderns.

Whether or not that spelling is correct, I may be permitted here to indicate three major reasons for reviving such concepts as that of the two ages, and that of Satan. First of all, the historian as a historian must make his goal that of entering fully into the thought-world of the period that he is studying. In the second place, a perennial source of misunderstanding the Bible is too great haste in translating the more alien patterns of thought into terms that are more congenial to our present outlook. Therefore, to use again those alien patterns is a needed check upon our self-centeredness and complacency. In the third place — and this is the most important reason — the New Testament categories (e.g., Satan) are still negotiable currency because they provide useful pointers to a reality that transcends the distinction between ancient and modern. Satan can and does work through both archaism and modernism because both are inherently self-centered, both are tools for adding to one's own superiority, both are ways of overstressing the significance of *chronos,* both are mediums through which the mind of the old age is grafted into the mind of the sons of that age. One indication of this perennial relevance of Biblical vocabulary is the experience of the Church itself. In its periods of renewal, ever and anon the Church rediscovers the peculiar pertinence of ways of thinking that it had supposed to be archaic; and in this rediscovery it has found a needed correction for its tendency both to archaize and to modernize.

INDEX OF SCRIPTURE PASSAGES

INDEX OF TOPICS AND AUTHORS

Printed in the United States
25117LVS00003B/154-171